the aromatic
garden
growing and using scented plants

the aromatic
garden

growing and using scented plants

JULIA LAWLESS

photography by CLAY PERRY

BARNES
&NOBLE
B O O K S
N E W   Y O R K

To Cara Denman for her guidance

PAGE 1: EXOTIC-LOOKING FLOWERS OF THE BALSAMIC-SCENTED
PINUS SYLVESTRIS. THE NEEDLES ARE USED TO PRODUCE PINE
ESSENTIAL OIL.
PREVIOUS: AN URN NESTLES AMONG THE AROMATIC PLANTS
AND ELEGANT TOPIARY AT ALDERLEY GRANGE, ENGLAND.
RIGHT: THE SCULPURAL OUTLINE OF BERGAMOT, A
REFRESHINGLY SCENTED HERB.

First published in Great Britain in 2001 by Kyle Cathie Limited

This edition published by Barnes & Noble, Inc., by arrangement
with Kyle Cathie Limited

2002 Barnes & Noble Books
ISBN 0-7607-3186-1

M 10 9 8 7 6 5 4 3 2 1

Text © 2001 Julia Lawless
Photography © 2001 Clay Perry
(for further copyright acknowledgements, see page 160)

Editor: Sheila Davies   Copy-editor: Sharon Amos
Designer: Paul Welti   Production: Lorraine Baird and Sha Huxtable

Printed and bound in Singapore by KHL Printing Co. Pte. Ltd.

Important Notice

This book contains information on a wide range of herbs that can be used
medicinally. It is not intended as a medical reference book, but as a source
of information. Before trying any herbal remedies, sample a small quantity
first to establish whether there is any adverse or allergic reaction.
Remember that some herbs which are beneficial in small doses can be
harmful if taken to excess or for a long period. The reader is advised not to
attempt self-treatment for serious or long-term problems without consulting
a qualified medicinal herbalist. Neither the author nor the publisher can be
held responsible for any adverse reaction to the recipes, recommendations,
and instructions contained herein, and the use of any herb or derivative is
entirely at the reader's own risk.

contents

Hardiness Zones (as described by the US Department of Agriculture)

North American gardeners are given guidance through a system of zones, of which zone 1 is the Arctic and zone 11 the southernmost part of the continent, where temperatures never reach freezing point. A plant may be hard to, say, zones 7-9, which means you can leave it outdoors all winter if you live in Texas, but not if you live in New York.

foreword

Perfume has the most extraordinary power to effect emotion and mood. It can also stimulate memory in ways varying from the intimate and nostalgic to the downright disagreeable. And most of this is based on the essential oils derived from plants, or synthesized in imitation of what they produce naturally.

Entire civilizations such as that of ancient Egypt (and, to some extent, medieval France) have based their religious and social functioning around perfume. In Britain, the importance of the aromatic in medieval times (when scent was thought to be the main defense against disease) seems to be re-emerging in a desire for perfumed products used in the household, in health care, and, of course, in the garden.

A few years ago, the Chelsea Physic Garden designed and planted a Perfumery and an Aromatherapy Border designed to show the variety of plant materials used in the perfume industry and the essential oils used in aromatherapy treatments. Subtitled "Thinking with your nose," this display has proved surprisingly popular. I am therefore delighted that Julia Lawless has expanded this notion into a practical guide to growing and using scented plants while placing their use in a sound historical context.

It is also good to know that any encouragement of the essential oil industry supports the economics of countries such as China, Brazil, Turkey, Indonesia, India, Morocco, and Egypt. And, unlike medicinal herbs (the vast majority of which are

ABOVE: THE EXQUISITELY BEAUTIFUL SINGLE PEONY, *P. PEREGRINA* (FROM ITALY AND THE BALKANS), HAS A RICH HONEY FRAGRANCE AND CAN BE SEEN HERE GROWING EN MASSE IN LONDON'S CHELSEA PHYSIC GARDEN.

taken from the wild), these materials are cropped, making their use far less of a conservation concern.

I wish the reader joy in the creation of a scented haven. May it stimulate only happy memories as you think with your nose…!

Sue Minter

CURATOR, CHELSEA PHYSIC GARDEN

introduction

I have been working in the field of aromatherapy and medical herbalism for more than 20 years, but is only within the past ten that I have had the opportunity to grow many of the plants I already knew so well from their medicinal, perfumery, and aromatherapy applications. In retrospect, it now seems a completely natural development: after all, at one time most herbalists would have grown or at least been familiar with the all plants in their apothecary. Growing scented plants and herbs has brought the whole field of aromatic medicine vividly to life for me and has helped transform my approach from one of theory into a direct experience of the inherent nature of the plants themselves.

Gradually I came to know the distinct character and temperament of the different plants: mint, for example, is a gregarious type that will take over the whole garden if not kept in check; wild thyme is tough and independent, used to putting up with difficult conditions; others, like chamomile and marigold, are mild and easygoing by nature and will even help look after other plants around them. Of course, many of the tropical plants familiar to the aromatherapist, such as sandalwood, clove, or rosewood, are impossible to cultivate in colder climates. Nevertheless, other exotic plants such as the madonna lily or the hardy jasmine species have adapted to more temperate climates, while tender species such as citrus trees and scented pelargoniums will thrive given the protection of a greenhouse or conservatory.

In the first scented garden that I designed, I took on an already well-established garden. At the back of the house was an overgrown *potager* with a pleached linden hedge running the length of the boundary. The vegetable garden was divided in half by a line of old espaliered apple trees. I was very grateful for these traditional features, which would have taken many years to establish if I had started from scratch. I did, however, change the overall layout of this section of the garden. On one side of the apple trees, closest to the kitchen, I created a traditional herb garden laid out around a standard variegated box in the center. Herbs were planted according to species, as in the old

RIGHT: THE MINATURE CLASSICAL ROSE GARDEN – *ROSA* 'DE RESCHT' AND SCENTED PEONIES ARE IN BLOOM.

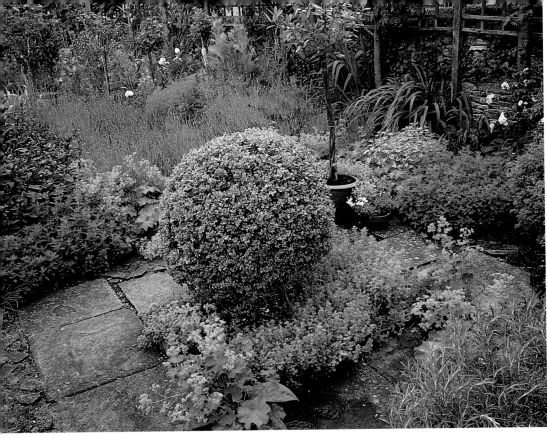

perpetually flowering cerise *Rosa* 'De Rescht' and the sumptuous, richly perfumed burgundy 'Dark Lady' (zones 5–9) as standard features. 'Louise Odier,' (zones 6–9) 'Comte de Chambord,' (zones 4–9) and David Austin's 'Cottage Rose' (zones 5–9) formed a backcloth of more demure, pink shrubs beneath. White tobacco plants

monastic physic gardens, with all the types of sage in one bed, thyme in another, and artemisias, lavenders, and mints, etc., each in their own bed. As time passed, I became more relaxed and interplanted old roses, peonies, and irises among the more classic medicinal and culinary herbs. I also allowed the fennel to self-seed freely, along with lady's mantle, marigold, and frilly pink opium poppies.

Then I planted a line of fragrant standard roses to further divide the herb garden from a scented cutting garden. Here I mixed aromatic bulbs, such as madonna and regal lilies, with scented annuals such as sweet williams, stocks, and heliotrope or cherry pie. Sweet peas were trained, rather unsuccessfully, up the wires of the old apple trees.

The front of the house was also largely overgrown, but here again there were redeeming features that were retained and incorporated into the new design. Two ancient wisterias graced the south wall near the entrance porch – although the white species (*Wisteria sinensis* 'Alba') (zones 5–9) flowered profusely with a divine perfume and the purple barely at all. I planted the rose 'Zéphirine Drouhin' (zones 5–9) in the semi-shade by the gate and the hardy jasmine (*Jasminum officinale*) (zones 8–10) to climb over the porch. A rather ragged box hedge formed a rectangular compound outside the front door. I fed and renovated it, and eventually it matured to form the basis for a miniature, classical rose garden with several

(*Nicotiana sylvestris*) (A) and a selection of fragrant peonies, the latter tending to become rather overblown, were also used to fill out the bed.

In the very dry, sunny raised bed against the porch I massed various varieties of cistus, including *C. ladanifer*, not only because they looked stunning tumbling over the old stone, but also because they were one of the few plants that seemed to thrive in such a free-draining site. On very hot days, they exuded a lovely rich, almost resinlike aroma – the so-called labdanum gum from cistus is used extensively in perfumery. The small patio area in front of the house was defined by a wooden arbor hung with the rosy-leaved rambling rose 'Albertine' (zones 4–9) together with a common honeysuckle *Lonicera periclymenum* 'Graham Thomas' and the pink-flowered jasmine (*Jasminum* x *stephanense*) (zones 8–10). They gave a lovely scent to the whole seating area, especially in the evening. Low-growing violets, old-fashioned 'Mrs Sinkins' (zones 5–9) pinks, and, close by the paving, hardy scented cyclamen (*C. cilicium*) (zones 6–9) sprung up at their base, flowering at different times of the year.

On the sheltered face of the house, I planted a spreading *Fremontodendron* 'California Glory,' which bore dramatic yellow flowers from spring until early fall (no scent, but gorgeous), together with the strange and exotic-looking evergreen chocolate vine (*Akebia quinata*), which has unusual vanilla-scented ruby-red flowers. Farther along I planted the exquisite evergreen scented clematis, *C. armandii* 'Apple Blossom,' which virtually covered the entire wall in a single season, plus *Trachelospermum jasminoides* – not a "true" jasmine yet bearing white star-shaped flowers with a pervasive jasminelike perfume and glossy evergreen leaves. A half-hardy honeysuckle (*Lonicera etrusca*) (zones 7–9) was trained around the bedroom window with the climbing white rose 'Souvenir de la Malmaison' (zones 5–8) for night scent. Since this was the most sheltered spot in the garden, I also risked planting slightly tender species at their feet, such as lemon verbena (*Aloysia triphylla*), the delicate fringed lavender (*Lavandula dentata*), a ginger plant (*Hedychium gardnerianum*), and the delicate pink Darjeeling daphne, *D. bholua*. All survived the winters (with a little help from thin spun polyester) – in fact, the lemon verbena turned into the most beautiful, healthy shrub with a very refreshing and uplifting perfume.

The greatest challenge was landscaping a sloping piece of land next to the seating area. In the end, this was developed into a number of different paved terraces beside stone steps leading down toward the greenhouse, with a wide bed at the bottom. Mediterranean mountain plants such as the French white lavender (*L. stoechas* f. *leucantha*) (zones 8–9), prostrate rosemary, santolina, and thyme were planted in gravel between the paving to create a naturalistic feel to the whole area. The wide bed was used to display larger scented specimens such as the fast-growing tree lupine (*Lupinus arboreus*) (zones 8–9), the hazy-blue spires of Russian sage (*Perovskia atriplicifolia*) (zones 6–9), the winter-flowering shrubby honeysuckle (*Lonicera fragrantissima*) (zones 5–8), and the more unusual burning bush (*Dictamnus albus*), with its strange minty aroma. The evergreen and highly decorative *Choisya ternata* 'Sundance' with its golden aromatic leaves and white scented flowers, dark green-leaved mint bushes (*Prostanthera cuneata*), and the dramatic sculptural form of a *Yucca gloriosa* (zones 7–10), with sharp daggerlike leaves and scented ivory flowers, provided year-round interest. Still larger shrubs such as the yellow-flowered Tibetan tree peony (*Paeonia delavayi* var. *ludlowii*) (zones 5–8) and the stunning reddish-orange variety *P. delavayi* (zones 5–8), together with the lovely orange-blossom *Philadelphus* 'Boule d'Argent,' (zones 5–8) the purple-leaved elder *Sambucus nigra* 'Guincho Purple,' and the fragile lilac (*Syringa* x *persica*) (zones 3–7) were sited

farther back beside the boundary wall. The whole bed was underplanted with bulbs and irises, including the spectacular scented tall bearded iris 'Langport Claret,' (zones 3–8) the popular daylily 'Golden Chimes,' (zones 3–9) and a selection of oriental lilies. The grassy area beyond was scattered with early spring-flowering bulbs – my favorite being the simple poet's narcissus (*N. poeticus*).

Some years later, I had the opportunity to develop a completely different kind of scented retreat right in the center of an urban environment. Here, my aims and possibilities were more challenging, since there was no yard, only a sunny balcony. I immediately decided to use the opportunity to try growing all sorts of tender species, because the city provided a warmth and level of protection that was out of the question in the open countryside. Mimosa (*Acacia dealbata*) with its yellow ball-like flowers, the graceful *Nerium oleander*, even the wax flower (*Hoya carnosa*) (T) survive outside all winter with the minimum of protection on the balcony – and indeed look better for it. Standard grapefruit and lemon trees, the former grown from seed, are over-wintered indoors, but have benefited from being out all summer. Inside, the exquisite gardenia (*G. augusta*), exotic scented orchids such as *Dendrobium nobilis*, (T) and the white waxy-flowered *Stephanotis floribunda* thrive as long as they are kept out of direct sunlight. Culinary and classical herbs including lavender, rosemary, parsley, and basil are grown in pots outside the kitchen window. Even in the center of a city, it is possible to create a scented sanctuary – a place to nourish the soul and soothe body and mind.

In the first half of this book, we will look at scented gardens throughout history and explore ways of creating a unique and personal fragrant environment. In Chapter 7, we will be looking at a number of specific aromatic plants in greater depth. I have been very disciplined in choosing each plant portrait for this section: apart from being used specifically to produce an essential oil, each plant must also add interest to a garden through its esthetic appearance and practicality. These specifically selected plants provide what I consider to be the basis of a modern aromatic garden – a beautiful (yet useful) haven of tranquility with an emphasis on the healing and transformational qualities of scent.

1 history of the scented garden

RIGHT: AN ENCLOSED COURT-
YARD AT THE FOURTEENTH
CENTURY ALHAMBRA PALACE,
GRANADA, SPAIN.

the persian garden as an image of paradise

The very concept of creating a scented garden is rooted in ancient history. From the earliest times, the culinary and medicinal properties of herbs and aromatic plants have made them a vital part of human existence. From material necessity to esthetic pleasure is a short step, and historical records suggest that the first scented gardens were planted within the enclosed courtyards of Persian palaces over 2,500 years ago.

ABOVE: A MINATURE PERSIAN GARDEN FROM A
FIFTEENTH-CENTURY WATERCOLOR PAINTING.

These gardens were made not only to delight the senses, but also to provide a spiritual sanctuary, quite apart from any practical benefits they conferred. Since the Koran taught that it was mankind's duty to conserve and revere nature as part of the divine creation, these sacred gardens were looked upon as a means of recreating and experiencing heaven on earth.

The term "paradise" derives from the Greek word *paradeisos*, which in turn was based on the Persian, *pairidaeza*, literally "surrounded by walls." This referred to an enclosed garden of pleasure… an earthly paradise where secular and sacred elements were intertwined. The classical Persian garden was constructed to a formal plan within a square or rectangle, having a fountain in the center from which four streams issued – one in each direction. The whole area was then carefully planted with fruit-bearing and fragrant trees, aromatic herbs, and

flowers, for the Persians required three main qualities in their paradise gardens: running water, shade, and scent.

Within the Islamic tradition, water was naturally considered to be a very precious element within the garden, since the surrounding area was frequently dominated by desert or wilderness. Shade, of course, was also essential as a place of refuge from the burning heat of the sun. The patterns of light and shadow created by decorative screens and doorways, which were frequently used to create different "rooms" within the overall layout, also played an intrinsic part in the construction of these traditional designs. Scent within the garden may seem by comparison to be less "essential" than the absolute necessity for water and shade. Yet for much of the ancient world, including Persia, perfume was held in such high esteem that it was virtually seen as being as vital to life as food or water! In the words of the prophet Mohammed:

Three things of the world which I love the most are women, perfume, and prayer.

In the Islamic esoteric text *The Jasmine of the Fedeli d'amore*, Ruzbehan describes the celestial world as being suffused with a wondrous scent that was associated with the presence of the divinity. The evocative power of perfume was also understood as the silent language of passion and human emotion, and was valued as a sacred tool of transformation. Scented plants, therefore, endowed the early Persian paradise garden with a very special quality by providing a direct "bridge" from the mundane to the heavenly and elevated it from being simply an earthly domain into a *pairidaeza* – a paradise realm. Like an oasis, these fragrant, fertile gardens came to represent a miraculous place of refuge or a haven within a hostile environment. Indeed, like most early gardens, they are found within courtyards or are surrounded by low buildings, rather than lying outside the domestic compound, simply because the outside world was such an unsafe place.

The Persian gardens also had strongly symbolic connotations and used intricate and exquisite patterns in their design. Like a microcosm of the universe, the formally constructed streams and

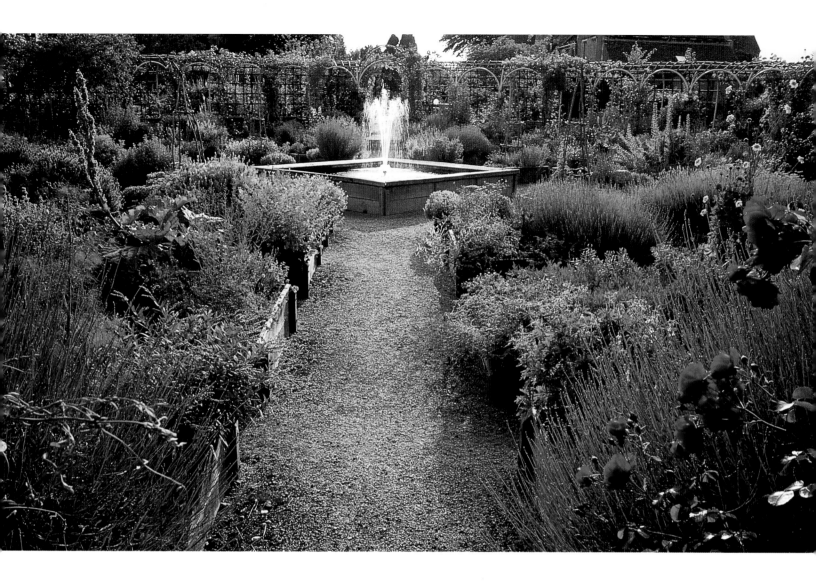

canals represented the rivers of life flowing to the four corners of the earth, while the fountain issued from the heart at the center. Cypress trees were associated with death and eternal life, while fruit trees, especially the orange, were planted in great numbers due to their rich and bountiful imagery. In Cordoba, the surviving tenth-century mosque gardens of the Court of Oranges still has 100 orange trees standing in perfect rows beside the water channels.

But above all, it was the fragrant rose that was held in the highest esteem and is still found in all Islamic-style gardens, especially since many legends link the rose with the prophet Mohammed. The famous Persian mystic Avicenna dedicated a whole book to the virtues and spiritual qualities of the rose. Roses and jasmine still abound in the gardens around the Taj Mahal in India, which shows a strong classical Persian influence.

Practical necessity and a highly refined esthetic sensibility were combined with a profound reverence for nature and a sense of the sacred to create a sanctuary – not away from the world, but within it. Earthly pleasure and divine inspiration partook of the same nature: thus, these early classical, scented gardens were built by the nobility of Persia not only to offer relief from the desert heat, but also to provide a secluded place for inner contemplation as well as for amorous dalliance! It is still possible to get a sense of the classical splendor of these ancient Persian masterpieces of design by visiting the Alhambra Palace in Granada, built in southern Spain for the Moorish rulers of the fourteenth century. Here, the soothing sound of water running over stone, the graceful images of trees and arches reflected in still pools, and the heady scent of roses, jasmine, and lilies wafting on the warm breeze retain their power to transport the soul to another world.

fragrant backdrop for the exotic flowering plants, herbs, and trees.

Cedar of Lebanon was also used to make the caskets for embalmed Egyptian kings because of its fine fragrance and great durability. Indeed, the ancient Egyptians were renowned for their knowledge and expertise on aromatic plants, especially regarding their medicinal, cosmetic and ritual applications. In gardens on the banks of the Nile, they cultivated sweet-smelling plants, herbs, and spices to provide fresh material for their daily requirements, since natural aromatic preparations were considered an intrinsic part of everyday life. One of the first depicted plant expeditions (c. 1495 B.C.), shown on a wall painting at Karnak, is in search of the incense tree for Queen Hatshepsut. The Egyptians' exuberant love of nature is evident from the carvings in their temples and their garlanded deities. No fewer than 256 different species are depicted on the walls of the "Botanical Garden," a room in the temple of Amun at Karnak.

The Egyptian priesthood also attached great importance to gardens as places of contemplation. Thus we find walled gardens attached to the temples as tranquil places of retreat. More importantly perhaps in botanic terms was the fact that known medicinal plants were grown in these temple gardens and form the earliest-known basis for the botanic garden. The Egyptian Papyrus Ebers manuscript, a *materia medica* written about 1552 B.C. (in the time of Moses), contains numerous descriptions of fragrant plants, aromatic remedies, and their methods of use. Saffron was employed as a condiment and perfume material; galbanum, mastic, and eaglewood were used for

early aromatic gardens

Some of the most famous early aromatic gardens are the Hanging Gardens of Babylon, which were built by Nebuchadnezzar II for his wife in the sixth century B.C. Greek descriptions of these fabulous gardens, which were supported on stone columns and irrigated by streams to keep the terraces moist, depict an image of paradise much like the Persian ideal, with running water, shade, and scent. Aromatic wood from the cedar of Lebanon was used extensively in building these gardens and must have created a highly fumigation and purification purposes; and cannabis or Indian hemp was used as a sedative and for its narcotic properties. The scented oil from the blue lotus was considered sacred and offered to the Pharaohs in their tombs along with narcissi and other aromatic materials. Frankincense and myrrh, especially, were considered invaluable plants throughout the whole of the ancient world, because their fragrant gum-resins formed the basis for most incense. The famous *kyphi* of Egypt, for example, was a liquid incense recipe whose fragrance, according to Plutarch, "allayed anxieties and brightened dreams and was made of those things which delight most in the night." This precious perfume was made from a mixture of more than 16 aromatic substances including juniper, cardamom, calamus, cyperus (a fragrant grass), mastic, saffron, acacia, cinnamon, peppermint, myrrh, and henna.

In Cairo, street sellers sang of henna, "Oh odours of Paradise: oh flowers of Henna": these were tiny white, very fragrant flowers that were also used to produce the enticing perfume *cyprinum*. Cleopatra drenched her Nile barge with cyprinum to create an aromatic greeting for Mark Anthony. Henna is also the "camphire" mentioned in the *Song of Solomon:*

A garden enclosed is my sister, my spouse; a spring shut up, a fountain sealed. Thy plants are an orchard of pomegranates with pleasant fruits: camphire and spikenard, saffron, calamus and cinnamon, with trees of frankincense, myrrh and aloes with all the chief spices. (Rosemary Verey, *The Scented Garden*)

The enclosed scented garden described in the Bible in the Song of Solomon depicts a sensual paradise where sacred and secular pleasure are united, and provides a model for the medieval *hortus conclusus*. Likewise, the Garden of Eden originally showed God and man in a state of complete harmony: in the Talmud, when Adam walked in the Garden of Eden on the first day, "he smelled wonderful scents and enjoyed beautiful sights." But this sense of blissful ease was not to last, for both

Judaism and Christianity refer back to the Garden as a place of original ease, a lost paradise, where humanity and nature were in accord with the divine, God.

In the beginning, God created a garden called Eden. Eden is traditionally located in Mesopotamia, probably in the northern part of the region since an apple tree was able to grow there without irrigation. Before the fall, Eden was a fertile, fragrant oasis of delight, magically calm except for the sweet sounds of water and laughter. Since the dawn of civilisation, human kind has ceaselessly endeavoured to recreate this mythical paradise. (G. Van Zuylen, *Visions of Paradise*)

This is doubtless the root of our search to create an arcadian paradise over the centuries: an attempt to recreate a sense of perfect harmony. This is even more relevant today when the pressure and problems facing both the individual and society at large seem to be increasing. Britain's Prince Charles finds his garden at Highgrove in Gloucestershire:

… a place of escape from the noise, rush and often the brutality of the world. It is a place where both humans and wildlife can take sanctuary. The garden in this way can become a glimpse of Paradise; a sacred space where humanity, nature and the Divine meet in harmony. (Martin Palmer and David Manning, *Sacred Gardens*)

the greek and roman legacy

The concise botanical knowledge and skill of the ancient Egyptians was developed by several outstanding Greek men of learning, many of whom studied at the great library of Alexandria. Herodotus and Democrates, who visited Egypt during the fifth century B.C. also transmitted directly what they had learned about perfumery and natural therapeutics from the Egyptian physicians. Hippocrates, who was born in Greece about 460 B.C. and is universally revered as the "Father of Medicine," prescribed various aromatic remedies; indeed, from Greek medical practice there is derived the term "iatralypte," from the physician who cured exclusively through the use of aromatic preparations. Later, Theophrastus (371–287 B.C.) described over 550 species of plants and the distinguishing nature of scents in his *Enquiry into Plants*, written about 340 B.C. Many familiar fragrant flowers and herbs are mentioned in this work, such as narcissi and lilies, but it is Dioscorides (A.D.40–90) who is better known for his *De Materia Medica*, which described the medicinal use of over 600 plants.

By the fourth century B.C., the Greeks were also cultivating flower gardens dedicated to the gods, and these in turn influenced gardening in Rome. Both the Greek and Roman visions of the ideal garden were influenced by the classical Persian paradise garden, and were usually laid out to a formal design with fruit-bearing trees, herbs, and running water. Many aromatic plants were named after nymphs or lovers in Greek legend, such as Artemis or Narcissus. According to myth, it was Apollo who taught the healer Aesclepius that the fragrant lily-of-the-valley could be used as a tonic for the heart. The favored flower of the Greeks, however, was the rose – the flower of Aphrodite, the Goddess of Love.

Sadly, under the Romans the rose later became a flaunted symbol of ostentation. Nero had his banqueting floors strewn with rose petals. Roses were also used in garlands for military heroes and were considered essential to everyday life. They also enjoyed a position of great prominence in the Roman garden, which was otherwise mainly given over to aromatic herbs. In their pursuit of sensuous pleasure, the Romans devoted an entire street in Capua simply for the manufacture of different types of scented substances, especially rosewater.

The Roman knowledge of herbs and aromatic plants was derived mainly from the Greeks, in particular from Dioscorides. Their horticultural knowledge also spread throughout the Roman Empire, and much of this knowledge was later preserved in the monasteries. During the conquest of Britain, the Romans carried with them a number of flowering fragrant fruit trees, such as the cherry, pear, quince, and peach, and introduced many other familiar plants from their colonies along the Mediterranean coast. Among these were such well-known ones as chervil, chives, parsley, rue, onion, fennel, rosemary, southernwood, borage, sage, and thyme. Such plants adapted well to more temperate climates and formed the basis for the "herbaries" or herb gardens of the great monasteries that sprang up all over Europe in medieval times. This herbal legacy bequeathed by the Romans also proved invaluable for the development of herbal medicine in Britain. The earliest English Herbal, written about the time of the Norman conquest and still preserved in the British Museum, owes its origin to a book written by a Roman doctor, Apuleius Platonicus.

the medieval monastic garden

During the Middle Ages, the monasteries not only served as spiritual centers for the community; they were also seats of learning. The study of plants was one of the main areas of intellectual endeavor, since herbal medicine was the most common method of treating illness. Concern for physical healing was a mark of Christian philosophy and thus based primarily on practical considerations. So the "cloister" garden developed, devoted to growing useful medicinal

ABOVE: THE CLOISTER GARDEN AT THE FIFTEENTH-
CENTURY MONASTERY EL PARRAL, SEGOVIA, SPAIN.

yet Rome still proved pivotal in its horticultural influence in Britain. Water was frequently found in these gardens, as in the early Islamic paradise gardens, and the monks could meditate on the elements. The formal ordering of the cloister garden was also conducive to a state of restful ease – a tranquil haven where the monks or nuns could find the peace that "passeth all understanding." Sometimes an orchard was planted at the sacred eastern end and was used as a place for contemplation on death and the eternal life. The "physic" garden was generally found north of the eastern end of the church, or sometimes in the cloisters or courtyards besides the church. The famous Benedictine monastery of St. Gall in Switzerland, founded in the year 610 A.D., served for centuries as an ideal model for monastic gardens throughout Europe. Here, the cloister garth provides the central feature or focal point of the whole design and was divided into four equal sections by footpaths:

*The garth is square, an ideal plan based on the description of the Temple built by the Israelites. (*Aben and de Wit, *The Enclosed Garden)*

Traditional cloister garths can still be found throughout Europe and America, for example at Wells Cathedral, Somerset, in England; at the Basilica of St. Francis, Assisi, in Italy; and at the National Cathedral in Washington, DC. Within the enclosure, as at St. Galls, there were generally two herb gardens: one was the physic garden or infirmary garden, planted with healing medicinal herbs, the second was the kitchen garden. Here, culinary herbs for the table, such as thyme, parsley, rosemary, and mint, would be grown, as well as vegetables – see Chapter 2. Information about medicinal and culinary herbs was exchanged extensively between monasteries over this period. Abbot Benedict of Aniane in Languedoc in France is known to have corresponded with his colleages in Germany and England, and exchanged medicinal plants with Alcuin of York around the year 800. In a letter to Charlemagne of France, Alcuin wrote of his hope that:

The French may learn the wonders of gardening from the British, so that a paradise – "a garden enclosed" – may flourish not just in York but also in

herbs and aromatic plants, as well as providing a place of contemplation for the monks.

This style of garden, known in medieval England as the "cloister garth," was a large, enclosed garden with a beautifully kept green lawn in the center of the monastery or cathedral. Surrounded by stone cloisters with a covered arcade, it provided a place where the monks could stroll in leisurely contemplation or sit at peaceful leisure and view the passing day.

These cloister garths were formally laid out, and often divided into four sections similar to Roman villa gardens. It was originally as a reaction against urbanized Rome that monastic Christianity had arisen with its keen interest in agriculture and gardening –

Tours, and that there might be "the plants of paradise" with the fruits of the orchard. (Palmer and Manning, *Sacred Gardens*)

At the same time, despite barbarian invasions, contact with the Islamic world encouraged migration of both ideas and plants from Spain and from the East. It was through the influence of the Byzantine church, however, that the Middle Eastern idea of the aromatic garden found its way into the very heart of European culture, initially in the form of a small paradise garden or flower garden. The flower garden generally lay behind the altar to the east of the church, which itself faced east – thereby facing Jerusalem and the rising sun. This garden was placed in the care of the sacristan – the monk in charge of sacred objects such as the high altar. This shows how important the medieval church considered aromatic and sweet-smelling flowers, which were valued both as symbolic votive offerings and for their intrinsic beauty.

This garden was usually round or semicircular in structure and provided the sacred aromatic flowers and herbs for decorating the altar. The idea of a walled, perfumed garden was symbolically associated with the Garden of Eden, the original paradise, and was upheld in biblical imagery such as in the *Song of Solomon*.

In 1260 Albertus Magnus, a Dominican monk, specified the requirements of a perfect pleasure garden in much the same terms as its Persian

ABOVE: A PROFUSION OF OLD FASHIONED-SCENTED FLOWERS, INCLUDING IRISES, SWEET ROCKET, AND ROSES, AT THE OLD CHAPEL GARDENS, ENGLAND.

counterpart, having a fountain at the center and being redolent with perfume....

... every sweet-smelling herb such as rue, and sage and basil, and likewise all sorts of flowers, as the violet, columbine, lily, rose, iris and the like ... behind the lawn there may be great diversity of medicinal and scented herbs, not only to delight the senses of smell by their perfume but to refresh the sight with their flowers.

These medieval monastic gardens had a strong sense of the symbolic connotations of plants, flowers, and trees. For example, lungwort (*Pulmonaria offficinalis*) was so called because its leaves, which are speckled and marked, were considered to resemble diseased lungs. Sweet violets represented humility, and the earliest of the cultivated lilies, the fragrant white Madonna lily (*Lilium candidum*), was linked with the Virgin Mary. Above all, the rose was held in the highest esteem. The red apothecary's rose (*Rosa gallica* var. *officinalis*), was also closely linked with the Virgin Mary and with Christ's blood. There was a widespread cult of planting "Mary gardens," which featured wildflower meadows: today they are echoed in Christian Marian gardens, which use statues of the Virgin Mary together with lilies and roses, her traditional plants.

the secular pleasure garden

The secular pleasure gardens were the domain of the nobility, and later in the Middle Ages became more linked with sensual delight than

LEFT: "SMELL" – ONE IN A SERIES OF DELICATE TAPESTRIES ON THE THEME OF THE LADY AND THE UNICORN.

contemplation of the eternal, as in the monasteries. These gardens were called *hortus deliciarum*, or the "garden of delight," a scented sanctuary where men and women could meet discreetly in a romantic setting as opposed to the sacred *hortus conclusus* of the church. Medieval courtly love, as we often see it depicted and described in poetry, was played out in these fragrant pleasure gardens. Much idealized romantic literature, such as the French allegorical poem *Le Roman de la Rose* (fifteenth century), contains descriptions of a lover meeting his lady in her private, secret garden and in this case, warning of the dangers of profane love.

...there was always an abundance of flowers. There were very beautiful violets, fresh, young periwinkles; there were white and red flowers, and wonderful yellow ones. The earth was very artfully decorated and painted with flowers of various colours and sweetest perfumes. (Guillaume de Lorris and Jean de Meung c. 1235–1280, from *Visions of Paradise*.)

These secluded gardens featured high trellising, overhung with fragrant climbers (often roses or sweet-scented climbers) and scented chamomile seats for lovers. Hidden rose arbors became the background for courtly love and romance in a highly stylized setting. They often contained a rose garden and a water feature such as a fountain, or a clear pool. Sensuality rather than spirituality became the vogue, and fragrant plants emphasized pleasure rather than

being transcendent vehicles to the Divine.

Ironically, according to Sue Minter, Curator of the Chelsea Physic Garden, the pleasure garden was originally a *"secret garden associated with the Virgin Mary. The garden represented her virginity and its flowers and fruits, the flowering of her virginity. It was paradise found, as against the paradise lost of the lost Eden."* (Sue Minter, *The Healing Garden*)

Clearly though, the sacred garden of Mary had lost its primarily religious connotations, and paradise found therefore appeared at this time in history to be linked more with worldly than divine love!

Medieval tapestries also frequently depicted courtly gardens with seasonal flowers growing wild in grass: "flowery meads," which were highly popular in the Middle Ages. These were places of relaxation and romantic dalliance, and included all the flowers seen throughout the year. Some of the most exquisitely beautiful tapestries showing flowery meads are those depicting a lady and a unicorn, from the series of *The Lady and the Unicorn*. Here the lady and her maid are shown fashioning a crown with clove-scented carnations or "gilliflowers," which were extremely popular at the time because of their spicy fragrance. Carnations were also associated with betrothal and marriage on account of their potent, seductive fragrance. These tapestries, hanging in the Musée de Cluny in Paris, were woven around 1500 and were known as *millefleurs*, meaning "a thousand flowers." They portrayed an abundance of sweetly scented flowers: roses, violets, wallflowers, pansies, and forget-me-nots. Flowering fruit trees and aromatic herbs were also shown, but always growing in the flowering mead, not in formal beds.

the renaissance influence

In the middle of the fourteenth century, the Italian poet Giovanni Boccaccio provided a link between the medieval garden and the splendors to come in his collection of tales, the *Decameron*. In one story, "The Valley of the Ladies," he describes a walled circular garden with a flower-studded lawn (the classical medieval *hortus conclusus*) with "a fountain of pure white marble." The statue at the center of the fountain issues forth a jet of water, which is circulated in cleverly wrought little channels, a forerunner of the art of hydraulics, a popular feature of the Renaissance.

The influence of the Renaissance, and its revived interest in classical antiquity, which began in Italy in the later part of the thirteenth century, influenced the whole of Europe. It brought with it not only profound changes in thought regarding buildings, but also garden and park designs. The basis of this was the classical Italian villa garden in which were found labyrinths, box topiary cut in elaborate designs, water and fountains showing Arabic influence, and pots filled with fragrant flowers. The Italian artist Giorgio Vasari described the Villa Medici, near Florence, as "the most magnificent and ornamental garden in Europe." The gardens of Villa d'Este at Tivoli, begun in 1550 and completed 30 years later, are undoubtedly the most spectacular of the Renaissance period with their elaborate fountains and intricate terracing. But Renaissance gardens were not simply grand statements of ostentation: in the beautiful Pallazzo Farnese at Caprarola, a *giardino segreto* or secret garden (a descendant from the *hortus conclusus*) provided a haven of tranquility and intimacy away from the vast sweeping vistas of the rest of the garden. In fact, the Renaissance gardens incorporated most of the features of medieval gardens: roses, scented arbors, grassy banks, fountains, walkways, hedged walls, and mounts. Aromatic box also was used extensively in topiary and for edging and hedging. The Renaissance garden was thus fundamentally the medieval garden within a classical and expanded form.

ABOVE: A FORMAL KNOT GARDEN, FROM ABOVE, AT SOUTHAMPTON UNIVERSITY MEDICAL GARDENS, ENGLAND.

In England, the Renaissance influence led to the establishment of the "formal" garden, which used geometrical shapes to show the domination of man over nature. Early Tudor gardens were characterized by the square knot garden, which was divided into four. Knot gardens had existed in the late medieval period, but it was with the Tudors and the influence of France, and later in the Elizabethan age, that knot gardens acquired supremacy. These gardens were placed below the principal room of the house or palace so they could be viewed from above to the best effect. They were a vital element of all royal gardens. In 1613, according to Gervase Markham in *The English Husbandmen*, there were two types of knots: the open knot which was planted with aromatic herbs such as thyme, hyssop, rosemary, or lavender, then simply filled with colored earth. The closed knots used the spaces between the knots to display single-colored flowers, such as violets, sweet williams, primroses, or gillyflowers. The knots show a very close relationship to embroidery and marquetry, with the

earliest designs found in Thomas Hyll's *The Profitable Art of Gardening* (1568). Looking down from above, these knots would have created a swirling, patterned aromatic display. A recent re-creation of a sixteenth-century knot garden at Barnsley House in Gloucestershire, England, is made of green and gold box, intertwined with germander.

By the sixteenth century, gardens in England, France, and the Netherlands shared many characteristics. Charles III and Henry II of France were deeply impressed by the Italian villas and their gardens, as was Henry VIII of England. They all saw the garden as a direct expression of the strength of the monarchy and regal power, and some of the most outstanding and magnificent gardens of the period were the great heraldic gardens. In England these were Hampton Court, Whitehall, and Nonsuch, constructed for Henry VIII. All three gardens display ornate painted and gilded wooden heraldry, symbols of the House of Tudor, together with aspects of the medieval garden such as fountains, roses, arbors, mounts, and walkways. Both Hampton Court and Whitehall showed a marked French influence. Whitehall had walkways lined with low-growing scented herbs (referred to as "spices" in descriptions of the time) and both had extensive orchards. Nonsuch no longer exists and was not completed by the time of Henry VIII's death, but was intended to be the most princely of all his palaces. The garden was a series of courtyards opening one onto the other, and according to Thomas Plattner in 1599, it was suitably named "for there is not its equal in England." In Elizabethan times, under Lord Lumley it became one of the most outstanding gardens of the times. Nonsuch had 12 arbors, a maze with unusually high hedges, an orchard, and a knot garden. Such royal gardens were gardens of pleasure with sweetly scented roses and fragrant fruit trees, besides the knots and formal walks. In 1509 Stephen Hawes, in *The History of Grand Amour and la Bell Pucell*, describes the early Tudor royal gardens:

Than in we wente to the garden gloryous, Lyke to a place of pleasure most solacyous.

It was largely through the influence of Catherine de Medici, wife to King Henry II, that Italian ideas were brought to bear on French gardening practices at this time. The key to the new French style was the ornamental *parterre* or garden bed, which was usually fashioned using intricate box hedging. Although knot gardens had been an intrinsic part of the Italian Renaissance garden, the French refined their design using

elaborate planting schemes in what came to be known as *broderie*, since they resembled a piece of finely made embroidery. These were best viewed from above, as were the English gardens of the Tudor and Elizabethan period, but here they were less romantic and more formalized and geometric in style than their British counterparts.

The first *parterre de broderie* was made by Jaques Mollet at the end of the sixteenth century at Anet, but the most prominent French garden of the period was the Paris Jardin de Tuileries commissioned by Catherine de Medici. Pierre de Nôtre designed the fabulous *parterres* nearest the palace, while his grandson André became one of the most influential garden designers in history. It was he who conceived the great gardens at Vaux, constructed on a major cross axis with a central fountain reminiscent of the Persian paradise ideal. Later, he provided the genius behind the gardens at the palace of Versailles, for the young Louis XIV. The Versailles gardens, whose grand formal layout corresponded to the four points of the compass, took the whole of Europe by storm: rulers in Austria, Germany, Spain, and even the Russian king, Peter the Great, wanted their own version of Versailles! Le Nôtre's influence reached as far as America, for Pierre L'Enfant's design for Washington, DC, is based on one of Le Nôtre's favorite themes – the *patte d'oie* or "goosefoot pattern," describing a series of radiating avenues.

Louis XIV, the Sun King, was in fact infatuated with all aspects of gardening. At Versailles he commissioned a special *potager* incorporating fruit trees, vegetables, herbs, and fragrant flowers – a project that took over five years to complete. He also personally sponsored plant expeditions to bring back specimens from the New World and Far East. Exotic plants would later inundate the whole of Europe as world horizons expanded over the following centuries.

LEFT: PORTRAIT OF AN AURICULA.
ABOVE: HIGH WALLS SURROUND THE PHYSIC GARDEN
AT FONTREVEUX ABBEY IN THE LOIRE VALLE, FRANCE.

The late sixteenth and seventeenth centuries saw French Protestants, the Huguenots, fleeing from religious persecution and settling in East Anglia, Lancashire, and southern England. They brought with them specialized gardening knowledge and many new scented flowers, and helped revive an interest in horticulture at the time that it was waning. They cultivated flowers specifically for their esthetic appeal and were known as "florists": their aim was to create perfect blooms with the best color and most fragrance. There were eight flowers in particular attributed to them: the hyacinth, auricula, carnation, pink, ranunculus, tulip, polyanthus, and anemone. To them we owe the wide diversity of pinks, carnations, polyanthus, and auriculas that can still be found in old gardens today.

Voyages of discovery now brought new species to Europe, including many well-known scented species such as narcissus and tuberose, which were propagated in the new botanical gardens. The Flemish botanist, Charles de L'Ecluse, was the first scientific horticulturalist and served as the superintendent of the Leiden Botanic Garden. He cultivated many exotic Middle Eastern bulbs and tubers, including hyacinths, irises, lilies, gladioli, sunflowers, and especially tulips – changing the face of northern European gardens forever. The ingenious devices and flamboyant designs of the late Renaissance gardens, together with the classical mystic of the medieval pleasure garden, virtually disappeared, for now plants were arranged strictly according to species and genus. The Italian gardens of Padua and Pisa were founded in 1543, and in the seventeenth century two great physic gardens were developed in England: one at Oxford, which became a botanic garden, and the other at Chelsea. The gardens at Kew in London were also originally a physic garden created in the eighteenth century by the then Princess of Wales. Other important botanical gardens were founded in Heidelberg, Montpellier, and Paris.

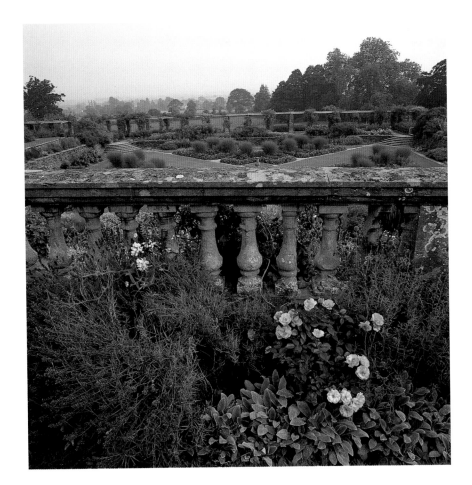

LEFT: A STRONG STRUCTURAL FRAMEWORK UNDERLIES THE LUTYENS-JEKYLL DESIGN AT HESTERCOMBE HOUSE, ENGLAND.

to the house, but fragrance was secondary to color and dramatic massed effect.

It was not until the nineteenth century with William Robinson, more renowned perhaps as a horticultural writer than a gardener, and Gertrude Jekyll, who combined both strongly esthetic and practical gardening knowledge, that sweetly scented planting came back into fashion in Britain and then America. William Robinson devoted a whole chapter to fragrance in his classic work *The English Flower Garden:*

A man who makes a garden should have a heart for plants that have the gift of sweetness as well as beauty of form and colour... No one may be richer in fragrance than the wise man who plants hardy shrubs and flowering trees... families of fragrant things.

In *The Wild Garden*, Robinson encouraged the natural development and respect of different plant forms, flowers, and foliage, and it was his insistence on informality and his concept of permanent planting that marked the beginning of the garden as we know it today. Although primarily known for her color-coded planting, Gertrude Jekyll was also responsible for reviving a number of fragrant old plants that had fallen out of fashion, including several old-fashioned rose varieties. Together they made an enormous impact on the development of English, European, and American gardens in the twentieth century.

Beginning in 1946, another British designer, Vita Sackville-West, began writing regular columns for the *Observer* in London and transformed the direction of contemporary gardening ideas. Her greatest masterpiece was undoubtedly the garden at Sissinghurst, still considered the most quintessential British garden, which was styled around a series of

contemporary influences

Sadly, by the eighteenth century, scented plants had become undesirable in fashionable gardens. This was due to the influence of the landscape movement, designed and implemented in Britain by "Capability" Brown, Humphrey Repton, and others from 1720 on. They systematically destroyed the old formal gardens of the earlier centuries, such as the Elizabethan garden at Longleat, to replace them with the landscaped garden. Scented flowers were banished from sight and were kept at a distance from the house or planted in walled flower gardens so as not to disturb the new sweeping designs. Later, when Repton and John Loudon did recommend plants to be grown closer to the house, they made no particular reference to scented plants, in comparison to the earlier enthusiasm and ardor of the sixteenth century writers. This decline continued throughout the nineteenth century in Britain with the Victorians' passion for brightly colored bedding. To the credit of the Victorians, however, they did bring flowers closer interconnecting outdoor "rooms." The inspiration for its design was derived directly from her love of Renaissance gardens, the medieval *hortus conclusus,* and from the magical walled gardens of Persia ablaze with color and endowed with wonderful scents. In many ways, Sissinghurst could be said to epitomize the ancient scented paradise ideal within a contemporary setting: the "white garden" especially, redolent with scent, is of international renown. Hidcote Manor Garden, in Gloucestershire, England, conceived by the American designer Major Lawrence Johnston who purchased the property in 1907, has also been an inspiration to gardeners internationally. Like Sissinghurst, the overall plan is based on a variety of garden "rooms" set around a central axis, and shows a definite Italian and French Renaissance influence.

The American landscape architect Nellie B. Allen (1869–1961) was particularly impressed by her visits to these English gardens, as well as Gertrude Jekyll's own garden in Surrey and Great Dixter in Sussex, laid out by Jekyll's collaborator, the English architect Edwin Lutyens. Allen's own specialties were knot gardens, geometrically designed enclosures bordered by green hedges and walled gardens that showed her love of the medieval *hortus conclusus* and the ancient

ABOVE: AN EXOTIC AMBIANCE CHARACTERIZES THIS EX-PRESIDENTIAL CALIFORNIA GARDEN.

scented Persian paradise gardens. An original watercolor design entitled *A Persian Garden* (1919), for example, shows an enclosed garden with a central pool set beside arched columns encircled by cypress trees. Ellen Shipman, who collaborated with Charles Platt on many famous gardens across the U.S., also employed the "walled garden formula," frequently using fragrant plants and symmetrical designs with a central sundial or fountain feature. Other Americans, including Helena Ely, Charles Gillette, Martha Hutcheson, Beatrix Ferrand, Louisa King, and Rose Nichols, were also influenced in their work both by the English traditional garden and by European designs – and in the case of Nichols (a better-known writer), by Moorish and Middle Eastern paradise gardens. But it is important to note that these are not the only gardening writers of the last one hundred years to have had an impact. Roy Genders' *Scented Flora of the World* first published in 1977, is a modern classic on fragrant plants, as is Rosemary Verey's *The Scented Garden* (1981), which covers a range of traditional and modern aromatic garden styles.

2 aromatic herbs for health & cooking

early herb gardens

Herbs have been used for thousands of years by all cultures alike and were the first plants to have been cultivated by mankind. The range of plants that we call herbs has, however, changed over the centuries in Europe. At one time, many familiar flowers such as pinks, peonies, roses, and irises were termed herbs, as were most of our common vegetables. In the sixteenth century, for example, carrots and onions were known as pot herbs, whereas lettuces and radishes were called salad herbs. Many aromatic plants, such as sweet woodruff (*Galium odoratum*) and meadowsweet (*Filipendula ulmaria*) were also grown purely for their household uses. Although a large proportion of herbs are scented and contain aromatic oils, this is not always the case – many herbs are not fragrant and do not contain any essential oils at all.

the medicinal or physic garden

It was in the medieval monastic gardens, however, that the first serious study of herbs took place in Europe and where herbs were grown for their medicinal, culinary, and aromatic properties. Herbal treatment was the earliest form of medicine, and consequently the main reason for growing herbs was for their therapeutic benefits. Before the advent of modern drugs, plant medicine was the principal way of combating all kinds of disease, including infections, injury – and witchcraft. The notion of the physic garden began in Europe from the sixth century on, when herb gardens were planted next to the infirmary in monasteries. Formal physic gardens were established in Italy in the sixteenth century, first in Pisa in 1543,

BELOW: THE PHYSIC GARDEN, BASED ON A DESIGN BY
GERTRUDE JEKYLL, AT KNEBWORTH HOUSE, ENGLAND.

then in Padua and Florence. Germany, France, Sweden, and the Netherlands followed suit, and the first physic garden in England was the Oxford Physic Garden, planted in 1621. After Edinburgh's Physic Garden, the Chelsea Physic Garden was founded in 1673. It is the only physic garden in Britain that has not been turned into a botanic garden and retains its original name.

The physic garden was usually a large plot with raised beds, intersected by paths, where herbs such as lavender, rue, sage, mint, and rosemary were each individually confined to a separate bed to make harvesting and identification easier. Both the physic garden and the cloister garth were based on this formal arrangement of paths and beds laid out in regular geometric shapes. The beds were often edged with pegged wooden boards to keep the soil in place, or fences of woven willow, and also featured low hedging of compact aromatic shrubs such as box, lavender, rosemary, or santolina. Many contemporary herb gardens are still based on these early physic garden designs, using either a grid or a cruciform structure – a simple cross with a central circular bed. (See Chapter 6: Planning an Aromatic Garden, for other traditional herb garden designs.)

From the Middle Ages on, significance was also given to the astrological connection between herbs and the parts of the body ruled by different planets. In his *Liber de Vita*, Marsilio Ficino (1433–1499) wrote that the sun ruled St. John's wort, rosemary, and chamomile; Mercury ruled dill, fennel, honeysuckle, and lily-of-the-valley, while Venus ruled mint, thyme, and violet. The relationship between herbalism and astrology lasted until the eighteenth century when a more pragmatic, scientific approach became prevalent.

The Doctrine of Signatures dates back even earlier, originally developed in the esoteric mystical schools of Alexandria. This idea connected the shape of a herb with its curative properties and was a doctrine much promoted by Paracelsus in the early sixteenth century. For example, wild pansy, with its heart-shaped, leaves was said to cure disorders of the heart, whereas plants whose leaves are kidney-shaped were thought to be good for the renal system.

Today, the main plants to include in a medicinal herb garden are those that can be used to make refreshing and digestive tisanes or herbal teas. These can be made at home from a wide range of plants, including linden flowers, chamomile, mint, sage, lemon balm, verbena, and fennel.

the aromatic herb garden

In the Middle Ages, scented herbs such as rosemary or lavender were widely used for alleviating damp musty smells and offsetting the effects of poor sanitation, as well as being employed in the sickroom for their antiseptic and disinfectant properties. Herbs such as the cinnamon-scented sweet rush (*Acorus calamus*) or sweet woodruff (*Galium odoratum*) were used for strewing on floors. Meadowsweet

(*Fillpendula ulmaria*) was a favorite herb of Queen Elizabeth I, who had it laid on the floors of her palaces. Others such as hyssop, lavender, sage, chamomile, and germander, which release their fragrance when trodden on, were very popular with the gentry and in churches. Bay leaves were also used to disinfect the atmosphere in churches, and chapels strewn with fresh bay leaves can still be found in Italy and parts of the Mediterranean. Professional perfumers were employed to fumigate rooms in Tudor England, while at the time of James II there was even a "Strewer of Herbs in Ordinary to his Majesty." In more modest cottages, sweet-scented apple wood was burned along with plowman's spikenard or nard (*Inula conyzae*) – a species of elecampane.

Aromatic flowers and herbal sprigs were also bound into small posies called "tussie mussies" to ward off sickness or infection, and to act as amulets while traveling. Herbs such as St. John's wort, rosemary, wormwood, mugwort, rue, and bay were all thought to have potent protective qualities, and were often planted near doors or hung by windows to ward off bad spirits. Bundles of dried herbs or aromatic powders were also used extensively to scent household items such as bedlinen, clothes, or furniture, as well as helping to keep insects and moths at bay. Potpourri was commonly made using the petals from an enormous range of flowers, including roses, bay, marjoram, rosemary and thyme, which all contain large proportions of bactericidal essential oils, were especially highly regarded in this respect, as were spices such as cloves, cardamom, cinnamon, and ginger.

marigolds, lavender, iris (orris), and lemon verbena. Perfumes, flower waters, and other cosmetic lotions concocted from specially cultivated plants were also popular, the recipes for which would be passed on from generation to generation (see Chapter 5).

In 1617, William Lawson wrote *The Countrie Housewife's Garden*. He not only described medicinal and culinary herbs, but also those which are especially valuable for the still room – where remedies, perfumes, soaps, potpourri, wines, and vinegars were prepared – and for the home. He recommended country women to have both a flower garden and a kitchen garden, and also advised mixing lavender and roses in with the vegetables. Lawson's *potager*-style arrangement, where vegetables, herbs, "still room" plants, and flowers for cutting are combined in an overall scheme, would make a good design for a modern aromatherapy garden.

the culinary herb garden

Aromatic culinary herbs have always been grown for their ability to flavor and enhance the preparation of food and drink. The preservative properties of plants were also considered to be invaluable before the advent of modern storage techniques, such as refrigeration, as were their aperitif and digestive properties. Many of the Mediterranean herbs such as

The health-giving properties of herbs have also played a part in their culinary application. In the late seventeenth century, for example, salads and herbs were considered highly important because scurvy was rife, due to a general lack of fresh fruit and vegetables in the diet. John Evelyn, the diarist, wrote a *Discourse on Sallets*, as they were known, saying that "raw Sallets and Herbs have been found to be the most sovereign Diet" to get rid of disease. "Sweet herbs" was a term that arose in the seventeenth century to describe sage, marjoram, thyme, hyssop, savory, and mint, grown in the kitchen garden, along with vegetables or "pot herbs."

The benefits of eating plenty of fresh vegetables, salads, and herbs are well recognized today, and herbs are being grown increasingly for their flavoring and therapeutic qualities. Apple mint, for example, is always useful in the kitchen and is highly aromatic. Sweet violet, pot marigold, and nasturtiums lend their flowers and leaves to salads or sweet dishes, while lemon balm, lemon verbena, and chamomile all make soothing, delicious tisanes. Angelica stalks can be candied and the leaves used in salads. Parsley and chives are invaluable for garnishing, while the subtle flavors of French tarragon and summer savory are excellent in sauces. For more exotic oriental cooking coriander (cilantro), caraway, and anise are indispensable, while juniper provides small black aromatic berries essential to game dishes. Sweet bay trees planted in containers can not only be used to mark the corners of beds or as a central feature, but along with such well-known kitchen herbs as thyme and marjoram, their leaves are intrinsic to creating a *bouqet garni.*

Herbs, of course, can also be grown for their esthetic appeal, quite apart from any medicinal or culinary usage. Although kitchen herb gardens are traditionally quite formally laid out, in the country garden culinary herbs are frequently mixed into informal beds. A modern kitchen herb garden can be based on a formally structured design, as in the early monastery gardens, or can follow a more relaxed country-garden style. The famous walled kitchen garden or *potager* at the seventeenth-century château of Miromesnil in France, for example, displays a mix of vegetables, herbs, and flowers giving the effect of "joyous simplicity and generosity." Alternatively, most culinary herbs can be grown in pots, tubs, or windowboxes which can be placed within easy reach of the kitchen door.

some kitchen herbs

In addition to the herbs listed in Chapter 7, there are a few other species to describe here that are especially valuable for their culinary and household applications.

Dill (*Anethum graveolens*) This is a hardy annual with attractive heads of golden flowers. Its leaves are similar to fennel and are delicious in salads and soups, as well as with fish. The seeds are very aromatic and can be used in wine vinegars or for making pickles. They

LEFT: FEATHERY DILL HEADS.
RIGHT: FRESH PARSLEY.

can also be steeped in water to soothe stomach upsets and hiccoughs.

Chervil (*Anthriscus cerefolium*) This herb is popular in French cooking. It enhances the flavor of other herbs and is frequently used in *bouquet garnis.* Traditionally, it is used in egg dishes and as a vegetable garnish. Its foliage is sweet, similar to aniseed. The plant has heads of white flowers and is a delicate annual that prefers light shade. Unlike dill, chervil seeds do not retain their germinating qualities long and should be sown as soon as possible after ripening.

Borage (*Borago officinalis*) This was a favored herb of the ancient world. The Romans brought it to Britain, and the Pilgrim Fathers carried it to New England in the early seventeenth century. Its leaves and flowers were steeped in wine to make a tonic – they are used today to flavor Pimms No.1. As its leaves and flowers have a mild cucumber fragrance, they are a pleasant addition to any cool drinks in summer. The blue flowers are very decorative in green or fruit salads, or floating on a fruit punch. They can also be candied. Borage is a hardy annual, easy to grow and self-seeds freely.

Parsley (*Petroselinum crispum*) This must be one of the most widely used of all culinary herbs. It is a hardy biennial, usually grown as an annual since its leaves are tough in the second year. Its seeds need moisture and warmth to germinate, and the plant likes fertile soil, preferably in full sun or dappled shade. A tip to help encourage the seeds to germinate is to pour boiling water into the earth before planting. There are different varieties: some are flat leaved and some curly. Parsley seeds are used to make essential oils. Medicinally, parsley tea is diuretic and can be used to treat bladder and kidney infections. In the kitchen it is very versatile, used for flavoring salads, soups, stews, egg, fish, and meat dishes – in fact, virtually all dishes that aren't sweet.

Salad burnet (*Sanguisorba minor*) This plant is ideal for salads as the delicate foliage has a mild cucumberlike flavor. It is tasty with vegetables like the ceiling to perfume and cool the air. It was also placed with the bedlinen to impart a fresh scent, and was used in potpourri. Its scent of newmown hay comes from its coumarin content and is most pronounced when the plant is dried. It intensifies the longer it is kept. Sweet woodruff has moth-deterrent properties and in dried form can be placed between book pages to remove musty smells.

asparagus or celery, and burnet leaves make an attractive garnish to a fruit salad or fruit cup. It is a decorative plant, too, for in sunshine the dull gray-green leaves take on a pink tinge. They last until winter, when they can also be used to flavor stews and sauces. Salad burnet grows very easily from seed, and the summer flowers are green and purple.

Sweet cicely (*Myrrhis odorata*) This is a delicate perennial herb. Its Latin name means literally "fragrant perfume." The crushed unripe green seeds were once used extensively for polishing furniture since they have a fine, nutty, aniselike aroma, and the plant is still used to make an essential oil used in perfumery work. Sweet cicely has light green, soft feathery leaves and umbels of white flowers, followed by distinctive long seed pods. It eventually reaches a height of about 3ft (1m) tall, but dies down completely over the winter. It is an attractive and useful addition to the kitchen garden: the sweet leaves can help to counteract acidity in some kinds of fruit. They can also be used to flavor soups and omelets.

Sweet woodruff (*Galium odoratum*) A delightful plant for the kitchen garden, sweet woodruff is one of the few herbs that prefer shade. It is a low-growing perennial with small white flowers, and although it is not a culinary herb, it has many household uses. The fresh leaves of sweet woodruff were once hung from

aromatic recipes

(The following recipes serve four people, unless otherwise specified)

HERBAL TEAS OR TISANES (WATER-BASED INFUSIONS)

Health-giving herbal teas or tisanes can generally be made using either fresh or dried plant material. Dried plant materials are more concentrated: 1 teaspoon of dried material equals about 3 teaspoons of fresh material. Fresh herbs are often more potent and are likely to have a higher medicinal value, but dried plants are more readily available all year round. Whenever possible, infusions should be made using fresh herbs or flowers as soon as they have been picked.

Dosage: use 1 teaspoon of dried herb or 3 teaspooons of fresh herb per cup of water. For very young children or elderly people, use half the dosage.

Simply place the herb in a china or enamel teapot and allow to steep for 10 minutes before drinking. For a more concentrated infusion, pour the water into an enamel pan and bring almost to a boil. Add the herbs and leave the pan on the heat for 10 minutes, maintaining the liquid just beneath boiling point. Drink immediately, adding honey to taste as required.

HERBAL VINEGARS AND OILS

Almost all culinary herbs can be used to flavor vinegars and oils. This has been done for centuries, particularly in Mediterranean countries. Some herbs are better suited to flavor vinegars, including basil, bay, chervil, chives, dill, fennel, garlic, juniper, lavender, lovage, marjoram, mint, oregano, rosemary, sage, savory, tarragon, and thyme. For steeping in oil, the best herbs are basil, bay, chervil, dill, fennel, garlic, juniper, lavender, lovage, marjoram, mint, parsley, rosemary, sage, savory, and thyme.

Herbal Vinegars

Use good white vinegar. Pound a handful of your favorite herb and bruise it well in a pestle and mortar. Add 1 pint (500ml) vinegar to 1 handful of herbs in a wide-necked jar, then seal. Leave for a week, then strain. Repeat the process if you want a stronger flavor. After the second week, strain to remove all the leaves and stems, and bottle the vinegar. Finally, add a few fresh sprigs of the herb for identification and a decorative effect.

Herbal Oils

Follow the method as above, but substitute the vinegar with a good-quality virgin olive oil or sunflower oil.

APPLE AND HERB SOUP

    1lb (500g) cooking apples, peeled and cored
    Celery tops, finely chopped
    $1/2$ cup brown sugar
    Cinnamon
    Cloves
    Shredded rind and juice of 1 lemon
    Fresh salad burnet leaves

Stew the apples, celery, sugar, and spices in 1 pint (500ml) water. When the apples are soft, add lemon juice and rind and cook for a few minutes longer. Leave to cool. Before serving, stir in some salad burnet leaves and decorate the soup with a few extra leaves.

DILL SAUCE

This is a seventeenth-century recipe.
    1 $1/2$ tablespoons butter
    1 $1/2$ tablespoons flour (wholewheat)
    1 $1/2$ cups hot broth
    2 tablespoons chopped fresh dill
    $1/2$ tablespoon lemon juice

    Salt and pepper
    $1/2$ tablespoon brown sugar
    l egg yolk

Melt the butter. Blend in the flour and hot broth gradually, stirring to keep a consistent mix. Add the dill, lemon juice, salt, pepper, and sugar. Cool the sauce slightly, then whisk in the egg yolk. This sauce is delicious served with roast meat, especially beef.

Good-quality bouillon powder is an acceptable substitute for homemade broth.

PESTO

    4 tablespoons chopped fresh basil
    3 garlic cloves, crushed
    2 tablespoons ground pinola (or walnuts)
    3 tablespoons grated Parmesan cheese
    5 tablespoons extra-virgin olive oil

Grind the basil, garlic, and pinola together in a pestle and mortar. Add the Parmesan cheese to form a thick paste. Slowly add the olive oil to the mixture, blending carefully. This pesto sauce can be heated gently before use with pasta or baked potatoes.

SPINACH WITH DILL

    Fresh dill (a generous handful)
    2lb (1.2kg) spinach
    4 shallots
    Butter
    Lemon juice
    Salt and pepper

Boil or steam the dill, spinach, and shallots together. Serve with butter and some lemon juice. Add salt and black pepper to taste.

HOT HERB SLAW

    $1/2$ cabbage, shredded
    2 tablespoons butter
    $1/2$ cup vegetable broth

ABOVE: HERB BUTTER IS ALSO DELICIOUS
SERVED WITH FISH.

RIGHT: LAVENDER HONEY MAKES AN IDEAL GIFT.

Fresh basil, dill, and oregano
3/4 cup natural yogurt

Sauté the cabbage in the butter for a few minutes,
then add the broth and small sprigs of each of the
herbs. Simmer for a few more minutes, then add the
yogurt. Cook for a moment longer, then serve.

RAVIGOTE SAUCE
(FOR BAKED CHICKEN OR POULTRY)

   1 cup meat broth
   1 tablespoon fresh tarragon
   1 tablespoon fresh chives
   1 tablespoon fresh chervil
   1 garlic clove, crushed

Remove the grease from the baking pan, but leave
the juice. Add broth, chopped herbs, and garlic clove.
Bring slowly to a boil. Serve with herbs in the sauce.

CREAMY BASIL SAUCE

   2 shallots
   1 cup heavy cream
   Handful of fresh basil

Chop the shallots and cook gently with the heavy
cream for a few minutes. Shred the basil finely and

divide into two portions. Stir one half into the cream
and shallot mixture and use the other to garnish the
sauce. This is delicious served with pork chops or
chicken breasts.

HERB BUTTER

   1 tablespoon fresh chervil
   1 tablespoon fresh chives
   1 tablespoon fresh tarragon
   1 tablespoon chopped shallots
   1 teaspoon lemon juice
   1lb (500g) butter

Steam the chervil, chives, and tarragon lightly for few
minutes. Drop the shallots into boiling water briefly,
then drain and blend with the mixed herbs. Blend the
herbs, lemon juice, and shallots with the butter. This
herb butter is excellent with vegetables, baked
potatoes, or roast meats.

LEMON VERBENA JELLY

   2 cups fresh lemon verbena leaves
   1/4 cup cider vinegar
   4 1/2 cups sugar
   3oz (75g) liquid pectin

Shred the lemon verbena leaves. Pour 2 1/2 cups of
boiling water over the leaves; cover and leave to
stand for 15 minutes. Strain the mixture and pour into
a saucepan. Add the cider vinegar and sugar, and
bring to a boil. Stir well. Add the pectin and boil
thoroughly for about 1 minute, stirring all the while.
Pour into sterilized jars and seal.

ANGELICA RATAFIA

This is based on a Victorian recipe.
1/2lb (250g) angelica stalks
2 pints (1l) good brandy
2lb (1.2kg`) brown sugar
1/4oz (7g) ground mixed clovers and cinnamon

Cut the angelica stalks into small pieces and steep in
the brandy. Add 1 pint (500ml) water and the brown
sugar, then mix in the spices. Stand for six weeks,
then filter and bottle.

LAVENDER HONEY

    1lb (550g) honey
    1 cupful lavender leaves

Pour the honey on the lavender leaves and heat gently in a double boiler, simmering for 30 minutes. Strain into warm sterilized jars and seal. Keep for at least a month before using. This honey is excellent for coughs and sore throats, and delicious with herb teas.

THYME AND LEMON SAUCE

    1 teaspoon coriander seeds
    2 tablespoons fresh thyme
    2 lemons
    1 tablespoon honey

Use a mortar and pestle to crush the coriander seeds and thyme. Squeeze the lemons and add the juice to thyme and coriander seeds with the honey. Blend thoroughly together. This sauce is particularly delicious with fish dishes.

ROSE PETAL WINE

    2 quarts (2l) scented rose petals
    4lb (2.5kg) sugar
    Juice of 1 lemon
    Wine yeast and nutrient

Mix the rose petals, sugar, and lemon juice together. Add 1 gallon (4l) boiling water. Steep until the water is lukewarm. Then add the wine yeast and nutrient. Leave the mixture in a warm place for one week to ferment. Stir once a day. Strain into a fermentation jar and put on an airlock. Once a firm deposit has formed, strain into a clean jar. When fermentation has stopped and the wine is clear, strain into clean bottles. Lay by for six months before drinking.

MINT PUNCH

    2 pints (1l) fresh mint
      leaves
    1/2 lb (250g) superfine sugar
      (or more to taste)
    2 cups grape juice
    Lemon juice
    2 pints (1l) ginger ale
    Mint leaves and glacé
      cherries to garnish

Grind the washed mint leaves in a bowl until soft. Dissolve the sugar in boiling water, add to the mint leaves, and steep for 10 minutes. Strain away the mint leaves, and add grape juice and lemon juice to taste. Check sweetness, and if necessary add more sugar. Add the ginger ale. Refrigerate until cold. In summer, serve with ice together with fresh mint leaves and glacé cherries as a garnish.

SPICY FRUIT TEA

    3 tablespoons whole cloves
    1 cinnamon stick
    1 cup dried orange peel
    1 cup dried orange mint
    1 cup chamomile flowers
    2 cups dried lemon verbena leaves

Grind the cloves and cinnamon to a fine mixture. Add to the orange peel and mint, then combine the mixture with the chamomile flowers and lemon verbena leaves. Store in an airtight tin. Add boiling water to the tea in the usual fashion and steep for 10 minutes before drinking.

BORAGE SUMMER WINE

    Fresh borage leaves and flowers
    White wine
    Sugar to taste
    Lemon slices

Steep the borage leaves in a small quantity of boiling water. Cool. Strain off the leaves. Add the cucumber-flavored water to white wine, sweeten with sugar to taste, and add a couple of slices of lemon. Serve with blue borage flowers as decoration.

3 a perfumery & aromatherapy border

RIGHT: IN THE SCENTED BEDS, PLANTS CASCADE ONTO THE GRAVEL PATH AT ALDERLEY GRANGE, ENGLAND.

origins of the border

Herbaceous beds, or borders, as we know them, are a relatively recent phenomenon. The term was defined by John Loudon in 1822, in his *Encyclopaedia of Gardening*. Two of the earliest examples in England, the birthplace of the classical herbaceous border, are at Lord Byron's family home at Newstead in Nottinghamshire and at Arley Hall in Cheshire. Of Arley, Gertrude Jekyll wrote in 1904: "Throughout the length and breadth of England it would be hard to find borders of hardy flowers handsomer or in any way better than those at Arley… It is easy to see… how happily united are formality and freedom." (*Some English Gardens*)

ABOVE: LUPINES, FORGET-ME-NOTS, AND CEANOTHUS FEATURE IN THIS FORMAL ARRANGEMENT OF BORDERS, PATHS, AND ISLAND BEDS AT LOSELEY HOUSE, ENGLAND.

Early frets and parterres The term "border," meaning a long perennial bed, derives from medieval times when beds were created around the edges of gardens. These beds were raised and edged with boards, no doubt the derivation of the "boarder" or border. In the seventeenth century, plants were grown not only in borders, but also in "frets," which were elaborate geometric border designs. Fruit trees and bushes were an important consideration in these gardens, grown so they could easily be picked. The earliest border plants included fragrant flowers such as primroses, saxifrages, double rocket, wallflowers, double stocks, and auriculas. The frets were planted with sweet-smelling lilies, hyacinths, peonies, tulips, iris, fritillaries, crown imperials, and daffodils.

Parterres also became popular in the seventeenth century. They were similar to frets, but the border designs were defined with narrow box edging. One of the finest remaining parterres is found at Het Loo in Holland. Here, fragrant florists' flowers – carnations, hyacinths, pinks, and auriculas – were very popular.

In the eighteenth century, selected flowers were highlighted as specimen plants. They were planted at intervals surrounded by bare soil to show them at their best. Indeed, the style was known as "sparse planting." The effect was completely artificial or contrived, and in no way exuberant or natural. Formality was the ideal. In the 1820s John Loudon held that: *Flowers in borders should always be planted in rows, or in some regular form... Every approach to irregularity, and a wild, confused, crowded, or natural-like appearance, must be avoided in gardens avowedly artificial.* (Tony Lord, *Best Borders*)

The Victorian influence The eighteenth century had also seen landscape-style gardens banish flowers to the walled garden, often set some distance from the house. It was only toward the end of the century that flowers began to come back into vogue and were brought nearer to the home, where they could be appreciated for their esthetic appeal. The first flower garden of this kind was created at Nuneham Park in Oxford, England, for the Earl of Harcourt. Here, flowers were used extensively in island beds and were planted *en masse* purely for effect. Borders had never been designed in such a relaxed or dense manner before, and they paved the way for the Victorians' love of colorful informal bedding. They were, in many ways, the precursor of modern borders, but differed from gardens today in that color was juxtaposed rather indiscriminately. Under the Victorians, although a more naturalistic style of planting took place, unfortunately the overall effect was often cluttered or crude. They also relied on the help of a large number of staff to maintain the beds of mainly annual plants.

The Victorian style of design was modest in comparison to the Edwardian. They tended to plant excessively large clumps of a single species on such a grand scale that the subtle contrast of one group of plants with another was lost. The emphasis was purely on using bold colors to create a dramatic effect – the enjoyment of perfume and scented plants were virtually forgotten. The Edwardian age in Britain, according to Lady Ashbrook at Arley, was "the most dreadful period of gardening; the vulgarity was horrendous, all show and ostentation."

Contemporary border design Fortunately, the excess of the Edwardian age and the questionable esthetics of the Victorians were dramatically changed by two garden writers, Gertrude Jekyll and William Robinson. Under their influence, fragrant and structural plants were reinstated, as border designs took on greater subtlety and style.

Jekyll gardened with a view to creating beautiful "pictures," and she encouraged planting with a single color or a limited range of colors and plants. She also lived in a period when labor was plentiful, which is not the case today. One drawback of her designs was that she often used a limited number of her favorite plants (such as lilies and carnations). These plants bloomed for a few weeks only: in large gardens this

was not a problem, but it can be very restrictive in smaller city gardens and even country gardens today.

Different types of border Borders generally run along a wall or hedge or mark the edge of a lawn. They were traditionally planted with hardy herbaceous perennials, but today any flowerbed in which there is variation in the planting heights can be called a border. In the early nineteenth century, large island beds became popular to display species of plants to their best advantage. These beds, which sit in the middle of the garden, without a wall or hedge as a backing, allow air and light to circulate more freely around each group of plants and thus encourage healthy growth. Such beds are suitable for larger gardens and can also be grouped in twos, with a path dividing them.

Borders can also be mixed, combining herbaceous planting with shrubs and small trees for structure, together with tender perennials, annuals, biennials, and bulbs. Shrubs and trees provide shaded areas in which to plant different species. Gertrude Jekyll used mixed borders, planting bulbs under trees and using shrubs to extend the flowering season. Borders can also be composed almost entirely of shrubs, interplanted with bulbs and perennials for seasonal display.

President Thomas Jefferson (1743–1826), famed as a landscape architect as well, traveled extensively throughout Europe and acknowledged the pre-eminence of English garden design at this time. For his home in Monticello, Virginia, he subsequently laid out a studied version of the *jardin anglais* with a serpentine walk, continuous adjacent mixed borders, and an abundance of oval island beds. But the real impetus for the rise of the English-style garden, with its proliferation of colorful flower borders, came from the French designer Gabriel Thouin. The new fashion for formal promenades and island beds spread throughout France during the nineteenth century – even Josephine, wife of Napoleon, declared that she, too, was entitled to a *jardin anglais* at Malmaison. Claude Monet, who began the creation of his much-painted gardens at Giverny in 1883, used paths bordered by wide mixed beds planted with masses of irises and old-fashioned fragrant favorites, including peonies, honesty, sweet rocket, and forget-me-nots.

favorite old-fashioned border plants

Old favorites for the border that are extremely fragrant include primroses, sweet rocket, wallflowers, tobacco plants, phlox, and stock (particularly night-scented stock). Many of these plants were used for display in the early frets, but as border plants they are best allowed to grow naturalistically, planted in clumps or small groups.

BELOW: HOPS FRAME THE PATH LEADING TO A GREENHOUSE, BORDERED BY SWEET WILLIAMS.

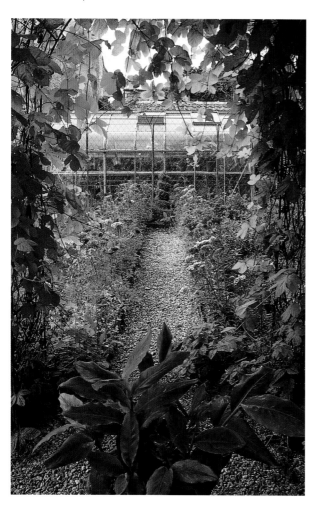

Winter/spring Primroses and the rest of the great family of *Primulaceae* (including cowslips, primulas, polyanthus, and auriculas) are some of the most obliging fragrant plants of the spring garden. Their flowering extends from late winter to late spring. They clump up and can be divided, and thus continually increase themselves. *Primula vulgaris*, the common yellow primrose, has a sweet mossy scent and is found growing wild in many parts of Europe – modern hybrids provide a range of color. In Elizabethan times, primulas or polyanthus were known as "jack-in-the-green." Primroses were very fashionable with the Victorians and were a favorite of Gertrude Jekyll: *All the scented flowers of the Primrose tribe are delightful – Primrose, Polyanthus, Auricula, Cowslip. The actual sweetness is most apparent in the Cowslip; in the Auricula it has a pungency, and at the same time a kind of veiled mystery....* (*The Gardener's Essential Gertrude Jekyll*)

Wallflowers (*Erysimum cheiri*) have been around for hundreds of years. They have a superb warmly pervasive, sweet-spicy scent and are easy to grow. Planted in single colors for impact or mixed, their jewellike colors have the rich beauty of Persian carpets or oriental spices. Wallflowers are used to produce an essential oil that is occasionally used in exotic perfumes.

Summer/fall In high summer herbaceous phlox are some of the most generously scented plants and are a mainstay of the summer border. Bob Flowerdew, well known for his organic gardening methods, calls them a subtle mixture of "sweet and musty." They come in swathes of color ranging from pink to violet, white to purple, through to lilac, crimson, or scarlet. White, mauve, and pink phlox tend to have a stronger fragrance than the brighter colors. The border phlox (*P. paniculata*) (zones 4–8), which originated in the northeastern U.S., is more common. It can grow up to 4ft (1.2m) high and is found in a range of colors. *P. maculata* (zones 4–8), known also as wild sweet william, is very pretty with lilac-pink very sweetly fragrant flowers. Both species flower from mid-to-late summer. If they are deadheaded regularly, they will produce a second crop of blooms in a few weeks. Furthermore, the plants clump up and can be divided after three years, thus multiplying your stock. They require a rich soil, and although they like the sun, they can thrive in light shade.

Sweet rocket (*Hesperis matronalis*), otherwise known as damask violet or dame's violet, is highly fragrant and obligingly self-seeds, providing a mass of tall plants throughout the border, topped with pretty white, lilac, or purple flowers. It is an old country-garden favorite and gives an air of softness to any scheme. Its delicious clove fragrance is particularly strong in the evening.

The tobacco plant (*Nicotiana alata*) comes from South America and is another headily perfumed border flower that can flower well into fall. Although a perennial, it is best treated as a half-hardy annual. Its tubular flowers range from white through to purple and red. *N. sylvestris* (A) boasts long white flower tubes, rather like a thin lily, and is visually more dramatic than *N. alata*, releasing an exotic fragrance in the evening. Both species like rich moist soil and grow equally well in sun or light shade.

Perhaps one of the finest fragrances of the summer border, though, comes from a plant that is almost ugly, gray and dull in the daytime, yet comes into its glory in the evening when its lilac flowers open and pour out the sweetest of clove fragrances. This is

the night-scented stock (*Matthiola longipetala*) (A), a small straggly annual from Greece. It is best planted with other richly scented stocks that are more attractive in the day such as the sweetly fragrant Virginia stock (see below), the hardy biennial Brompton stock (*M. incana*) (A), or the ten-week and seven-week stocks, which are half-hardy annuals. These can range from white and rose through to lilac, apricot, and yellow in color. The white perennial form of *M. incana* lasts for years and is very fragrant.

Virginia stock (*Malcolmia maritima*) carries white, rose, lilac, and red flowers during the summer. These plants flower for up to two months at a time and start blooming only a month after sowing, so it is possible to have a long flowering season by sowing seed successively. Of the different varieties of stock, Francis Bacon wrote in his seventeenth century *Of Gardens* that they have a penetrating clove scent which "is far sweeter in the air (where it comes and goes like the warbling of music) than in the hand." Other traditional favorites like violets and pinks are covered in Chapter 7.

the rose garden

One of the most highly prized of scented shrubs is without doubt the rose. In the fragrant border, roses are essential. They have long been used in the production of essential oils, perfumes, and rosewater. Sappho, the Greek poet (c. 600 B.C.), is credited with composing this verse in praise of the rose:

*Would Jove appoint some flower to reign
In matchless beauty on the plain,
The rose (mankind will all agree)
The rose the Queen of Flowers should be.*

The Queen of Flowers Roses are essential for any aromatherapy garden. The Arabs were the first to discover how to distill the petals with water in the ninth century and soon after began producing rose water on a vast scale. Rose oil is still considered one of the most important of all scents in perfumery work, while its healing qualities are just as highly

valued in modern aromatherapy practice as they were thousands of years ago.

Classical rose gardens As a versatile border shrub, the addition of roses will enhance almost any garden, and there is now such a choice available that it is possible to find a fragrant variety to thrive in even the most inhospitable of situations. The cerise, raspberry-scented, thornless rose 'Zéphirine Drouhin,' for example, will tolerate a dry, shady position.

Classically, roses lend themselves to a formal planting plan, where a whole area is devoted to the appreciation of their unique beauty and perfume. Formal rose gardens reached their zenith in France under the auspices of the Empress Josephine, who established an important collection at her home, La Malmaison, in the late eighteenth century. By the time she died, she had collected more than 250 varieties, which were laid out in formally designed beds.

A classical rose garden still features in many historic gardens, often outlined by box hedging, although its interpretation can vary in style from the formal to the romantic. In the former, the roses are grown as specimens in their own right, whereas in the country-garden style of the latter, they tend to be mixed or underplanted with other old-fashioned fragrant plants such as dwarf lavenders and pinks. A number of herbaceous flowers also mingle happily with roses in an aromatic border and traditionally complement their beauty, including sweet rocket, peonies, irises, and lilies. Roses also combine well with herbs in a *potager* or kitchen garden, mixing notably with lady's mantle, lemon balm, lavender cotton, catnip, and chives – an excellent companion partnership since the latter seem to help prevent disease on the roses. (The use of a range of herbs in the perfumery border is described in Chapter 7.)

Roses in mixed borders In large gardens, the most striking effects are achieved by planting groups of three or more of one variety or species of rose together. In a smaller garden there may not be space for more than a few individual specimens. Even if it is not possible to devote a specific area of the garden to roses, there is sure to be a place for a single rose. According to Rosemary Verey, most old-fashioned

roses in fact look best grown in association with other plants in a more relaxed type of border setting. She advises, however: *In choosing varieties it is important to bear in mind that many bloom only once and that the foliage of some is rather drab after flowering, while others have attractive leaves and hips in autumn. It is wise, therefore, as in garden planning generally, to have other features nearby to attract the eye away from plants which are past their best, towards a different focal point.* (The Scented Garden)

Fragrant evergreen shrubs such as the mint bush, choisyas, and daphnes can provide enduring structure to a border of otherwise deciduous shrubs such as roses. The additional underplanting of spring bulbs will immediately expand the season in which any garden can be enjoyed, and is easy to accomplish. A carefully designed layout that maintains the overall structure, such as the use of clipped box hedging around the edge of the beds or a focal point, such as

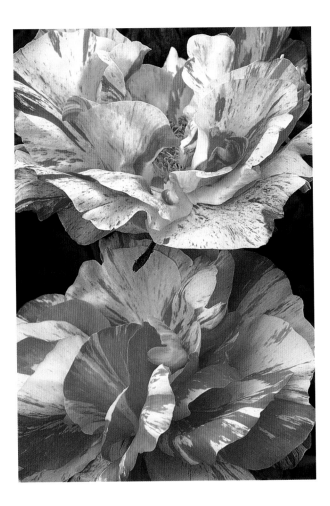

a sundial or fountain, is the most consistent way to provide year-round interest.

The original wild rose species Today there are thousands of different varieties of rose in cultivation, but among these, some are especially outstanding for the sweetness of their perfume. One of the most exquisite of the early roses is the wild eglantine rose or sweet briar (*Rosa rubiginosa*) (zones 4–9), immortalized in Elizabethan poetry. Although it has a very simple form, its delicious applelike fragrance and hardy growth have ensured its long-lasting popularity. Vita Sackville-West thought a hedge of sweet briar *"one of the most desirable things in any garden... after rain the scent is really and truly strong in the ambient air. You do not need to crush a leaf between your fingers to provoke the scent: it swells out towards you of its own accord, as you walk past, like a great sail filling suddenly with a breeze off those Spice Islands which Columbus hoped to find." (The Illustrated Garden Book)*

The original wild roses, at least 150 in number, are ancestors of all the roses we know today. One of the most important and ancient of the very early European roses is the French Rose or Rose of Provins (*R. gallica* var. *officinalis*), otherwise known as the

apothecary's rose; in the Middle Ages it was widely used by physicians for its medicinal properties. It has velvety, pinkish-crimson petals and a rich, sumptuous perfume. Derived directly from *R. gallica* var. *officinalis* is the striking striped rose, known as Rosa Mundi (zones 4–9) (*R. gallica* 'Versicolor'), romantically named after the mistress of King Henry II, Fair Rosamund. Gallica roses might well have been taken to England during the Crusades, although their exact date of provenance is unknown.

Most Gallicas are very resilient, fragrant bushes and flower over the midsummer period. They range in color from deep pink to purple or crimson. One of the best of the Gallicas is the crimson-purple 'Charles de Mills,' (zones 4–9) with an exotic fragrance. Another outstanding Gallica is 'Duc de Guiche' (zones 4–9), which is a double, dark crimson-purple. 'Tuscany Superb,' (zones 4–9) a sport from Tuscany, is deep crimson.

Damask roses Damask roses (*R. damascena*) (zones 4–9) were brought to Europe from Damascus by the Crusaders during the twelfth and thirteenth centuries. They, together with the Albas and Centifolias, are some of the most important roses in the production of perfume and rosewater. The Persian rose 'Ispahan' (zones 4–9) is a superb light pink, and famed for blooming six weeks longer than other old shrub roses. Nancy Steen, a New Zealand-based authority on old roses, extols its virtues thus: *a paragon amongst Damask Roses is Ispahan, Rose d'Isfahan or Pompom des Princes – a rose that grows wild on the hills of Persia... When this Damask Rose is in full bloom, literally thousands of perfect flowers weight down the long arching branches until the bush looks like a fountain or shower of several shades of pink.* (D. Kellaway, *The Virago Book of Women Gardeners*).

Alba roses

The Alba rose dates back to the Middle Ages and is one of the hardiest, with colors ranging from pink to white. 'Alba Maxima,' (zones 3–9) otherwise known as the Jacobite Rose or the White Rose of York during the War of the Roses, is a very ancient and vigorous ivory-white rose with a superb scent. 'Alba Semiplena' (zones 3–7) is a close relative, famous for its fragrance and grown in Bulgaria for distilling attar of roses. Perhaps the most beautiful of the Albas, though, is 'Queen of Denmark' (zones 3–9) – more correctly known as 'Königin von Dänemark.' Sweetly scented pink blooms bestow a strong, warm fragrance, making it an indispensable rose for the aromatic border.

Centifolia or cabbage roses

Centifolia roses are a richly perfumed group of old double roses that thrive in warm climates. *Rosa centifolia* (zones 4–9) means literally the rose of a hundred petals. Identified in Holland in the sixteenth century, these roses

RIGHT: THE SUMPTOUSLY FRAGRANT 'CHARLES DE MILLS,' (ZONES 4–9) AN OLD GALLICA ROSE SPECIES.

were immortalized by Flemish painters of the seventeenth century. A sport of *R. x centifolia* grown extensively in France and Morocco for commercial extraction purposes is known as 'Rose de Msi' (zones 4–9); its rich fragrance has a narcotic, aphrodisiac quality. Sissinghurst boasts a very beautiful, abundant 'Chapeau de Napoleon' (zones 4–9) (syn. *R. x centifolia* 'Cristata'), another pink Centifolia with a strong balsamic scent, which stands out even among its illustrious neighbors. 'Tour de Malakoff,' (zones 4–9) also known as the Taffeta Rose has flowers that turn from bluish-pink to violet and then lavender. It has a superb perfume. According to rose expert Graham Stuart Thomas, "there is nothing like it in horticulture... with flowers that take one's breath away."

Portland roses

The Portland rose is named after the Duchess of Portland, thought to have brought the rose from Italy to England in the eighteenth century. The rose is of unclear parentage, although some claim it is a cross between a Damask and Gallica with a China

'Constance Spry' (zones 5–9), which has a strong myrrh fragrance; and 'Heritage' (zones 5–9), with pink peonylike blooms. For yellow roses, 'Graham Thomas' grows very tall and is hard to beat for its deep golden color as well as its Tea-rose fragrance. 'Golden Celebration' (zones 5–9), with even deeper yellow blooms, has an exquisite fragrance. The dark red rose 'The Prince' (zones 5–9) is spectacular, and 'Falstaff' (zones 5–9), a new red rose, promises to be one of the most beautiful and fragrant of the English reds.

rose. Unlike most old-fashioned roses, Portlands are both repeat flowering and highly fragrant, possibly due to their Damask origins. One of the most beautiful of the Portland roses is 'Comte de Chambord,' (zones 4–9) originally bred in America, but renamed after the Comte in France. It has deep pink, highly fragrant, and full flowers. *Rosa* 'De Rescht' is also well perfumed with deep crimson flowers and is one of the best of the repeat-flowering roses because it is free of any disease.

Bourbon roses Shortly after the Portland rose appeared, another very beautiful and fragrant class of recurrent roses arose from the southern Indian ocean: the Bourbons. Their fragrance frequently has overtones of raspberry. Perhaps one of the loveliest Bourbons is 'Louise Odier' (zones 5–9), which has deep pink, cupped petals and flowers continuously in the summer. 'Madame Isaac Pereire' (zones 5–9) is one of the largest and most vigorous of the Bourbons and is a delightful deep pink, with a hauntingly fragrant perfume. 'Souvenir de la Malmaison,' (zones 5–9) named after Empress Josephine's garden in Paris, is pale pink with a very strong perfume. Unfortunately, it does not like rain. Of the white Bourbons, 'Boule de Neige' (zones 5–9) is an excellent highly fragrant shrub, with camellialike blooms.

New English roses Of the new class of repeat-flowering English roses created by David Austin, some of the most memorably scented and reliable are 'Gertrude Jekyll' (zones 5–9), which is a soft pink, exceptionally fragrant rose used in perfumes;

Other Roses It is not possible to deal with all the other classes of roses, except to mention briefly Tea roses for their fragrance and Rugosa roses. Tea roses arrived in England via the East India Company along with cargoes of tea in the nineteenth century. John Harkness, grandfather of the famous British rose grower, Jack, extolled their virtues: "If the rose be the queen of flowers, the Tea-scented Rose may be regarded as the queen of queens, for undoubtedly they are in refinement and delicate beauty superior to their robust and more highly coloured relatives." Moss roses, such as the exceptional 'William Lobb' (zones 4–9), are often highly scented due to their Damask/Centifolia origins.

A perfumed border should always contain the hardy Rugosa roses, with their cloverlike fragrance. 'Roseraie de l'Haÿ' (zones 3–9) is perhaps the best known of these hardy, aromatic shrub roses that make ideal hedging. The flowers are deep purple-crimson and smell of almonds. The most scented of the Rugosa roses is probably the single white *Rosa rugosa* 'Alba' (zones 3–9) and the double white 'Blanche Double de Coubert' (zones 3–9). Rugosas flower throughout the summer and have fine hips in the fall.

other fragrant border shrubs

A number of traditional shrubs that mingle happily with roses in the fragrant border and complement their beauty (including choisya, daphne, and orange-blossom) are listed below. Others, such as cistus or rock rose, lavender, and myrtle, are described in Chapter 7, together with recommended varieties.

Buddleia A common yet very reliable shrub, which has panicles of honey-scented flowers borne over a long period. It is a good wall shrub, growing to a considerable height, and enjoys a sunny sheltered position and flowers from midsummer to early fall. Buddleia is rich in nectar and is often referred to as the butterfly bush. *B. alternifolia* (zones 6–9) originated in China and is a graceful shrub with lilac flowers. *B. davidii* (zones 5–9), one of the more familiar species, ranges in color from dark purple through to violet and reddish purple. A particularly striking shrub is *B. d.* 'Black Knight,' which has flowers in a rich dark violet. *B. fallowiana* var. *alba* (zones 8–9) carries creamy white flowers, as does *B. d.* 'White Bouquet.'

Choisya *C. ternata* is a neat and beautiful hardy evergreen shrub, also known as Mexican orange blossom. Invaluable for the scented border, it has the virtue of flowering twice, in the spring and in the fall, although with fewer flowers. The scent is delicious, redolent of orange blossom and carried by white starlike flowers. In addition, its glossy green leaves release an astringent fragrance when squeezed. This is an easy plant to grow. 'Sundance' has bright golden leaves, whereas 'Aztec Pearl' has green leaves and almond-scented flowers.

Daphne Sweetly clove-scented, daphnes fill the garden with their glorious scent in early spring. Out of the 50 daphnes available, some of which are evergreen and some deciduous, about half have exquisitely scented flowers that can be smelled from a yard or two away. Perhaps the easiest to grow is *D.* x *burkwoodii* 'Somerset' (zones 5–8), which has pink

ABOVE: A WHITE GIANT YARROW (*A. GRANDIFOLIA*) WITH THE WINE-RED CLIMBING ROSE, 'GIPSY BOY.'

clusters of flowers. *D. odora* is strongly scented, while one of the most familiar is *D. mezereum* (zones 5–7), a native of Britain that bears pink or white flowers. The showy *D. bholua* var. *glacialis* 'Gurkha,' comes from Nepal, but grows only on the West Coast. It's mauve-pink flowers are powerfully fragrant, as are those of *D. b.* 'Jacqueline Postill.'

Deutzia These are deciduous shrubs, that carry white, pink, or purple flowers. They bloom from late spring to early summer and are native to the Himalayas, China, Japan, and Central America. One of the finest species comes from western China: *D. longifolia* 'Veitchii' (zones 7–8) has lilac-pink flowers until the middle of the summer. For summer blooming, one of the best shrubs is *D. setchuenensis* var. *corymbiflora* (zones 6–8) with starry white flowers. *D. compacta* (zones 6–8) has an almond scent with white flowers developing from pink buds.

Mahonia Mahonias are magnificent architectural plants bearing spiky evergreen foliage and yellow flowers. The scented species smell of lily-of-the-valley. The genus falls into two categories: those that are taller and prefer some shade are originally from Asia; the smaller species from America prefer more sun. *M. japonica* (zones 6–8) is native to China and has fragrant lemon-yellow flowers borne from late fall until early spring. Another excellent mahonia bearing fragrant bright yellow flowers is *M.* x *media* 'Lionel Fortescue' (zones 7–9). *M.* x *m.* 'Charity' (zones 7–9) is also popular, but its lily-of-the-valley fragrance is not as pronounced. *M. aquifolium* (the Oregon grape) (zones 6–9) comes from western North America and is a small shrub with yellow honey-scented flowers followed by blue-black berries.

Peony Peonies are invaluable in the early summer border; many are scented and range in color from white to crimson. Two delightful pink fragrant peonies are *P. Lactiflora* 'Sarah Bernhardt' (zones 4–8) and 'Marie Crousse' (zones 4–8), while 'Duchesse de Nemours' (zones 4–8) is a good double-scented white. For a stunning single white variety, *P. Emodi* (zones 6–8) is my favorite. Peonies flower early in the season along with the first roses of summer and can be used to fill in spaces under other shrubs.

Philadelphus This is one of the most fragrant shrubs in the midsummer border. Its scent is like that of orange blossom, hence its common name of mock orange. One of the most highly scented is the double variety, *P.* 'Virginal' (zones 5–8). *P. coronarius* (zones 5–8) is one of the most common species. It carries single white flowers and has been grown in gardens since the sixteenth century. It is a country-garden favorite and has a very powerful fragrance. *P.* 'Beauclerk' (zones 5–8) has single white flowers with a more delicate scent, but is still delightfully fragrant. Most of these shrubs are tall, but *P.* 'Manteau d'Hermine'(zones 5–8) is suitable for growing at the front of the border.

Rhododendron These form some of the most strikingly beautiful and dramatic shrubs, a small number of which are sweetly scented, including azaleas. They range in size from small bushes to large trees. The most common species in woodland gardens, and one of the most fragrant, is *R. luteum* (zones 6–9), the yellow deciduous azalea from the Caucasus, which fills the spring air with its honeysuckle fragrance. *R. atlanticum* (zones 5–9), with small white or sometimes pink-flushed flowers that have a rich rose-spiced scent, comes from the eastern United States. Originally from the Himalayas is a subspecies of *R. maddenii*, introduced to Europe in the nineteenth century by Sir Joseph Hooker – *R. m.* subsp. *crassum* (zones 6–8), which is very beautiful, and white flushed through to pink.

Skimmia This is a small, compact, evergreen spring-flowering shrub from the Himalayas and eastern Asia. It is happy to grow in shade and in containers. Male and female flowers with a powerful fragrance are borne on different plants, and both are needed if you are to get bright-colored red winter berries. *S. japonica* (zones 7–9) can grow up to 4ft (1.2m) high. For fragrance, the best cultivar is *S. j.* 'Fragrans,' a male plant with white flowers and a scent like lily-of-the-valley. *S. j.* 'Rubella' is another male skimmia and is good in winter gardens since it carries red buds in the winter that open out into yellow flowers in spring. For the front of the border, a smaller skimmia such as *S. j.* subsp. *reevesiana* 'Robert Fortune' is ideal, usually growing less than 3ft (1m) high. It is native to China, and unlike other skimmias, its white spring flowers are hermaphrodite and are also sweetly fragrant.

Viburnum This is one of the best genera of highly fragrant shrubs for the scented border. *Viburnum* comprises around 150 species, both evergreen and deciduous, many of which have a sweet honey scent. Some flower in late fall through the winter to early spring, while others flower in spring. An old favorite of the spring-flowering species is *V. carlesii* (zones 5–8), which is native to Japan and Korea. Its flowers are initially pale pink turning to white and are deliciously fragrant with a scent like daphne. *V. farreri* (syn. *V. fragrans*) (zones 6–8) has the virtues of being free-flowering, highly scented, and hardy. Another lovely viburnum is *V. x bodnantense* (zones 7–8), which blooms through winter with rose-flushed fragrant flowers that fade to white. This is probably the finest of the winter-flowering viburnum, with a fragrance that is honey scented and suffused with almond. *V. x burkwoodii* (zones 4–8) is semi-evergreen and is good in city gardens since it does not mind pollution. Its pink-budded white flowers are sweetly scented with the clovelike fragrance of old-fashioned pinks, and it flowers from midwinter to late spring. *V. odoratissumum* (zones 8–9) has fragrant white flowers, but prefers a mild climate or to be planted against a warm wall.

Wintersweet *Chimonanthus praecox* or wintersweet is a deciduous shrub from China. Its yellow flower bells are stained purple, with a wonderfully sweetly spiced scent. Rosemary Verey evocatively describes it as reminiscent of jonquil and violet. Wintersweet brightens up the border in the middle and latter part of winter. To get the full benefit of its sweet winter fragrance, plant it close to the house, preferably near a wall. The more heat it absorbs in the summer, the

ABOVE: A FORMAL WALK RUNS BETWEEN MIXED BORDERS OF HERBS AND SCENTED SHRUBS, DESIGNED BY LUTYENS-JEKYLL AT HESTERCOMBE HOUSE, ENGLAND.

more abundant will be the flowers in winter. In the border, wintersweet is best planted at the back, because it is distinctly uninteresting in the summer.

Witch hazel *Hamamelis mollis*, or Chinese witch hazel, is the most common and popular witch hazel. Its flowers have a fresh, spicy-fruity scent and are carried from early winter to early spring. These deciduous hardy shrubs are excellent for the border in winter, when they scent the garden with their unusual yellow or reddish flowers. *H.* 'Brevipetala' has deep autumnal yellow flowers with a heavy sweet perfume; *H. x intermedia* 'Pallida' (zones 5–9) has a lighter yellow flower with a strong, sweet yet delicate fragrance. Another powerfully scented variety is *H. japonica* 'Zuccariniana' (zones 5–9), which has pale lemon-yellow flowers. For fall color, the leaves of *H. x i.* 'Jelena' turn scarlet, orange, and red, while the flowers themselves appear almost orange. The distilled extract that is obtained from *H. virginiana* (zones 3–8), known as witch-hazel water, is widely used as a treatment for sprains and bruises, and as an astringent cosmetic lotion.

4 fragrant exotica & container plants

ABOVE: GLASSHOUSE AT CHATSWORTH, ENGLAND.
RIGHT: THE DRAMATIC INTERIOR OF THE STONE-BUILT CONSERVATORY AT FLINTHAM HALL, ENGLAND.

the birth of the conservatory

As far back as the Romans, grapes and vegetables had been protected from inclement weather with special structures. In Pompeii the ruins of early greenhouses have been found dating back nearly two millennia. Yet the conservatory as we know it today originally grew out of the orangery – initially a temporary wooden structure used to protect orange trees from frosts and cold weather. Growing oranges as a status symbol became fashionable among the aristocracy of Europe in the fifteenth century.

These delicate scented trees needed protection from European winters, especially as the fashion for the exotic oranges and citrus fruits moved north toward the colder climate of Britain.

Greenhouses and orangeries The original wooden structures, described by John Evelyn as "wooden tabernacles," were initially known as "greenhouses" because the evergreen orange trees were referred to as "greens." The orange trees were moved out of the orangery during the summer months to a prominent position in the garden where their beauty and fragrance could be enjoyed, and then returned to the greenhouse for the winter.

Traditionally, orangeries were constructed using a wooden frame with a solid roof and stone walls. This changed in the nineteenth century when the tax on glass was removed, resulting in a boom in the construction of glasshouses. This, combined with engineering advances and the use of cheaper iron, led to the birth of the modern conservatory, or solarium, which quickly usurped the place of the traditional orangery. A conservatory was, literally, a room in which to "conserve" plants in cold weather.

The fashion for orangeries waned still more as different tropical plants were introduced that required more light. By the nineteenth century, too, plants were being grown more for their decorative and exotic value rather than simply for pragmatic reasons. Glasshouses were necessary and valuable as a means of extending the growing time of certain plants throughout the year, and fragrant roses were particularly popular in this respect. Frequently built to adjoin the quarters of the lady of the house, a conservatory provided a selection of exotic scented flowers that could be enjoyed from the privacy of the boudoir. Subsequently, they evolved into palatial glassed structures and often became magnificent additions to grand homes, housing exotic plants and giant palms to impress visiting guests. Initially, all the great glasshouses were privately owned, like the huge conservatory at Chatsworth, Derbyshire, in England, and the fabulous glass houses at La Malmaison in France and Wilhelmshöhe in Germany.

The great glasshouses Gradually, however, great glasshouses began to appear in public parks and botanical

LEFT: MASSIVE TREE FERNS IN THE TEMPERATE GLASSHOUSE AT KEW GARDENS, LONDON, ENGLAND.

ABOVE: A MATURE ORANGE TREE WITH SCENTED PELARGONIUMS, FUCHSIAS AND OTHER TENDER PLANTS, IN THE GREENHOUSE AT GUMBY HALL, ENGLAND.

gardens devoted to the study and conservation of plant life. The early nineteenth century saw the building of several magnificent and striking glasshouses such as the Palm House for the Berlin Botanic Gardens (1821), the great Palm House at the Royal Botanic Gardens, Kew (1848), and the sumptuous Winter Gardens in the Champs Elysées, Paris (1846). By the second half of the nineteenth century, after the building of the magnificent Crystal Palace in London in 1851 (based on the conservatory at Chatsworth), the glasshouse ceased to be the preserve of the rich and titled. It was now the newly wealthy middle classes and industrialists who built conservatories in an attempt to recreate tropical paradise gardens. These paradises naturally contained the exotic scented plants of warmer climes, including now-familiar tender species such as scented pelargoniums.

The first part of the twentieth century saw a decline in the popularity of the conservatory as the cost of labor rose and hardy plants replaced exotic ones in fashionable society. It took until the late 1970s and early 1980s for conservatories to come back into fashion, coinciding with a growing interest in exotic plants. Today solaria are extremely popular, extending an existing house, providing a link with the outside world and, most importantly, providing a place to winter more tender and exotic flora. In a world that increasingly seeks to recreate different garden styles from around the world, they are essential.

the plant hunters

We take for granted the exotic fragrant plants at our disposal nowadays, but it was only as recently as the eighteenth and nineteenth centuries that the range of aromatic plants was radically extended with the introduction of new species from abroad. This was the great period of the plant hunters. Thanks to the efforts of these intrepid explorers, many of the exotica found in European and American gardens today come from as far afield as Tibet, Burma, China, Japan, and the West Indies. It was a dangerous business, which prompted the botanist Carl Linnaeus to write in 1737: *Good God. When I consider the melancholy fate of so many of botany's votaries, I am tempted to ask whether men are in their right mind who so desperately risk life and everything else through the love of collecting plants. (P. and W. Musgrave and C. Gardener, Plant Hunters)*

BELOW: SIR JOSEPH BANKS (1744-1820), ENGLISH EXPLORER AND NATURALIST, BY SIR JOSHUA REYNOLDS.

Perhaps one of the best known of these explorers was Joseph Banks, who brought back dried specimens of 1,300 new species from a three-year round-the-world trip with Captain Cook in the 1770s. Banks subsequently became the first director of Kew Gardens and sent out professional plant hunters in his footsteps: men like Francis Masson, a Scotsman who went to South Africa, the West Indies, Azores, and Canary Islands; and David Douglas, another Scotsman, who collected plants in the Pacific Northwest. The Douglas fir is named in his honor.

The plant hunters who brought countless new species of plants to Europe throughout this period were generally male: bachelors were preferred, with virtues such as "honesty, sobriety, activity, humility and civility," according to Sir Joseph Banks. Bougainville, Cook, Bonpland, and von Humboldt were prominent among the intrepid male European explorers. It was an English woman, however, who documented many of the exotic plants from foreign climes, in her paintings. Her name was Marianne North, and she was one of the great plant collectors of the Victorian age. A private income and excellent connections to influential officials of the British Empire such as viceroys, rajahs, and governors, allowed her to travel freely and gave her access to plants as far afield as the Far East, Jamaica, Brazil, Tenerife, India, South America, South Africa and Australia. She financed the Marianne North Gallery at Kew Gardens in London, to which she donated her paintings.

Through the influence of the plant hunters, many new annuals, perennials, shrubs, and trees were introduced from far-flung shores and entirely changed the face of gardening. Thousands of new species became available to the public, and many of these plants, particularly North American natives, were suitable for outdoor cultivation as well as for the conservatory or greenhouse. Now it was possible to have a range of plants for a seasonal display ranging from spring to early fall and even winter planting. It was a radical change from earlier centuries.

pots and container plants

A practical way to enjoy many tender or semitender species is to grow them in pots or containers that can be moved indoors or outside as the temperature dictates. This movable system of gardening greatly extends the flexibility of the growing season for the gardener. For example, containers planted with scented lilies can be plunged into a bed to add drama, fragrance, and color whenever there are gaps. Fragrant containers set near an open window in summer or on a balcony adjoining a bedroom will permeate a room with their perfume. The additional joy of containers is that they can be removed instantly once the flowering season of the plant is over. With the wide range of scented plants available both for the conservatory and more general container planting, there is the possibility of an ever-changing garden.

Aromatic plants can provide us with fragrance throughout all the seasons, so there is never a moment when we cannot bend down and smell some sweet-scented flower. We must also be aware, though, never to overload any planted area or a conservatory with too many fragrant plants or the effect will be overpowering. Aromatic planting does not preclude planting nonfragrant plants or even lightly scented varieties.

Spring containers Spring brings evocative fragrances that remind us that the long, cold, dark days of winter are over. First the wild primroses, sweet

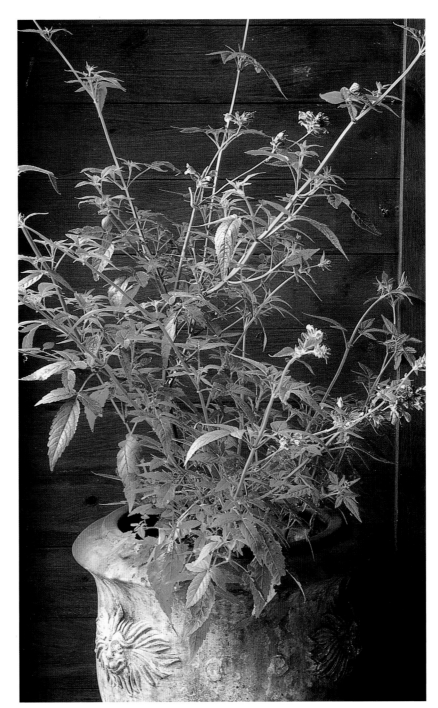

ABOVE: THE LEAVES OF BALM OF GILEAD (*CEDRONELLA CANARIENSIS*) HAVE A STRONG EUCALYPTUSLIKE SCENT.

violets, and snowdrops delicately show their heads; sweet-smelling cyclamen, daffodils, and the richly scented jonquil narcissi follow. Irises, the hardy daphne, skimmia, and lily-of-the-valley all perfume the early fresh days of the year, made more evocative by flowering cherries, decorative crab apples, and other fruit trees. It would be difficult to imagine spring without flowering bulbs and fruit tree blossom. Some dwarf trees can be container grown.

ABOVE: THE COMMON PRIMROSE WITH ITS SWEET, MOSSY SCENT – A WELCOME HARBINGER OF SPRING.

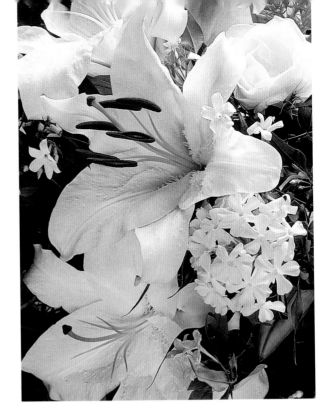

ABOVE: FRAGRANT AND STATELY, LILIES ARE AMONG THE MOST VERSATILE OF CONTAINER PLANTS.

Hyacinths (see page 117) are the most exotic of the fragrant bulbs and make a rich statement planted in containers with narcissi and daffodils. Some of the best narcissi for pots are the old Tazetta, such as *N.* 'Canaliculatus' (zones 5–9) and 'Minnow' (zones 5–9), which are sweetly scented with small flowers. Found in the wild in Spain and France and growing right through to the Far East, these narcissi are equally at home in pots or left to grow in the wild garden. Bulbs can be "forced" for midwinter flowering displays. The widely grown grape hyacinth, *Muscari armeniacum,* with its bright azure-blue, bell-like flowers, mingles happily with sweet-smelling yellow primroses, which flower at the same time. Scillas are also pleasing scented additions to any spring or summer planting; the rich blue Siberian squill, *S. siberica* (zones 5–8), is an early-spring flowerer, as is the paler blue *S. mischtschenkoana* (syn. *S. tubergeniana*) (zones 6–9), which has dark blue veins.

Freesias have a rich, sweet fragrance that can perfume an entire room in the spring or winter, and are usually enjoyed as cut flowers. In a solarium their life is lengthened considerably and their sweet fruity fragrance enjoyed for much longer. These half-hardy flowers come from South Africa, where they grow freely outdoors, but they need a minimum temperature of 50°F (10°C). White and yellow varieties include *F.* 'White Swan,' which is very fragrant, and *F.* 'Yellow River.' For a mauve double freesia, plant *F.* 'Romany.'

Tulips are not generally scented, but there are a few fragrant species worth planting for a spring display. The dwarf tulip *Tulipa humilis* (zones 4–6) has sweetly scented magenta-pink flowers and is best grown as a pot plant. The lady tulip (*T. clusiana* syn. *T. aitchisonii*) (zones 4–7) has striking white fragrant flowers, striped pink with crimson or purple bases. The naturally occurring variety *T. c.* var. *stellata* has white flowers with yellow bases. Bright yellow *T. sylvestris* (zones 4–8) is a very fragrant old tulip, grown in gardens since the sixteenth century. 'Black Parrot' (zones 4–7) is a striking deep purple scented cultivar.

Small cherry trees can be grown in large pots and make a delightful spring show. Try one tree per pot of the small, pink, double-flowered cherry *Prunus triloba* 'Multiplex' (zones 6–8), underplanted with grape hyacinths or primroses. Alternatively, the downy cherry (*P. tomentosa*) (zones 2–7) is a small, pale pink flowering cherry shrub that has lovely green leaves turning to deep maroon. Scented azaleas, some hardy and others tender, also make a striking feature in good-sized terracotta pots and have the advantage of colorful fall foliage (see page 50).

Miniature lilac, *Syringa meyeri* var. spontanea

ABOVE: NARCISSI AND DAFFODILS CAN READILY BE FORCED FOR MIDWINTER AND EARLY SPRING DISPLAYS.

ABOVE: ENDEARING AND EASY TO GROW IN POTS, FRAGRANT SWEET PEAS ARE LOVED BY ALL.

'Palibin,' is a hardy mauve-pink variety that is perfect for planting in pots since it does not grow taller than 5ft (1.5m). Very fragrant with hints of violet, it flowers in late spring and early summer. It can be underplanted with snowdrops, scented crocus, or hardy spring-flowering cyclamen. The popular pot plant *C. persicum* is only suitable for the conservatory, requiring temperatures of 50–60°F (10–15°C) in the winter months. It flowers from late fall through to early spring. The blooms range from white through to pink and purple, and are sweetly scented with overtones of lily-of-the-valley.

Summer containers The warmth of summer brings with it an abundance of fragrant bushes such as the frothing white mock orange blossom (*Philadelphus*) and a wide range of old-fashioned highly perfumed roses, particularly the Damasks. Climbers such as the heady jasmine and honeysuckle pour their perfume out upon the air, as do the more humble plants like phlox, stocks, wallflowers, tobacco plants, and pinks, all of which can be grown in pots or containers.

Popular plantings for summer pots or window-boxes include scented pelargoniums and nasturtiums (*Tropaeolum majus* – see page 155). Petunias are lightly scented and provide a wide colorful range of tubular flowers for many months right up to the fall. Phlox and pinks (*Dianthus* – see page 110) combine well with fragrant pink and white verbena. Herbs are also ideal for container planting and often work well planted together in combinations – slightly tender species such as the delicate lavender *Lavandula dentata* or summer savory can easily be protected from frost when planted in pots. Sweet-smelling violets such as *Viola cornuta* Lilacina Group, which produce masses of flowers over several months, are ideal for hanging baskets. Lilies are the most imposing of all the container plants. Richly perfumed, most flower in the middle of the summer (see page 127). Small scented rose bushes are particularly attractive, especially when grown as standards and underplanted.

Sweet peas (*Lathyrus odoratus*) are an old favorite and look delightful grown up a small trellised wigwam in a large pot. They are powerfully scented – especially the cultivars 'Gigantic,' 'John Ness,' and 'Vogue.' Heliotrope is another old favorite especially loved by butterflies. Also known as cherry pie for its cherry-scented flowers, the old-fashioned varieties range from deep mauve *Heliotropium* 'Chatsworth' (zones 9–10) to white *H.* 'White Lady.' The flowers of both heliotrope and sweet peas are used to produce essential oils occasionally used in high-quality perfumes. Tobacco plants (*Nicotiana alata*) provide sultry summer-evening scent, as does night-scented stock (*Matthiola longipetala*, syn. *M. bicornis*). The humble sweet alyssum (*Lobularia maritima*) is useful as a sweet honey-scented annual to fill out pots or hanging baskets. Its color ranges from white through pink to purple.

Fall containers Fall may not have the abundance of full summer, but there are still a number of sweet-smelling plants that are aromatic in the later part of the year and suitable for pots and containers. A number of the summer-flowering plants continue through into the fall: tobacco plants and mignonettes (*Reseda odorata* – see page 142), stocks, blue woodruff (*Asperula orientalis*), and sweet peas that are sown late. The fragrant autumn clematis *C. flammula*, with its starry white flowers, and *C. rehderiana* (zones 6–9), carrying cowslip-scented pale yellow flowers, can be planted in pots or windowboxes, with trellising to allow them to climb. Many herbs are still flourishing: purple sage, rosemary, and lavenders – particularly the decorative French lavender (*Lavandula stoechas*) – all look good in the fall.

Bronze fennel (*Foeniculum vulgare* 'Purpureum') adds height and architectural interest to a container with its delicately feathered foliage, as does the more strictly defined and striking sweet bay tree (*Laurus nobilis*), which can be pruned into a number of shapes. The classic round ball is always pleasing at the entrance to a doorway, but other shapes can add different emphasis to a group of planters. Autumn-flowering cyclamen are very sweetly perfumed: *C. cyprium* (zones 6–9), a delicate white-flowered carmine-headed species, flowers from fall through to spring; *C. caucasicum* (zones 5–9) is another winter- flowering species.

Tuberose (*Polianthes tuberosa*) is a tender perennial from Mexico. According to the poet Shelley, it was "the sweetest flower for scent that blows," and it later became a great favorite of the Victorians. It bears its tubular ivory flowers in the summer and fall, and requires plenty of water during the growing season. The intense exotic scent from the flowers is employed to produce an "absolute" used in perfume making. The bulbs should be dried off in the winter and stored in sand, then replanted in pots in spring. An even more powerfully scented variety is the double tuberose 'The Pearl.' Although it can be moved outside in the summer into full sun, it requires a minimum year-round temperature of 60°F (15°C).

Winter containers Although choice is limited, there are still some plants that are fragrant in the dark months of the year and can be planted in containers. Evergreens such as sweet or Christmas box (*Sarcococca*) have honey-scented flowers through to late winter. The dwarf form, *S. hookeriana* var. *humilis* (zones 6–9) is suitable for containers and carries creamy-white fragrant flowers followed by black berries. For pinkish flowers, plant the larger *S. h. digyna* (zones 6–9), which grows up to 4ft (1.2m) high. Winter-flowering cyclamen have been already mentioned for fall containers. Yellow mahonia will perfume the air from midwinter through the winter and on into early spring with its lily-of-the-valley fragrance, while skimmia, viburnums, and daphne can be relied on through winter into spring for fragrant flowers.

Early honey-scented snowdrops push their delicate blooms through in late winter, as do the delicately perfumed *Iris reticulata* (zones 5–8) and the grassy-leaved *I. unguicularis* (zones 6–9). There are also delightfully sweet-scented shrubs like yellow wintersweet, witch hazel, and sweet briar, all of which can be grown in tubs. Crocuses can bring a late winter fragrance – white flowers with yellow-ocher centers are carried by *C. chrysanthus* 'Snow Bunting' (zones 3–8), while *C. c.* 'E.A. Bowles' (zones 3–8) is a late winter- or early spring-flowering crocus with scented rich yellow flowers. Other fragrant crocuses to flower in late winter or early spring include bright yellow cloth-of-gold crocus (*C. angustifolius*) (zones 3–8); yellow *C. ancyrensis* (zones 5–8); lavender-blue fragrant *C. c.* 'Blue Pearl' (zones 3–8); and the pale lemon-yellow *C. c.* 'Dorothy' (zones 3–8). For mauve or purple scented crocuses, plant *C. laevigatus* (zones 5–8).

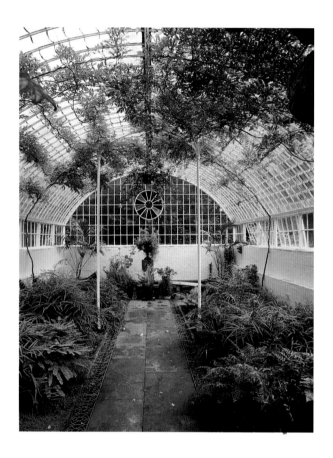

To create more interest in winter, plant box (*Buxus sempervirens*) and other aromatic evergreens, such as the low-growing flaky juniper (*J. squamata* 'Blue Carpet') with its aromatic blue foliage, or wintergreen (*Gaultheria procumbens*) with its fragrant white spring flowers, together with flowering bulbs.

fragrant exotica for the sunroom

The following tender fragrant plants need to be overwintered in a temperate to warm solarium.

Babiana stricta The baboon flower is so called because its corms are favored food for baboons. The flowers, which bloom in late spring, range in color from cream, yellow, and blue to violet. They have a sweetly penetrating scent similar to that of freesias. Lift the corms in the fall and repot each spring. They like sun and require a minimum temperature: 50°F (10°C).

Boronia These plants come from Australia. They are evergreen shrubs bearing highly scented flowers with a citrus overtone. One of the best varieties is *B. megastigma*, which flowers in late winter and early spring. It has lemon-scented brownish-purple flowers, which are ocher-colored inside. In the summer the shrubs can be taken outdoors as they like sun. The flowers are used to produce an exotic "absolute" used in oriental perfumes. Minimum temperature: 45–50°F (7–10°C).

Bouvardia This is a small deciduous or semi-evergreen shrub from Mexico and South America, whose blooms emit a glorious fragrance akin to jasmine and honey throughout summer until the winter. In warm weather the pots can be moved outside. Plants should be pruned in early spring after flowering. Minimum temperature: 50–65°F (10–18°C).

Brugmansia, More commonly known as datura or angel's trumpets, these plants have intensely perfumed trumpetlike flowers, which are borne in profusion throughout the summer and early fall, and are especially fragrant at night. A native of the Andes and South America, these evergreen or semi-evergreen shrubs make a strikingly dramatic addition to any solarium, and despite their exotic appearance, do not require high temperatures, although they must be kept free of frost. Datura can grow as tall as 10ft (3m) and bear as many as 200 blooms on a single plant. Highly perfumed white flowers are carried on *B. suaveolens*, redolent with the fragrance of lilies and narcissi. *B. arborea* (syn. *D. arborea*) and *B.* x *candida* (syn. *D.* x *candida*) are also white. *B. sanguinea* has yellow and orange-red trumpets. It grows to 6ft 6in (2m) high and flowers from late summer to winter. For a violet (or white) highly fragrant datura, try growing *D. inoxia*. Plants can be placed outside in light shade in the midsummer months, but require plenty of water. After flowering and with cuttings taken, the plant should be severely pruned. Beware of red spider mite, particularly with *B. suaveolens,* and note also that all parts of the plant are poisonous. Minimum temperature: 45–50°F (7–10°C).

Brunfelsia This is a striking and easy-to-grow evergreen aromatic shrub for the solarium. It comes from tropical South America and blooms obligingly for long periods during the summer months. The most common variety is *B. pauciflora* (syn. *B. calycina*), which has large, scented, deep violet flowers that fade to white over three days. *B. latifolia* carries scented pale mauve flowers while *B. undulata* has fragrant white blooms. The most exotic perhaps is

the night-scented *B. americana* or lady of the night, which carries pale yellow, spicily scented blooms that fade to a creamy white. These shrubs like a humid, warm atmosphere, but can be planted outside in the summer, preferably in shade and away from strong sunlight. Minimum temperature: 55°F (13°C).

Buddleia This a group of aromatic shrubs is named after an early eighteenth-century botanist, Rev. Adam Buddle. Generally they are very hardy, but there are several species suitable for a cool conservatory. Two of them are highly scented evergreens with creamy-white blossoms and a honeylike aroma, which have the added advantage of blooming in winter and early spring: *B. auriculata* (T) from southern Africa and *B. asiatica* (zones 8–9). *B. colvilei* (zones 8–9), discovered in Sikkim by Joseph Hooker, needs protection when young and is therefore ideal for the solarium. It has large deep red flowers. The orange ball buddleia (*B. globosa*) (zones 7–9), which went to Europe from Peru in 1774, has large yellow spherical flowers that

ABOVE: STEPHANOTIS IS A TOLERANT, EVERGREEN
HOUSEPLANT WITH WAXY, RICHLY SCENTED FLOWERS.

are sweetly fragrant. This species can sometimes
benefit from winter protection and is a colorful addition
to any conservatory. Pots can be placed outside in the
summer. Minimum temperature: 40°F (5°C).

Camellia These are evergreen shrubs that in general
are only faintly scented – the majority have no scent at
all. Yet there is one suitable for the solarium; it has
fragrant white flowers, tinged with pink. *C. sasanqua*
'Narumigata' (zones 7–9) is an attractive evergreen
shrub with shiny dark green leaves. It should be grown
in ericaceous medium and watered with rainwater in
hard-water areas. Minimum temperature: 40°F (5°C).

Clethra arborea From Madeira, this is known as the
lily-of-the-valley tree. It is evergreen and carries very
fragrant white flowers throughout late summer and
fall. If it is placed outside in summer, make sure it is in
light shade. Minimum temperature: 40°F (5°C).

Dregea sinensis (syn. *Wattakaka sinensis*) This is a
delightful evergreen climber bearing honey-scented
creamy flowers streaked with pink in the summer

months. It blooms profusely and is a rampant grower,
and needs to be cut back in the fall. In the summer it
can be moved outdoors to a sheltered position.
Minimum temperature: 40°F (5°C).

Hoya Otherwise known as wax flowers, these come
from Australia, and China. They are suitable for a
warm sunroom and prefer light shade. *H. carnosa* (T)
is a vigorous evergreen climber growing up to 12ft
(3.7m) and bearing penetrating spicily sweet white
flowers (which fade to pink) with deep pink centers. It
is easy to train and is a decorative, heavily perfumed
addition to the conservatory. Another white hoya with
purple-red markings is *H. australis* (T), which can also
produce pink fragrant flowers. Minimum temperature:
55–60°F (13–15°C).

Mandevilla laxa (syn. *M. suaveolens*) The Chilean
jasmine is a tender, deciduous or semi-evergreen climber
from Argentina and Bolivia. Its flowers are like jasmine, but
much larger, and are deliciously sweet scented. It should
be planted in a large tub, as it does not like to be grown in
a small pot – unlike the common jasmine, which thrives
with its roots slightly confined. Prune lightly in the spring. It
can be moved outside in summer to light shade.
Minimum temperature: 45°F (7°C).

Nerium oleander This is a sweetly perfumed
Mediterranean shrub, also found in southwestern
Asia, which usually carries white and pink almond-
scented blossoms through the summer and fall,
although there are also scarlet and yellow varieties. *N.
o.* 'Album Plenum' is a fragrant double white, while *N.
o.* 'Roseum Plenum' is a double rose-pink. In the
winter oleanders need a cool conservatory, although
they enjoy being outside in summer if kept well
watered. Note that all parts of the plant are poisonous.
Minimum temperature: 50°F (10°C).

Orchid This is one of the largest plant families, with
17,500 different species that are found in every
continent except the cold Antarctic. Many are very
powerfully scented with exotic overtones of fruit and
spice. Orchids generally need moisture and consistent
warmth. In summer they require shading from hot
sunshine and can be grown successfully in a

sunroom, provided they are planted in a soilfree medium that is well drained, and are given frequent mistings and plenty of water. *Encyclia* is a spicily scented genus of orchid – *E. fragrans* (T) is particularly fragrant and *E. citrina* (T) is lemon-scented. Some of the popular *Cymbidium*, such as *C. tracyanum* (T) and *C. eburneum* (T), are perfumed with a fruity fragrance, reminiscent of apricots. More floral scents are found in the species of *Cattleya* with *C. loddigesii* (T) smelling powerfully of gardenia and *C. velutina* scented with the heady fragrance of hyacinth. Other scented orchids belong to the *Dendrobium* (T) and *Angraecum* (T) genera. Minimum temperature: 60°F (15°C).

Plumeria rubra This small and exotic frangipani tree, originally from Central America, now grows freely in southern Africa and subtropical climes. Its fruity-sweet perfume comes from white, pink, orange, or yellow blossoms that appear continuously throughout the year. Eventually it will grow about 10ft (3m) high. Minimum temperature: 55°F (13°C).

Stephanotis floribunda The Madagascar jasmine is a tender evergreen climber with a heavy, sweet fragrance borne by small, waxy, star-like white flowers, which appear from late spring until early fall. This climber enjoys a moist atmosphere, but can be placed outside in summer if it is kept in light shade. It should be misted frequently and the growing medium kept moist. Minimum temperature: 55°F (13°C).

RIGHT: ORCHIDS ARE THE ARISTOCRATS OF THE HOTHOUSE. MANY ARE FRAGRANT, INCLUDING THE SCENTED *CYMBIDIUM* 'MARY MILLER' (T).

5 secrets from the still room

RIGHT: EVEN TODAY, A STILL ROOM
SERVES TO PRESERVE THE SCENTS OF
SUMMER INTO THE DARKER WINTER DAYS.

the first perfumes

Perfume has been in use for more than 8,000 years. Ancient records suggest that the earliest perfumes were found in the East and Far East, especially in India, China, and Japan. The Egyptians were renowned for their perfumery expertise, as were the Greeks and Romans in the Western world. The word perfume literally means "through the smoke," from the Latin *per fumare*: burning fragrant plants and woods as incense and for fumigation was the earliest type of perfume. Scents, incense, and spices played an intrinsic role in the daily rituals of all these ancient civilizations: for use in religious rites, especially those concerning death; for the maintenance of health and hygiene; as well as for esthetic purposes and for sensual pleasure.

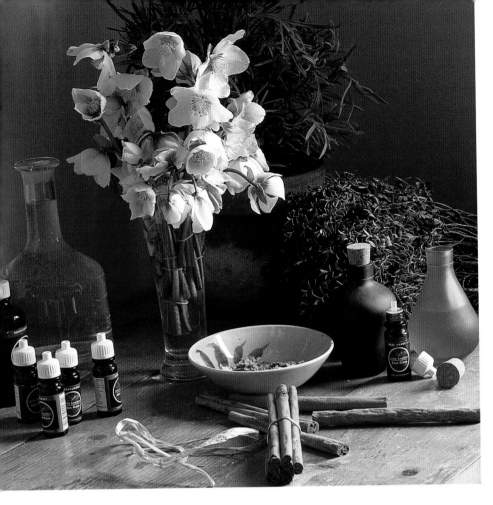

ABOVE: AROMATHERAPY OILS ARE INVALUBLE FOR THE STILL ROOM AND ARE WIDELY AVAILABLE NOWADAYS.

Aromatics were believed to have the ability to alter states of consciousness, both by lifting the spirits and by driving out evil influences in cases of mental illness. Frankincense, for example, has the capacity to transform moods and is used extensively in the Catholic Church. German research in the 1980s has shown that it contains a substance called trahydro-cannabinole, which directly affects the imagination.

The Egyptians, in particular, were masters of aromatic alchemy, the art of making fragrant elixirs that could bring about an altered state of consciousness – like their famous perfume *Kyphi*. For them, scent was a link with the divine, and they referred to perfume as "fragrance of the gods." Both the Greeks and the Romans also used perfumes and aromatic oils extensively and had considerable understanding of their psychotherapeutic properties. The physician Marestheus maintained that certain scents, such as rose or hyacinth, had uplifting and euphoric qualities, while Hippocrates recommended a daily massage with aromatic oils to promote a healthy body and mind, and to prolong life.

The Arab world and the Orient likewise enjoyed a passion for scent, although they had different ingredients at their disposal. Perfume materials such as sandalwood, cedar, and jasmine, together with a whole array of spices such as cardamom, ginger, and clove gave the oriental products a rich and sensual allure. These aromatic raw materials of perfumery, being both costly and in great demand, were among the first items to be traded between East and West. Clay pots used for distilling essential oils from plants, dating back to 3500 B.C., have been found in Mesopotamia, but it was not until the eleventh century under the Arab physician Avicenna that the art of distillation was perfected. This new process of steam distillation was critical to the development of perfumery as a whole, and it was from Arabia that knowledge of aromatics and perfume-making was first brought to medieval Europe.

All early perfumes were made wholly from natural ingredients, using fragrant petals, seeds, roots, or bark, together with scented gums and resins, as well as a small number of products derived from animals, such as musk. The first body perfumes were called unguents and were a type of ointment made by simply immersing the aromatic material in an oily or fatty base – a process called "enfleurage." Later, fragrant essential oils were extracted from the raw material in a variety of ways – by simple pressure (as is the case with most citrus oils), or by steam distillation (most essential oils are still made in this manner). As the formulation and production of perfumes became more sophisticated, they took on a whole range of different forms, including scented powders, flower waters, aromatic infusions, and room fresheners, as well as concentrated essences. Then with the discovery of the alcoholic extraction process in the fourteenth century, the art of perfumery assumed a new finesse.

The first books explaining perfumery techniques began to appear at the beginning of the sixteenth century in Europe, and it became common for women to prepare their own perfumes in a special still room – literally, a distillation room.

origin of the still room

The still room was used primarily for making aromatic substances of hygienic and medicinal value, and secondarily for making flavored vinegars or oils and aromatic wines and cordials, as well as for drying culinary herbs. In larger houses there was often another room used solely for the drying of herbs, but in smaller households both activities happened in the same place. The task of making these home remedies, fragrant waters, perfumes, cosmetics, scented soaps and candles, moth repellents, and potpourri was carried out by the ladies of the household, and often required a certain skill. Most of the recipes for still-room preparations were handed on orally, but some "receipts" have been preserved by families recording their medical and perfumery knowledge. Mary Doggett in 1682, for example, noted down one of the finest recipes for a "sweet bagg" using a mixture of orris, rosewood, coriander seeds, oranges, cloves, lemon peel, damask leaves, marjoram, juniper, sweet flag, and cypress roots.

Roses were used extensively for making flower waters, while linens, stationery, and clothes were scented with aromatic herbs such as lavender. A fragrant cosmetic water made from lily-of-the-valley and known as "aqua aurea" was used as a beauty aid, while myrtle flowers were used to make a popular skin tonic called angel flower water. Scented water was also frequently sprinkled on the floors of Elizabethan rooms, which were usually strewn with scented rushes or bay. The lemon-scented juice from the leaves and stem of lemon balm or the seeds of sweet cicely were used to polish heavy oak furniture and flooring, imparting their sweet perfume to the wood.

Scented woods and herbs were burned to prevent the spread of infection, but also to help get rid of musty smells. The Deanery of St. Paul's Cathedral in London was fumigated twice a week with aromatics such as rue or angelica root during the Great Plague of 1665. Potpourri was made from a wide range of flowers and petals, in both dry and moist form. Indeed,

ABOVE: HERBS SHOULD ALWAYS BE DRIED IN A DRY, AIRY PLACE – EITHER LOOSE OR IN BROWN PAPER BAGS.

over the following centuries in Europe, homegrown aromatic plants and herbs were used to make a wide range of different perfume materials, and this did not change until the mid-nineteenth century with the birth of modern perfumery.

Modern perfumes developed from the discovery and use of synthetic fragrances. While fragrances from natural compounds make up a well-documented and traditional inventory, synthetic scents, which only emerged 150 years ago, can provide a limitless source of cheaper and reliable "notes" or fragrances. Chemistry's first inroads into classical perfumery date from 1830 when cinnamon, aniseed, and pine revealed their secret aromatic ingredients: cinnamic acid, anethole, and borneol. Ten years later, the face of perfumery was dramatically changed again with the discovery of aldehydes – the key to the formula of Chanel No. 5. Since then, the scientific approach to perfumery has taken over to the extent that virtually all commercial perfumes and toiletry products on the market today are made almost entirely from synthetic materials.

An increasing number of people, however, are developing an adverse reaction to the mass of chemicals that surround us in the modern world, and are seeking out products that are 100 percent natural. The growing interest in the field of aromatherapy is having a notable effect on the perfumery world, with many cosmetic and perfumery houses moving toward a more natural emphasis. All perfumes are now described in botanical terms such as "floral," "mossy," "woody," or as containing jasmine, rose, or oakmoss,

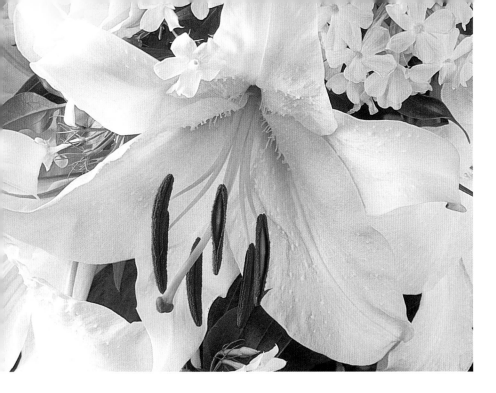

emerges some time after the first impression; the base note is the heavy element, which helps fix the higher notes and stop them from evaporating too quickly. Individual scents can also be classified into these three groups. Lemon, pine, and eucalyptus may be called top-note oils; middle-note essences range from geranium to marjoram and lavender; while base-note fragrances include frankincense, sandalwood, and benzoin.

A more comprehensive classification of scent was made in 1893 by Count von Marilaun, who arranged flower perfumes into six main groups based on the main chemical constituents present in their essential oil – the part of the plant that gives each its specific fragrance – including the indoloid, aminoid, benzoloid, terpenoid, and paraffinoid groups. However, this categorization was still not sophisticated enough to cover all plant-based fragrances and was later expanded to include ten separate flower-scent categories, four leaf categories, and two main wood or bark categories. In brief, they are as follows:

Flowers

1 Indoloid group Generally purple or brownish flowers that all have a meaty smell – *Trillium erectum* (zones 4–9) and a number of fritillaries.

2 Aminoid group Generally dingy white or cream flowers that have a fishy smell – *Pyracantha* and *Sorbus* species.

3 Heavy group Mostly white or pale cream flowers containing some aminoids, which smell sweeter and more floral from a distance, but at close quarters they can take on an overpowering, unpleasant smell of putrefaction – *Lilium candidum, Polianthes tuberosa, Osmanthus*, some members of the *Syringa, Philadelphus,* and *Daphne* genera and types of narcissus and jonquil.

4 Aromatic group Mainly white, yellow, or pale pink flowers with a pleasing balsamic, vanilla, or almondlike fragrance – *Cyclamen creticum, Clematis montana* (zones 6–9), *C. flammula*, several *Lonicera* species,

the classification of scent

Scents are wide-ranging. They were originally defined by Theophrastus as falling into two categories, good and evil, and only distinguished by degrees using such terms as pungent, powerful, faint, sweet, or heavy. They were subsequently redefined by Linnaeus in the eighteenth century into further subdivisions, such as fragrant, aromatic, or ambrosiac – the good categories; or alliaceous (smelling like garlic), foul or hircine (goatlike) – the bad categories. In the following century, a more sophisticated classification was used by Rimmel in his *Book of Perfumes*, in which he identified eighteeen different aromatic groups, including anise, balsamic, jasmine, citrine, rosaceous, sandal, spicy, tuberose, and violet.

Also in the nineteenth century, a Frenchman named Piesse instigated a new approach to perfumery work by classifying odors according to the notes in a musical scale. His vision continues to provide inspiration in perfumery work today, since fragrances are still defined as having "top," "middle," and "base" notes. The top note has a fresh light quality, which is immediately apparent; the middle note provides the heart of the fragrance, which

for example. Meanwhile, the aromatherapy industry itself is moving in the direction of mainstream perfumery by becoming more sophisticated and far-reaching in its impact, thus producing a merging of the two disciplines.

Choisya ternata, heliotrope, sweet peas, pinks, and carnations, plus leaves of *Liquidambar orientalis* (zones 8–9).

5 Violet group Plants that have self-fertilizing flowers with a violet scent, quickly fading to a mossy undertone – *Iris reticulata*, several *Acacia* species, plus of course purple violets and orris root (*Iris florentina*).

6 Rose group Flowers of variable color having a lovely sweet-floral, almost fruity fragrance that is not cloying – Damask roses, *Pelargonium capitatum* (T), *Iris hoogiana* (zones 7–9), *Paeonia suffruticosa* (zones 3–8), and types of magnolia.

7 Lemon group Citrus scent is more often found in leaves than flowers – *Rosa bracteata* (zones 4–9), *Oenothera odorata,* and *Nymphaea odorata*; lemon eucalyptus, lemon verbena, lemon balm, and lemon thyme leaves.

8 Fruit-scented group A wide-ranging class of flowers, some scented like oranges ('Wedding Day') (zones 5–9) roses; or pineapple (gorse and *Cytisus battandieri*); or apples (*Rosa wichurana* and leaves of *R. rubiginosa*) (zones 4–9).

9 Animal-scented group Included here are musky-scented flowers –valerian, crown imperial (*Fritillaria imperialis*) (zones 5–9), *Rosa moschata* (zones 7–9), and musk hyacinth (*Muscari muscarimi*) (zones 7–9), plus the leaves of the burning bush (*Dictamnus albus*).

10 Honey group These are sweeter than the musk scents, but can be cloying – clover, meadowsweet, honeysuckle, and various *Buddleia* species.

Leaves

1 Turpentine group Rosemary

2 Camphor group Sage, wormwood, eucalyptus, thyme, catnip, and bay.

3 Mint group All mints, some types of eucalyptus, geranium, and thyme.

4 Sulfur group Onion, garlic, chives.

Woods

1 Aromatic group *Cinnamomum camphora* (T).

2 Turpentine group *Pinus sylvestris.*

For a more in-depth analysis of the chemical makeup of particular essential oils present in various plant species and their value in aromatherapy, see *The Illustrated Encyclopedia of Essential Oils* (Julia Lawless, Thorsons).

However we define fragrance, its impact on us is profound. It creates a "sweet intoxication in the soul" and has been used by lovers and mystics alike from time immemorial. Could we but see these varied fragrances in the form of different colors, it would be a remarkable sight in the fragrant garden. Robert Bridges puts it eloquently:

…if odour was visible as colour he would see the summer garden aureoled in rainbow clouds. It is easy to imagine that the butterflies on a summer afternoon are caught up in a golden bowl of light in which scent and colour are inextricably linked. (Butterfly Gardener)

still-room recipes

DRYING HERBS AND FLOWERS

For drying purposes, flowering plants should always be picked with a good-length stem, just before they

BELOW: LAVENDER IS ONE OF THE MOST VERSATILE STILL-ROOM HERBS, WITH MANY DIFFERENT SPECIES.

come into full bloom, on a warm day. The best time of day for picking is the early morning after any dew has vanished: it is essential that all plants are completely dry before harvesting; otherwise, they will start to become moldy. Check that all parts of the plant are healthy and discard any rotten or discolored bits. Leaves should be cut when they are young and fresh; seeds should be left to sun ripen as long as possible on the plant before they are gathed.

Many plants benefit from being trimmed back in this way as a matter of course since it encourages healthy growth to clip off all the flowering stems before the fall. (In the case of tender plants, however, major pruning should be left until spring.) Harvested material should then be hung in small loose bunches in a dark, ventilated place – an old cupboard or a dry shed is ideal – or laid out on newspaper-lined trays and slid under the bed or a chest of drawers. Alternatively, loose bundles of three or four cut stems can be placed in brown paper bags, with the neck left open and hung on a rope line. A very gentle heat (from an open fire or warm cupboard) can help speed up the drying process, but intense heat is destructive to the plants' properties.

After a few weeks, check that the flowers and herbs are completely dry and brittle to the touch. Store seeds, leaves, and flowers in airtight jars or in paper bags secured at the top. Don't throw away the woody stems of aromatic plants: use them as incense or burning perfume (see below).

BURNING PERFUMES

Bundles of dried rosemary, lavender, sage, juniper, and cypress have been used for thousands of years as natural incenses, to perfume and purify the air. Simply dry the herbs, bind into bundles, and throw them onto open fires or barbecues. Other aromatic materials such as orange peel, pine cones, or citrus leaves, enhanced with added essential oils, can be used to perfume the house on special occasions.

HOME-DISTILLED ESSENTIAL OILS AND FLOWER WATERS

It is possible to make you own minute quantities of

essential oils at home using an enamel kettle (or a pressure cooker) and some rubber tubing. Pack the plant material in the kettle until it is full, then cover it with water. Attach a piece of rubber tube about 5ft (1.5m) long to the spout. Pass the rubber tubing over a bowl of ice set on a chair and then place the end of the tube in a glass container on the floor. Put the kettle on a heat source and slowly bring it to a boil. Let it remain just below simmering level until the water has virtually disappeared from the kettle. Repeat several times as required. Using an eye dropper, draw off the essential oil from the top of the condensed liquid in the glass container. The remaining flower water can be used as a skin tonic or light perfume.

EAU-DE-COLOGNE AND TOILET WATERS

Fill a small bottle with your chosen material, such as lily-of-the-valley flowers, rose petals, lavender or elder

LEFT: PETALS SHOULD ALWAYS BE GATHERED IN
PERFECT CONDITION AND USED IMMEDIATELY.

flowers, or citrus leaves, picked on a dry day. Top up
the bottle with pure vodka and leave for a week. Strain
and replace the flowers weekly for as long as the fresh
flowers or leaves are in season. Eventually, the alcohol
will be saturated with the scent of the flowers or herb,
and can be used as a concentrated eau-de-cologne. A
violet perfume can be obtained by mixing 2oz (50ml) of
vodka with $1/2$oz (12g) of dried orris root, which has been
finely chopped, in a glass jar. Seal and leave for one
week, when the alcohol will have a strong violet scent.
For a lighter toilet water, mix the concentrated solution
with at least an equal amount of witch-hazel water.
Decant into a decorative bottle with an airtight stopper.

HOME PERFUMES (ENFLEURAGE AND MACERATION METHODS)

Pack a small glass jar with fresh flower material, such
as jasmine, lilac, or lily. Always chose petals or flowers
that are in good condition. Fill the jar with jojoba oil and
let it stand for 24 hours. Put the plant material in a
cheesecloth bag and squeeze the oil back into the jar.

Repeat the process
using fresh plant
material every day for
at least one week.
Eventually this will
produce a very
concentrated
enfleurage-style
perfume or unguent.
Essences of lily-of-
the-valley, jasmine,
violet, and tuberose
are best captured this
way since their
fragrance is
destroyed by heat.

An alternative
method, which is
quicker but does not
preserve the true
scent in quite the
same way, is to use
an oil maceration process. Put a quantity of ordinary
coconut butter (sold in supermarkets) in an enamel
pan and place on a low heat so it turns to liquid. Place
the fresh plant material in the enamel pan together
with the melted coconut butter and stir gently for
about half an hour. Strain the coconut oil and plant
matter quickly and let it to cool. Repeat if a stronger
scent is required. The solid coconut butter can be
used as a perfume since it will be saturated with the
fragrance of the plants used.

AROMATIC BODY OILS (OIL-BASED INFUSIONS)

Scented oils have medicinal uses as well as culinary.
For example, infused lavender oil can help bring relief
to aching limbs; chamomile-infused oil can help
stomach ache; marigold oil is good for irritated skin.

Use good-quality oil like sweet almond oil or
apricot kernel oil. Fill a screw-topped jar two-thirds
full of oil. With a pestle and mortar, bruise a good
handful of your chosen herb, using the ratio of 2oz
(50g) plant material to 1 pint (500ml) of oil. Add about
1 tablespoon of white wine vinegar to the herbs and
add both crushed herbs and vinegar
to the oil. Seal tightly and shake well. Leave the jar on
a hot windowsill or, in winter, near a heater. Shake the
jar once a day for about three weeks. Test the oil by
rubbing it on your skin. If the fragrance lingers, the oil
is ready. If not, crush more herbs and repeat for
another couple of weeks. Then strain and bottle.

DRY POTPOURRI

There are numerous potpourri blends available. Several
recipes are included below, but experimenting with
different homegrown combinations can be exciting.

Elizabethan blend:
2 cups dried mixed rose petals
1 cup dried verbena leaves
$1/2$ cup dried lavender flowers
$1/2$ cup dried mint leaves
$1/2$ tablespoon orris root powder
Half a nutmeg, grated
20–25 drops rose essential oil
20–25 drops lavender essential oil
Decorative rosebuds

ABOVE: AN ELIZABETHAN POTPOURRI BLEND
WITH VERBENA, ROSE BUDS, LAVENDER, AND
MINT LEAVES.

Lapis lazuli blend:
With its fresh coloring and fragrance, this potpourri
blend works well in a bathroom.
2 cups yellow rose petals and buds
1 cup dried delphinium flowers
1 cup dried marjoram flowers
1 cup dried blue hydrangea flowerets
1 cup dried scented geranium leaves
1 cup dried larkspur flowers
1 cup dried bachelor's buttons
1 cup tiny sprays of dried blue sea lavender
1 cup dried chamomile flowers
1 cup dried lavender flowers
1 cup dried eucalyptus leaves, crumbled
2 teaspoons orris root powder
2 teaspoons cumin powder
10 drops oakmoss essential oil
10 drops cypress essential oil
20 drops rose essential oil
10 drops black pepper essential oil

Oriental blend:
This blend is spicy and sensual, which makes it
ideal for the bedroom.
2 cups dried pink rose petals and buds
I cup dried lavender heads
1/2 cup star anise
1/2 cup dried money plant seed heads
2 teaspoons orris root powder
2 teaspoons crushed whole cloves
10 drops sandalwood essential oil
5 drops geranium essential oil
10 drops jasmine essential oil
20 drops lavender essential oil
5 drops vanilla essential oil

Basic method:
Dry selected petals, buds, and leaves by laying them
on trays lined with sheets of newspaper. Slide under a
bed or chest of drawers away from the light. After a
few weeks, check that all the materials are dry and
seal in brown paper bags for later use.

Measure out and blend the essential oils into a
small glass bottle. The ratio to use is 100 drops of
essential oil to every 8 cups dried plant materials.

Use a pestle and mortar to grind together all the
dry powdered materials with the orris root powder,
which acts as a fixative. Add half the total quantity of
essential oils to this mixture. Blend in well.

Keep aside a few decorative potpourri ingredients,
but put the main carrier ingredients into a storage
container like a large jar and add the rest of the
essential oil blend. Mix thoroughly. Gently blend in the
powdered materials. Seal the container and leave to
mature in a dark place for between two and six weeks.

Display in a wide ceramic bowl or glass dish,
arranging the decorative ingredients (such as rose
buds) decoratively on top.
Alternatively, you can pack
the potpourri in clear
cellophane bags and seal
with a decorative ribbon to
present as a gift. Potpourri
can also make a decorative
base for presenting other
presents such as soap, bath
bags, or massage oils.

PERFUMED WASH BALLS

For centuries plants have been used to perfume toiletries. Lavender has been used for its clean, fresh fragrance since Roman times, while soapwort provided an early form of soap. As a sign of respect, rosewater was used in the East to bathe the hands and feet of visitors after a long journey. In medieval Europe, it was customary at major feasts to place great bowls of rosewater or other herbal waters at the table for guests to wash their hands. Later, scented wash balls made from Castile soap and blended with rosewater and other herbs such as lavender, cypress, or rosemary were prepared in the still room. This modern version makes a delightful gift.

> 1 cup unscented toilet soap, grated (or assorted
>   soap ends)
> 2/3 cup rosewater
> 5 drops lavender essential oil
> 5 drops pettigrain essential oil
> Food coloring (optional)
> Loose lavender flower heads
> Tissue paper
> Narrow ribbon

Grate the soap using a fine grater. Add the rosewater. Put the mixture in a bain-marie and heat gently until the mixture thickens. Take off the heat. Add the essential oils and food coloring if desired. Blend together with a pestle and mortar. Let the mixture dry out slightly, then take a small handful of the paste and roll into a neat ball. Repeat, making a number of balls until the soap mixture is used up. Before they harden, wet your hands with some rosewater and polish the balls to a smooth finish. Decorate with loose flowers and wrap the balls in colored tissue paper and ribbon for a professional finish.

HERB PILLOWS

These derive from the practice of stuffing mattresses with scented plants. The Roman emperor, Nero, reputedly slept on a mattress filled with fragrant grasses and dried rose petals, while Charles VI of France preferred lavender for scenting his bed and pillows. This recipe for a sleep-inducing herb pillow has a floral, slightly spicy bouquet. Other suitable

ABOVE: TRADITIONAL WASHBALLS ARE COMING BACK INTO VOGUE WITH THE DEMAND FOR PURE INGREDIENTS.

herbs that could be used are chamomile, lemon balm, woodruff, marjoram, and mint. For making larger pillows, use dried hops to add bulk, but be sure that at least half the contents are fragrant herbs.

Ingredients:
1 cup dried lavender
1 cup dried lemon verbena
1 cup dried hops
1 cup dried rose petals
1 lightly crushed cinnamon stick
1 tablespoon dried cloves
5–10 drops lavender essential oil
5–10 drops bergamot essential oil

Pillows:
2 pieces of batting about
   8in (20cm) square
2 pieces of plain cotton
   fabric about 8in (20cm)
   square
2 pieces of fabric for the
   case (silk, cotton,
or linen), about 8in (20cm)
   square
Ribbons, lace, or tassels
   for decoration

Mix together the dried
herbs, cinnamon, cloves, and essential oils of lavender
and bergamot in a dark container. Seal and leave for
one to two weeks in a cupboard.

Place a piece of batting on each piece of plain
cotton fabric and sew around all the sides. With the
cotton sides together, sew around three sides. Turn
right side out. Stuff the aromatic herb mixture into the
sachet through the remaining open side. Stitch up the
fourth side carefully.

Now make the outer case of the pillow the same
way. Place the right sides of the fabric together,
sewing around three sides and turning right side out.
Leave the fourth side open. Hem the edges of the
open side to finish. Close with ribbon ties, or use
snaps. Decorate the pillow with lace, tassels, or
ribbons. Slip the sachet inside.

For children, cut two equal-sized remnants of
material into the shape of a frog, snake, or rabbit, sew
together, and stuff with lavender or other scented
herbs for them to take to bed or place under their
pillows. Since most children like its sweet scent, a soft
lavender toy can be a great aid in helping to dispel
anxiety and provide a restful night's sleep.

SWEET BAGS
Sweet bags are small sachets of powdered aromatics
that have been used for centuries to perfume gloves,
linen, and scarves. They were also used to scent
stationery, handkerchiefs, and underwear.
Traditionally, Indian shawls were scented with
patchouli oil, not only for its exotic fragrance, but also
for the very practical reason that it protected the cloth

**ABOVE: HERB PILLOWS CAN BE STUFFED WITH A
VARIETY OF AROMATIC LEAVES, AND MADE IN A RANGE
OF DIFFERENT SIZES, STYLES, AND SHAPES.**

against moths. All kinds of powdered herbs, petals, or
spices can be used in making sweet bags, although
those with insect-repellent properties such as
lavender, artemisia, or lemon balm are among the
most traditional plants used. The sweet bag below is
based on an eighteenth-century recipe.

Ingredients:
Handful each of dried lavender, dried marjoram,
   dried lemon peel, dried
4 cups orris root powder
Orange peel and dried rose petals
30 drops essential oil (10 each of cypress, clove,
   and nutmeg)

Bags:
5 cotton pads
5 circular placemats
8in (20cm) in lengths of ribbon, 3in (7.5cm) wide

Using a pestle and mortar, crush the dried herbs to a
rough-textured powder. Add the orris root powder.
On each cotton pad, put two drops of each of the
essential oils. Put these, together with the crushed
herbs and orris root mixture, into a sealed jar or tin for
one week to infuse.

Divide the herb mixture into five portions, including

a cotton pad with each. Make the sweet bag by folding each mat in half, then wrapping it into a cone shape. Sew the edges of the outer layer to make the cone secure. Fill it with the herb mixture, then pull the inner folds of the cone together to enclose the mixture. Sew together. Alternatively, use ribbon folded into an envelope shape, stuffed with herbs and then stitched to secure.

TUSSIE MUSSIES

Tussie mussies are small scented posies that were used to combat unpleasant smells at a time when washing was a luxury. Like the pomander, they were used to deter infection as well as for the enjoyment of their fragrance. In medieval times, fragrant herbs were used to prevent the spread of contagious diseases: rue, sage, wormwood, rosemary, and lavender in particular were employed in this respect. The herb posies were frequently hung from the belt as a protection when traveling.

Later, under the Elizabethans, tussie mussies became an object of romance, and herbal posies were exchanged between lovers, with different flowers carrying their own secret message. For example, roses declared love, while lavender meant silence. Marigolds signified happiness, and marjoram wished fruitfulness on the recipient. The Victorians formalized the arrangement of the tussie mussie, making the herbs, flowers, and leaves more deliberately concentric. As its symbolism and the use of its secret language faded, it became simply an offering for special occasions.

A Tussie mussie still makes a unique and charming gift today, and can be given as a gesture of intimacy.

A fresh tussie mussie:
Freesias, blue hyacinths, roses
Pinks, primulas, common primroses
Mint, fennel, marjoram
Rosemary, chives
Raffia

Make small posies from a selection of flowers and herbs. Bind the stems together with raffia.

DRIED TUSSIE MUSSIES

You can also make tussie mussies from a selection of dried herbs and flowers by binding the stems together with floristry wire. Push each posy through the center of a paper doily and secure it with a decorative ribbon. For extra fragrance, add a few drops of essential oils such as lavender or geranium into the middle of the posy. Place in a sealed brown paper bag. Keep away from light and heat for at least two weeks to allow the oils to infuse.

BATH BAGS AND SACHETS

In aromatherapy, a few drops of lavender oil added to a warm bath before retiring has been shown to help prevent insomnia. Indeed, lavender has been used for bathing since Roman times, and its name is generally thought to have derived from the Latin *lavare* – to wash. To maintain the tradition, make yourself a simple cotton bag approximately 4x6in (10x15cm) with a drawstring opening, so it can be re-used easily. Then collect fresh flowers and leaves of lavender from the garden, together with other aromatic herbs such as lemon balm, lemon verbena, or rosemary if desired, directly before the bath. Attach the fresh-scented sachet to the hot faucet by the drawstring while the water is running. Children especially like concocting their own bath blends, and the scent is better than you will find in any commercial or dried preparation.

AROMATIC WREATHS

An extremely decorative way to display dried (or fresh) herbs is to make them into a simple wreath or garland. Make a base using thick florists' wire: form it into a circle three strands thick and no more than 12in (30cm) in diameter. Using fine wire, bind together small bunches of herbs that dry well such as lavender, oregano, bay, or yarrow. The inclusion of some decorative leaves or a few rose buds can also add interest. Attach the bunches one at a time to the wreath base using wire or strong thread, laying each new bunch so it overlaps the former and conceals the wiring. Gradually work your way all around the wreath, always laying the bundles in the same direction, until the circle is completed and full. Finally, attach a decorative ribbon to hang it.

6 planning an aromatic garden

scents and sensibility

Creating an aromatic garden is primarily about utilizing fragrant plants that contain essential oils and which have been used for their medicinal, perfumery, cosmetic, and generally healing properties over the centuries. Such a garden can not only look beautiful and meet our day-to-day practical needs, but may also provide a sanctuary or refuge from the stresses of everyday life. Ideally, an aromatic garden will provide a place where our connection with nature, our senses, and our instincts can come to life and be rejuvenated.

Like our home, our garden is a powerful reflection of how we feel about ourselves, the people with whom we share our lives, and our place in the world. Creating a "green" area within our home environment can be a nourishing and healing experience in itself – whether this is just a small patio area, a balcony, or a yard, a larger space with lawns, trees, and traditional beds. In fact, our immediate environment affects us in all sorts of ways, via all of our senses. We need only to think of the way in which different natural sounds can affect our mood and responses... the sound of rain, running water, silence, or, at the other extreme, a thunderstorm.

The scents associated with a particular place also have a profound effect on how we feel. Our sense of smell is directly related, via our brain's chemistry, to our emotional response to any given situation or person. In other words, it links us directly to our most primitive instincts about what makes us feel safe or threatened, sad, or happy. This explains why our reaction to a certain fragrance or perfume can transport us instantly to a specific place, or through association to a particular person or memory. It is also the reason why incense has been used as an intrinsic

ABOVE: SHIRLEY CHARGILL'S BEAUTIFUL ENGLISH GARDEN SHOWS HOW OUR OWN GARDENS CAN BE A NATURAL EXTENSION OF OUR HOMES.

part of religious or spiritual rites for thousands of years, in both the East and the West. Although perhaps we do not often notice them consciously, smells are one of the key ways in which we orientate ourselves on a sensory level. If we look at the way in which we respond to scent in our daily lives and apply this to our garden, it is vital to assess what kind of effects we require. This may depend on a whole range of things such as the kind of job we do; our passing moods – if we require stimulation or relaxation; the type of family we belong to or the social life we lead; and what kind of person we are by nature. How do we go about dealing with all these issues?

In this chapter, we will look more closely at individual requirements and the types of aromatic features that can be incorporated into an existing garden. We will also explore the ways in which fragrance has traditionally been employed in gardens throughout the ages, as well as in more contemporary garden designs.

starting from scratch

There are many elements that need to come together to make a successful aromatic garden design. Naturally, the character and fragrance of the plants themselves are of paramount importance. At the initial planning stage, however, some fundamental considerations need to be addressed before selecting specific plant varieties. These can be briefly summarized as: personal preferences and requirements; permanent or established factors; and specific style and design considerations.

Personal preferences and requirements. "A garden is a place in which to live outside," says the contemporary garden designer David Stephens, and it needs to reflect our everyday lifestyle. Apart from any esthetic considerations and before even starting to design our aromatic garden, we need to take into account some very practical considerations to do with lifestyle, resources, and personal taste. Ask yourself: how much time do I want to spend looking after the garden? (will it be high or low maintenance?); what do I want to do in it? (relax, entertain, etc.); who is the garden for? (children, adults, visitors, animals, etc.); when do I want to use it? (morning, afternoon, evening?); at what times of year do I want to enjoy it? (mainly spring, summer, all year?); how much money do I want to spend on it?; what kind of gardening do I like? (flowers, vegetables, pot plants, etc.).

Permanent or established factors
Very few gardens are created from a bare patch of earth. More often it is a matter of taking on an existing garden and adapting or changing it in ways to suit one's own individual requirements. With an aromatic garden, it is a question of reviewing what fragrant plants and features there are already in the garden, and what you wish to retain or change to make a more

dramatic or personal statement. Established views or paths need to be taken into account. Practical issues must be considered, such as making sure that there is good access between the kitchen and a dining area if you like to entertain outdoors.

Examining your existing garden also means looking at the space on a three-dimensional plane. For example, a steep slope might be used for terraced aromatic beds or a series of steps planted with fragrant low-growing herbs. Arches may be used to connect different "rooms" or to make a very interesting design feature within the overall plan.

Much of garden design is about making patterns, and these patterns must relate both to the house and to the surrounding area. To make an assessment of your own garden, start by drawing an individual plan or sketch of the whole plot, including the position of the house and its views onto the surrounding landscape. This can be done by simply drawing a series of inter-connected circles, each representing a different feature or area within the garden, with arrows

BELOW: EXISTING FEATURES AND NEW IDEAS ARE BEST SKETCHED OUT INITIALLY, USING A FEW SIMPLE LINES.

LEFT: THIS FORMAL DESIGN AT BURFORD RECTORY INCORPORATES MANY FEATURES INCLUDING ROSE ARCHES, HERBS, AND FRUIT TREES.

or furnishings. The proliferation of gardening books and magazines, as well as popular gardening programs on television and radio, can provide fertile ground for new ideas. Gradually, with such diverse information to hand, it is possible to build up a picture of your own style and design ideas and make your own aromatic scented garden a reality. These are some of the most obvious design choices:

❖ traditional or contemporary (or a mixture of both)
❖ open plan or divided into "rooms"
❖ formal or informal (or a mixture of both)
❖ ecological or horticultural
❖ minimalist or varied
❖ plant-orientated or predominantly hard-structured

An aromatic garden should be memorable, meaningful, and rich. There should be surprises and secret places, areas of stimulation and excitement, relaxation and intimacy. With the aromatic garden, we return to the ancient idea of the garden as a sanctuary – a fragrant refuge from the cares of the world. The notion of an intimate walled garden harboring sweet-smelling plants is implicit in the very early sacred gardens of the Persians, with their emphasis on running water, shade, and scent. Focal points such as a pool with fragrant water lilies, a geometric herb bed, or a well-placed urn or sculptural piece are all traditional themes that can be re-interpreted in a contemporary fashion.

With a view to breaking down your garden into different areas, a number of garden schemes and suggested plantings, together with specific aromatic garden features, are described. These can be selected and adapted according to your existing garden. (For designing a rose garden, see Chapter 3).

indicating views or routes of movement. It is important also to take into account the following basic considerations: type of soil; position and location (sunny, shady, exposed, etc.); which parts of the garden are successful and which are not. Consider the views from different aspects of your existing garden and think about movement through the garden, including circulation routes. Do they connect satisfactorily? Finally, make a working scale drawing.

Gardening implies that one is controlling nature. If you do not intervene, a garden quickly reverts to wilderness. But you need to decide to what extent you want to control nature. At one extreme, there is the precision of the knot garden, and at the other, there is the luxuriant fragrant country-garden style that emphasizes and even encourages the self-seeding of wild species in a naturalistic and random fashion.

Specific style and design considerations Only after having assessed your existing site can you move on to issues of style and design preferences. Inspiration for aromatic gardens can be found in a wide variety of places: from the historical influence of the early Persian walled gardens to famous traditional gardens such as Hidcote or Sissinghurst in England; classical châteaux such Miromesnil or Villier in France; to the newly laid out Central Park gardens in New York, totally redesigned by the American artist Lynden Miller within the past 15 years. Besides visiting various gardens open to the public or gardening shows and exhibitions, inspiration can also be found outside the field of garden design – from paintings, interior design,

designing an herb garden

When planting an herb garden, it is important to bear in mind what the main purpose will be. Do you want herbs mainly for their aromatic, culinary, or medicinal properties, or a mixture of all three? Today, herbs for cooking are generally more useful than the medicinal herbs that formed the backbone of the very early herb gardens. There are also esthetic considerations: you might use a mix of culinary and medicinal herbs simply for the dramatic display they provide. Either way, it is probably best to start by drawing up a list. Choose a design that appeals to you, and arrange the herbs accordingly, depending on height or the color of their foliage and flowers and, in the case of culinary herbs, their accessibility to the kitchen and ease of picking. (See Chapter 2 for a guide to suggested herbs and flowers.)

Generally, herbs are shown off to their best advantage in a formal structure. But if you prefer a more informal style, the herbs can simply be incorporated into flowerbeds for a naturalistic or romantic effect. Here are a few different ways in which you can design your herb garden.

Wheels or circles A popular way to plant herbs is to arrange them in the shape of a wheel or in concentric circles. In the nineteenth century, real cartwheels were used: herbs were planted inside the spokes and the raised hub created a circular border. Try sketching imaginary spokes from a central circular bed, defining them with brick or short wooden slats. Plant herbs between the spokes using one particular species in each segment – for example, different types of sage, santolina, or lavender.

Circles of herbs are simpler to design and require two to three concentric circles radiating out from a closed center. Keep the taller herbs such as angelica or fennel in the center. Then plant medium-height herbs –

lavender or rosemary – in the next ring. Add low-growing herbs to the outer ring, such as chamomile and thyme. Stepping stones between each circle give easy access to the plants. The outside of the circle can then be planted with a low hedging of box or santolina, with entrances from the four points of the compass into the inner circles.

The ladder Although not as organically pleasing to look at as either the wheel or circle, the ladder allows easy access and is therefore practical for picking purposes. It is a long bed where individual clumps of herbs are planted together, separated by either stone, brick, or wooden pathways, representing the rungs of a ladder. Low-growing herbs which are evergreen, such as oregano, marjoram and thyme, work best and help keep the ladder consistent in its design. Limiting the number of herbs used creates maximum visual impact: for example, a ladder could be made using simply a collection of differently colored

BELOW: A DRY AND DELIGHTFULLY UNCONTRIVED WALLED HERB GARDEN AT NORTHBOURNE COURT, ENGLAND.

ABOVE: THIS STRIKING KNOT GARDEN AT ABBEY HOUSE
USES A SNAKELIKE DESIGN OF CONTRASTING COLORS.

flowering thymes, each offering different scents.

Species to try include: caraway thyme, *Thymus herba-barona* (zones 6–8) (purple flowers/good with beef); *T.* x *citriodorus* 'Silver Posie' (zones 7–8) (variegated leaf/bouquet garni); *T. serpyllum* 'Pink Chintz' (zones 4–8) (pink flowers/attracts bees); *T. s.* 'Russetings' (zones 4–8) (dark pink/salads and soups); *T. richardii* (zones 6–9); *T.* 'Peter Davis' (zones 6–9) (gray-green foliage, mauve flowers/stews, sauces, stuffings); wild thyme, *T. serpyllum* (zones 4–8) (low growing, purple flowers/medicinal usage); *T.* 'Hartington Silver' (zones 5–9), syn. *T.* 'Highland Cream' (golden-green foliage, pale pink flowers very decorative); golden thyme, *T. citriodorus* 'Aureus' (zones 5–9) (gold leaves, /medicinal and culinary usage); *T. s.* 'Lemon Curd' (zones 5–9) (lemon-scented leaves, pink flowers/versatile culinary herb); *T.* 'Doone Valley' (zones 6–9) (citrus-scented variegated leaves/medicinal usage).

A knot garden A knot garden represents the most formal and structured planting of herbs and is very labor intensive. Designs can be extremely complicated or adapted for ease. You can draw on the sixteenth-century designs of Gervase Markham or the seventeenth-century manual *La Maison Rustique* for inspiration. Traditional knot gardens are either closed or open, and tend to follow set plans, although any abstract pattern can, in fact, be used. Arabic or Indian geometric designs can also be a rich source of ideas. In reality, it is often better to modify elaborate designs to something more basic. Simple design ideas are often the most effective and are easier to execute, but it is still important to sketch your plan on paper first before planting.

Herbs suitable for a knot garden include rosemary, hyssop, santolina, lavender, and wall germander, but smaller subshrubs such as thyme, dwarf curry plant, and sage can also be used. Evergreen box has always been a classic and looks elegant. It is much favored by the British gardening writer and historian Sir Roy Strong, who uses it extensively in his designs. Patterns can then be interplanted either with loosely structured herbs or with flowers such as old-fashioned roses, madonna lilies, carnations, or irises. Alternatively, the gaps between the interweaving design threads can be filled with gravel or colored stones. Very striking knot gardens can be based on simple repetitive designs that gain impact from the restrained use of a single species such as box or santolina.

Chamomile seats Chamomile seats were very popular in Elizabethan times in England and can be a most attractive feature in the herb or aromatic garden. To build one, either slice into a steep bank of earth or use an existing raised bed. If neither is available, create a seat by laying down two parallel low brick walls, then block in the ends to form a rectangular shape. To create the seat's back and arms, plant the fragrant bright green box *Buxus sempervirens* 'Suffruticosa,' although it will take a few years to reach full maturity. Alternatively, grow the shiny laurel *Prunus laurocerasus* 'Otto Luyken' (zones 6–9), which has the merit of growing fast and is outstanding for its foliage and white flowers. Fill in the brick retaining walls with earth, and plant it with the non-flowering, apple-scented chamomile *Chamaemelum nobile* 'Treneague.' Once the evergreen hedge surrounding the seat has matured, keep it closely clipped as an elegant frame.

scented arbors

A chamomile seat can be used to create the basis for an intimate scented arbor. A rustic wooden seat can be equally enchanting, situated beneath an arching trellis covered with sweet-smelling rambling roses and other fragrant climbers such as jasmine or honeysuckle. In the sixteenth and seventeenth centuries, arbors of hawthorn and honeysuckle arching over a seat were popular, and created romantic corners in the garden. Honeysuckle particularly enjoyed an ascendency in Elizabethan times. The word "arbour" derives from *herbe*, a place where sweetly perfumed herbs or plants grew. Today, it can provide a quiet refuge and place of contemplation or intimacy deep within the fragrant garden.

Climbing and rambling roses Climbing and rambling roses such as the deep rose-pink, thornless 'Zéphirine Drouhin' or the more fragile yet very graceful-looking 'François Juranville' (zones 4–9), with its fresh apple-scented, crushed-silk blossoms, can be planted together with clematis. The old rambler 'Albertine' (zones 4–9) can furnish the bower with a coppery-apricot flushed frame and is highly scented. The lovely soft pink once blooming 'Constance Spry,' although a new rose, retains the charm of the old cabbage roses in its appearance. It has a rich myrrh fragrance and spreads well, although it needs to be closely trained. 'Blairii Number Two' (zones 5–9), a Bourbon, is also a very beautiful and fragrant pink rose that climbs well. If not in your scented arbor, be sure to find a place in your garden for this lovely rose.

ABOVE: A ROMANTIC ALLEY OVERHUNG WITH SCENTED CLIMBERS LEADS TO AN ISLAMIC-STYLE PAVILLION AT DAVID AUSTIN'S ROSE GARDEN IN ENGLAND.

For white climbers, it is hard to beat the beautiful climbing Tea rose 'Sombreuil' (zones 7–9) with its deeply perfumed double flowers. Other reliable fragrant white climbers are 'Madame Alfred Carrière' (zones 6–9), which is happy to grow in shade, and the ramblers 'Albéric Barbier' (zones 4–9), which is easy to train, and 'Félicité Perpétue' (zones 6–9), which cascades freely with a primrose scent over a trellis.

Of the perfumed red climbers, perhaps one of the best is 'Guinée' (zones 5–9), which is a dark, velvet crimson. The climber 'Etoile de Hollande' (zones 6–9) is a deep crimson Tea rose with a very strong floral fragrance. For a more brilliant crimson, try planting the Hybrid Tea 'Allen Chandler' (zones 5–9), which is an excellent flowerer. Climbing 'Ena Harkness' is another Hybrid Tea rose that is very popular, with crimson-scarlet blooms. 'Alexandre Girault' (zones 4–9) is deep rose-pink with copper tones; it holds its color well in the sun and has a heady, fruity perfume.

Of the yellow scented roses, 'Mermaid' (zones 6–9) flowers prolifically throughout the summer months with large single blooms, but can grow very high. 'Céline Forestier' (zones 7–10) is a repeat-flowering, primrose-yellow noisette rose with flat blooms, suitable for growing in a smaller arbor. *R. banksiae* 'Lutea' (zones 7–10) is a vigorous double yellow rambler that can be most attractive with a

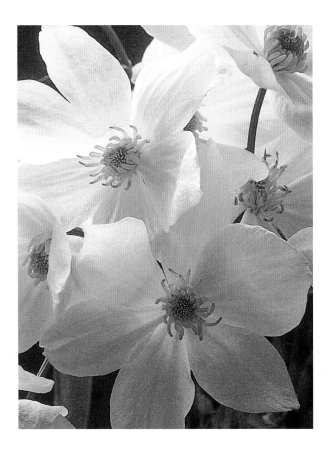

LEFT: THE FRAGRANT CLEMATIS 'SNOWDRIFT' IS ONE OF THE FIRST TO FLOWER IN THE SPRING.

musky scent, but it will need to be kept in check. 'Goldfinch' (zones 5–9) is another rambler which is very fragrant and has the advantage of producing attractive red hips in the fall.

Fragrant clematis A scented bower will happily mingle roses and clematis as natural companions. Be sure either to plant fragrant clematis that will complement the roses, or those that will provide a lovely color contrast, for example, violet clematis with pink roses. Note, though, that it is unwise to plant *C. montana* with climbing roses as this prolifically growing species will swamp them. Most of the large-flowered clematis are not scented, but a number of the smaller-flowered species are delightfully perfumed.

You can plant several clematis, each flowering in different seasons. The following clematis will not completely engulf a scented arbor, but be ruthless about pruning those that are indicated as prolific growers. Low-growing *C. Integrifolia* 'Hendersonii' (zones 3–7), with its pale blue scented blooms, flowers from midsummer into fall, while *C. recta* (zones 3–7) produces masses of small, creamy-white, sweetly scented flowers in summer, as does the vigorous *C. terniflora* (syn. *C. chinensis*) (zones 4–9) which flowers in late summer to early fall. Almond-scented *C. flammula*, the fragrant virgin's bower of Elizabethan times, is another white clematis that can

be enjoyed from late summer to fall. *C. triternata* 'Rubromarginata' (zones 5–9) (syn. *C. flammula* 'Rubra Marginata') also flowers from late summer to fall but with small, fragrant rosy-pink flowers. For a slightly scented, violet-blue clematis that flowers throughout summer, plant *C.* x *aromatica* (zones 5–9), while the pale blue *C.* x *jouiniana* (zones 4–9) produces masses of scented flowers in the early fall.

Later to flower is the lemon-scented *C. serratifolia* (zones 5–9), which carries yellow flowers in the fall, as does the yellow *C. songarica* 'Sundance' (zones 5–9). The heavenly pale yellow *C. rehderiana* (zones 6–9), the nodding virgin's bower with its bell-shaped flowers, has a scent reminiscent of cowslips, and flowers from late fall into early winter. This is a very vigorous clematis and needs to be kept well pruned. Another autumn-flowering clematis is *C. terniflora* (syn. *C. maximowicziana*), which requires plenty of warmth and sunshine but rewards enthusiasts with masses of small, creamy fragrant flowers. In late winter and early spring, the starry small white-flowered evergreen *C. armandii* 'Snowdrift' can be relied upon to perfume the cold air. *C. a.* 'Apple Blossom' has very pale pink flowers and blossoms at the same time.

Other scented clematis are more rampant: for early summer flowering, choose *C. montana* var. *rubens* 'Elizabeth' (zones 6–9), which is a sweetly scented, pink clematis, or *C. m.* 'Odorata,' a pale pink clematis. Both are best grown on large frames, on walls, or up trees. *C. m.* var *wilsonii* is a fragrant white montana that flowers prolifically in summer and can grow over 33ft (10m) high. *C. m.* 'Alexander' bears large white flowers in summer and is powerfully scented.

Other scented climbers Other suitable climbers for the scented arbor or for growing through trellising or over arches would be various types of honeysuckle and jasmine (see Chapter 7), and wisteria. Star jasmine (*Trachelospermum jasminoides*) does not actually belong to the jasmine family, but it is an exquisitely scented, twining evergreen climber that carries clusters of delicate white to cream, five-

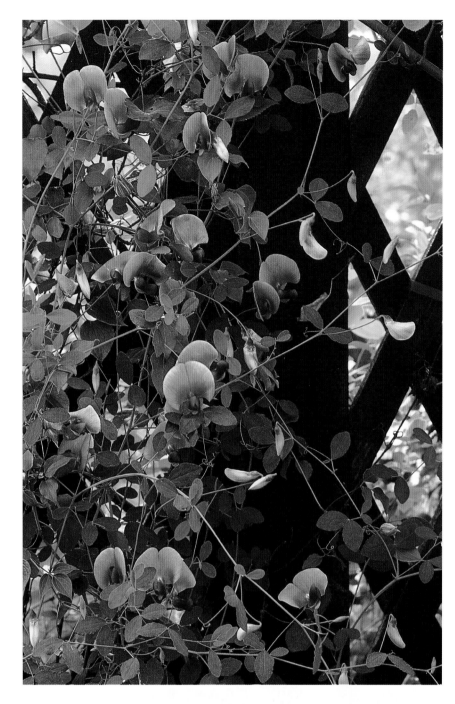

RIGHT: THE EVERLASTING
SWEETPEA IS A PERENNIAL
FAVORITE WITH GARDENERS.

petaled flowers during the late summer months. Fairly hardy, it has the advantage of lovely dark, glossy green leaves. *T. asiaticum* (zones 7–10) is another species with cream flowers that turn yellow in summer.

Wisteria must rank as one of the most beautiful, decorative, often invasive, hardy deciduous climbers. A member of the pea family, (Papilionaceae), the most fragrant species, *W. sinensis* (syn. *W. chinensis*) (zones 5–8), comes from China. Heavily vanilla-perfumed pale violet or lilac racemes are borne by *W. sinensis* 'Prolific' in the spring. *W. sinensis* has a white form, 'Alba,' which is even more scented, and *W.* 'Caroline' (zones 5–8) is a deep blue variety. The Japanese wisteria, *W. floribunda* 'Alba,' (zones 5–9) flowers in early summer with white blossoms that are more lightly scented. Other *W. floribunda* varieties include the violet and blue 'Multijuga,' purple 'Violacea Plena,' and rosy-pink 'Rosea.' The Chinese and Japanese wisterias are the two most widely planted species of this highly ornamental plant. With its gnarled stems, this climber is hard to beat in its flowering glory. Striking contrasts can be achieved by mingling lilac wisteria with yellow climbing roses. In full maturity, a plant can easily cover the wall of a house and is therefore more suitable to grow over arches or against walls than the more restricted area of an arbor. The only drawback of this splendid climber is that it takes about five years to flower.

More unusual and lesser-known fragrant climbers include the deciduous or semi-evergreen twining

Akebia quinata, otherwise known as the chocolate vine on account of its unusual deep brownish-purple, vanilla-scented flowers. It likes a sunny, sheltered position. *Actinidia* by contrast prefers shade, although it can be planted in full sun. The best-known variety is the Kiwi fruit or Chinese gooseberry (*A. deliciosa,* (zones 7–9) syn *A. chinensis*), which is a very vigorous climber that can reach up to 100ft (30m) or more. Small scented white flowers are borne by *A. arguta* (zones 3–8) and *A. kolomikta* (zones 5–8) in the early summer. These both grow to approximately 20ft (6m) high.

Cionura erecta (syn. *Marsdenia erecta*) carries fragrant clusters of five-petaled ivory flowers in the summer. It is a semi-hardy deciduous twining climber that prefers a sunny wall for protection. Small, fragrant, cream flowers are produced by the hardy evergreen climber *Kadsura japonica*, which is adorned with deep purple and red foliage in the fall. This climber grows best in semi-shade. For scented pale violet flowers in mid- to late spring, the evergreen *Stauntonia hexaphylla* is a hardy climber that later bears purple edible fruit if conditions are warm. Although frost hardy, it is happier planted in a sheltered sunny position and grows to 33ft (10m) high.

focal points and features

All gardens require focal points to attract the eye toward a specific view or provide enduring structure within the overall scheme. A piece of sculpture or a stone sundial can provide such a feature, which endures all year round. A decorative urn planted with a seasonal display of scented plants or an evergreen topiary specimen, such as a clipped bay, are other ways of endowing the fragrant garden with an aromatic focal point. (Container planting is described in Chapter 4.)

BELOW: THE PERFECT FORM OF THE LOTUS, OR WATER LILY, HAS ALWAYS SYMBOLIZED PURITY IN THE EAST.

Water features A water feature can be one of the most charming areas of the scented garden. Whether you choose to have an easily installed, preformed pond, a tiny water barrel, a wildlife bog garden, or a more elaborate concrete pool, you need to consider carefully what suits you best. Safety is a consideration if you have young children, and cost can be another factor. Esthetically, you may prefer to have a raised water garden or an elegant fountain as a central feature, providing a melodic cascade of water. Creating a waterfall can even be as simple as a diverting a narrow stream of water over several stone steps using a basic electrical pump and tube mechanism. Whatever your choice, water in your garden, enhanced with sweetly scented plants, will provide you with a cool and soothing haven.

Planting an aromatic water garden can be very straightforward. The most striking fragrant plants are the aristocratic water lilies from the genus *Nymphaea*. Exotic *N. odorata* from North America is particularly fragrant and happy to grow in still water. The most intensely perfumed variety is the large, white-petaled *N. o.* var. *gigantea*; abundant smaller, white starlike fragrant flowers adorn *N. o.* var. *minor*, whereas *N.* 'Odorata Sulphurea Grandiflora' is a sweetly perfumed yellow variety. For scented pink varieties, plant the beautiful rose-pink 'Rose Arey,' 'Masaniello,' or the soft pink 'W.B. Shaw.'

An unusually scented yellow water lily, suitable only for large ponds, is the brandy-scented *Nuphar lutea*, otherwise called brandy bottle. *Nymphaea* 'Gladstoneana' (T) is an excellent white tropical water lily, deeply fragrant, with voluptuous peonylike blooms.

Other fragrant plants for the water garden are *Acorus calamus* or sweet flag, which has cinnamon-scented leaves and was used for strewing floors in medieval and Elizabethan times. It is still used to produce an essential oil used in perfumery work. The lilac water violet (*Hottonia palustris*), the pale golden-yellow water iris (*Iris pseudacorus*), and the vanilla-scented, white-flowed water hawthorn (*Aponogeton distachyos*) are all suited to small pools. The rampant water mint (*Mentha aquatica*), with its mint-scented mauve flowers should be planted with caution and is perhaps best kept contained in buckets. The borders of a pond can be planted with the delicately scented yellow cowslips (*Primula veris*), the lemon-scented Himalayan cowslip (*P. sikkimensis*) (zones 4–8), or the giant Himalayan cowslip (*P. florindae*) (zones 3–8), which thrive in damp conditions.

Scented lawns and meadows Before the advent of grass lawns as we know them today, all lawns were fragrant. In the early seventeenth century, they were planted with either perennial chamomile or thyme, although other herbs were sometimes used. Francis Bacon in *An Essay of Gardens* (1625) extolled the virtue of three herbs that perfumed the air: "But those which Perfume the Aire most delightfully, not passed by as the rest, but being Troden upon and Crushed, are Three: That is Burnet, Wilde-Time and Water-Mints. Therefore, you are to set whole Allies of them, to have the Pleasure, when you walke to tread."

Salad burnet (*Sanguisorba minor*) has a cucumber scent; thyme can range from a lemony to a pine scent with small flowers of either pink, white, purple, or mauve; while mints have a pungent refreshing scent and soft leaves. A small fragrant herb lawn can be laid out in front of a scented arbor, as part of your herb garden, or as a feature in its own right. Use pennyroyal (*Mentha pulegium*) instead of water mint, chamomile (*Chamaemelum nobile* 'Treneague'), salad burnet, and creeping thymes such as *Thymus serpyllum* (zones 4–8) *T. praecox* (zones 5–8). These wonderfully fragrant carpets can be used in much the

ABOVE: THE RECTANGULAR POOL IS SOFTENED BY LUSH PLANTING IN THIS INTIMATE ENGLISH WATER GARDEN.

same way as a grass lawn, for according to Shakespeare, the more chamomile, thyme, and burnet are trodden on, the faster they grow.

For a wilder effect, meadow plants such as the apple-scented German annual chamomile (*Matricaria recutita*), the fragrant wild tulip (*Tulipa sylvestris*), the sweetly scented purple saffron crocus (*C. sativus*) (zones 5–8), and even the lovely madonna lily (*Lilium candidum*) can be naturalized in grassy areas. The flowery meads of medieval times (see also Chapter 1) incorporated a wide range of species in these romantic gardens, including violets, wallflowers, forget-me-nots, fragrant aquilegia, pansies, and pinks. There are also many species of scented jonquil, crocus, and narcissi which will spread in wild grassland and look stunning in the spring. Be careful not to cut the grass and leaves down for at least four to six weeks after the plants have finished flowering to avoid disappointment the following year.

A woodland area A number of scented plants are integral to woodlands, some so well loved that we could not imagine spring without them. Snowdrops and bluebells, violets, sweet woodruff, and those most beautiful of plants, the Christmas or Lenten roses. One of the earliest plants in the winter garden

ABOVE: A WOODLAND GLADE IN SPRING, WITH SNOW-
DROPS AT GREENEND GARDENS, SUFFOLK, ENGLAND.

that brings fragrance when there are still frosts and
snow about is the honey-scented, delicate snowdrop.
Happiest in dappled shade and humus-rich moist soil,
it is a hardy little plant, which steadily multiplies,
especially the common European snowdrop,
Galanthus nivalis (zones 3–9): snowdrops are most
dramatic planted in great sweeps under shrubs or
trees. The double form *G. n.* 'Flore Pleno' flowers in
late winter and early spring, and is suitable for winter
flower arrangements. *G. elwesii* (zones 3–9), which
comes from the Balkans and Turkey, is honey
scented, as is the strongly scented *G.* 'S. Arnott'
(zones 4–9), while *G. allenii* (zones 6–9) carries
almond-scented flowers in the middle of winter. The
earliest to flower is the autumn snowdrop, *G. reginae-
olgae* (zones 6–9), and around Christmas, *G. gracilis*
(zones 3–9) carries flowers that smell of violets.

Evergreen hellebores look lovely alongside
snowdrops; their dark leaves set off to perfection the
snowy whiteness of their companions. Ideally suited to
woodland planting, hellebores prefer dappled shade

with moist soil and are fully to half hardy. The stinking
hellebore (*Helleborus foetidus*) (zones 6–9) flowers in
the late winter and early spring, carrying pale green
bells edged in deep red. The variety 'Miss Jekyll's
Scented' has a scent similar to lily-of-the-valley, as
does the tender *H. lividus* (zones 8–9), while the
yellowish-green flowered *H. odorus* (zones 6–9) is also
fragrant. The Christmas rose, *H. niger* (zones 4–8),
carries white flowers in the coldest months, as does
the Lenten rose *H. orientalis* (zones 4–9), although the
latter flowers have little scent and can range in color
from ivory to the deepest maroon. Hellebores self-
seed freely and should be divided in the fall.

In late spring, the fragrant bluebell carpets temperate
woods, casting a violet-blue hue, which is especially
lovely in light green beech woods. The English bluebell
(*Hyacinthoides non-scripta* (zones 4–9), (syn. *Endymion
non-scripta*) usually bears blue balsamic-scented, bell-
like flowers, but they also occasionally produce pink or
white flowers, as does the Spanish bluebell (*H.
hispanica*) (zones 4–9), which carries larger flowers but
is virtually unscented. Both species are prolific self-
seeders and can be invasive in a bed but are perfect for
woodland settings. They are hardy and can be grown

from bulbs planted in the fall. A semi-shaded site is best in moist soil; full sun will bleach out the intense blue of these delicate-looking plants.

Violets thrive in grassy areas under trees and like dappled shade. With the exception of Parma violets, they are hardy and like cool moist conditions. Many lilies are also suited to planting in woodland conditions – see Chapter 7 for recommended species of both.

aromatic trees

Deciduous trees For late spring and early summer fragrant gardens, lilac is an old favorite. *Syringa vulgaris* (zones 4–8), the common lilac, is sweetly scented and has been grown in Europe since the sixteenth century. It can be found in all colors ranging from blue and white through to deep crimson-red, lavender, and purple. One of the finest of the common lilacs is *S. v.* 'Katherine Havemeyer,' which has lavender-purple flowers that fade to lilac-pink on opening. Another excellent lilac is the magnificent white *S. v.* 'Vestale'; *S. v.* 'Madame Lemoine' is another lovely old white lilac. But it was the lovely double white lilac *S.* x *persica* 'Alba' (zones 3–7), a strongly fragrant Persian, that was the favorite of John Rea, the early garden writer. It was cultivated originally in ancient India and Persia. *S.* x *josiflexa* 'Bellicent' (zones 4–7), produces sweet-smelling rose-pink flowers: a marvelous sight in any bed. For a lilac that blooms abundantly from spring and then intermittently until the middle of fall, the small scented rose-pink *S. pubescens* subsp. *microphylla* 'Superba' (zones 5–8) is highly recommended. Fragrant flushed-pink flowers are borne by *S. sweginzowii* (zones 6–7), a lilac introduced from western China

at the end of the nineteenth century.

Another charming flowering tree or shrub for the smaller garden is the genus *Styrax*, of which the dainty *S. japonicus* (zones 6–8) is deservedly regarded as the most elegant. Related to the snowdrop tree, *Halesia*, and known in North America as the snowbell tree, it carries bell-shaped scented white flowers in late spring and early summer that are best viewed from below. It grows to about 20ft (6m) in 20 years. *S. j.* 'Pink Chimes' is the pale pink variety. Like magnolia, it should be planted where it is

BELOW: A TWISTED MAGNOLIA BLOOMS BESIDE A WILD-FLOWER MEADOW IN EARLY SUMMER.

ABOVE: THE PALE BLOOMS OF *SAMBUCUS NIGRA*
'GUINCHO PURPLE' ARE SET OFF BY ITS DARK LEAVES.

protected from morning sun. The more powerfully perfumed variety is from Japan, *S. obassia* (zones 6–8), carrying fragrant white flowers in the early summer. This is a taller tree growing to approximately 30ft (9m) in 20 years. Aromatic benzoin is obtained from a tropical member of the genus, *S. benzoin* (T).

The black cottonwood (*Populus trichocarpa*) (zones 5–9), native to North America, is one of the finest and fastest-growing of the balsam poplars, exuding a powerfully fragrant balsamic scent. The fresh buds can be added to potpourri. Another highly fragrant poplar is the aromatic *P.* 'Balsam Spire' (zones 4–9), which is a narrow tree. The balm of Gilead or Ontario poplar (*P. candicans*) (zones 5–9) possesses the same fragrance and can be an attractive addition to the aromatic garden, while *P. balsamifera* (zones 5–9) is used to produce an exotically scented essential oil for perfumery.

The creamy clusters of starlike flowers of elder carried in spring and summer have a musky scent and can be used to make cordials, wine, and elderflower champagne. A healing tisane can also be made from the flowers. In the fall, the berries of the common elder (*Sambucus nigra*) (zones 5–8) can be used to make wine. They are also used to produce an essential oil used in perfumery. One of the most ornamental elders is the hardy golden *S. n.* 'Aurea,' which needs full sun to bring out the color of its leaves. Equally beautiful is the purple-leaved, *S. n.* 'Guincho Purple.'

For the larger garden, the linden or lime (*Tilia*), is a highly fragrant deciduous tree with delightful fruity-scented creamy-yellow flowers. It can grow up to 80–100ft (25–30m), and its main drawback is that the aphids it attracts cause dripping honeydew that can spread mold. In addition, some linden flowers can be toxic to bees. *T. x euchlora* (zones 3–7), the Crimean linden, is a beautiful tree, with very fragrant greenish-white flowers and does not attract aphids; its flowers, however, do cause this adverse effect in bees. The same is true of *T. tomentosa* (zones 6–9), also known as the silver linden, for its leaves appear to have been painted silver underneath. A linden tree suitable for smaller gardens is *T. mongolica* (zones 3–7), which has lovely yellow leaves in the fall as well as fragrant creamy flowers in summer. Linden essential oil is used in aromatherapy in much the same way as lemon balm, being soothing and rejuvenating.

Evergreen trees Stately trees such as the evergreen species of magnolia can be used as an elegant and striking feature in the aromatic garden. *M. grandiflora* (zones 7–9) is one of the best, originally from the southeastern U.S. It is a handsome tree with dark glossy leaves and great saucer-shaped flowers, powerfully lemon-scented from summer into the fall. These trees are best planted in semi-shade and can reach up to 100ft (30m). One drawback is the length of time it takes for flowers to be produced, although some varieties flower sooner than others. *M. g.* 'Goliath' produces its ivory-white flowers when it is young, as does *M. g.* 'Samuel Sommer.'

Astringent medicinal scents reminiscent of balsam or turpentine, belong to the *Pinaceae* and *Cupressaceae* families. These include the spruce, fir, cedar, cypress, juniper, and pine trees, all of which are used extensively to make fresh-scented essential oils. The upright Italian cypress (*Cupressus sempervirens*) (zones 8–10) makes a dramatic statement that captures the essence of the Mediterranean, while the giant cedar of Lebanon (*Cedrus libani*) (zones 7–9) and the Atlantic cedar (*C. atlantica*) (zones 6–9) are only suitable for the larger landscape.

The pine tree family comprises about 100 evergreen trees with resin-scented cones and foliage, many of which are suited to a smaller garden. The scented cones were originally used to flavor ale and wine, and were known as pine-apples. The Scots pine (*Pinus sylvestris*) is perhaps best known for its aromatic resin, which is used to extract essential oil of pine and as a source of turpentine. The Weymouth or white pine (*P. strobus*) (zones 4–9), taken to Britain from North America in the eighteenth century, is an elegant ornamental pine with green leaves striped with silver. The cones are literally saturated with fragrant resin. Smaller pines are the low-growing trees or shrubs, the mountain pine (*P. mugo*) (zones 3–7) and its various cultivars: *P. m.* 'Ophir' and *P. m.* 'Winter Gold' both have golden foliage in winter.

Tender species The fast-growing *Eucalyptus* genus is generally best suited to warm climates, although some can survive cold weather. The foliage of *E. citriodora* (zones 9–10) emits a lemony fragrance, but as a young plant it needs to be grown in conservatory conditions in colder climates. Oil of eucalyptus is obtained from the leaves and twigs of the frost-tender Victoria blue gum (*E. globulus*) (zones 9–10) and *E. citriodora* (zones 9–10) among others. Several other species, however, are hardier: the Tasmanian snow gum (*E. coccifera*) (zones 8–10) can survive most hard winters. Its crushed leaves emit a strong peppermint aroma; also winter hardy are the cider gum *(E. gunnii)* (zones 8–10), which has aromatic silvery-blue leaves; the yellow gum (*E. johnstonii*) (zones 9–10), which can grow to over 75ft (23m); and the beautiful snow gum *(E. pauciflora* subsp. *niphophila)* (zones 8–10), which is one of the hardiest and boasts a beautiful smooth trunk, colored cream, gray,

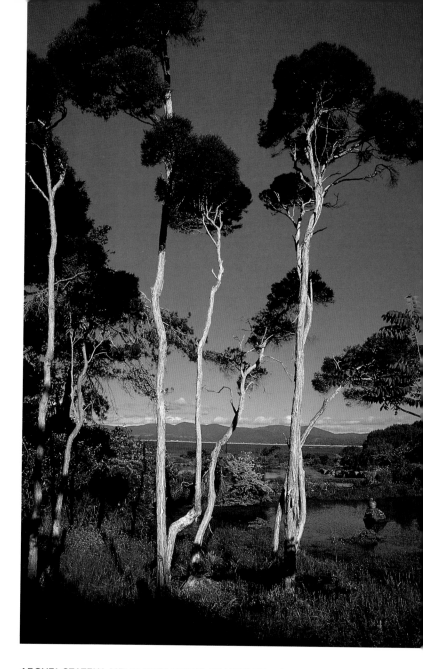

ABOVE: STATELY *MELALEUCA* TREES AT HAWLEY HOUSE GARDENS, TASMANIA – MANY PLANTS IN THE TEA TREE FAMILY ARE USED TO PRODUCE ESSENTIAL OILS.

and light green and compared to the skin of a python.

Melaleuca is a tender aromatic genus native to Australasia and Southeast Asia. The narrow-leaved paperbark tea tree (*M. alternifolia*) (T) from Australia is the smallest of the tea trees, growing to no more than 23ft (7m) in height. It has bright green needlelike leaves and tiny yellow or cream "bottle-brush" flowers and thrives in swampy areas. The fragrant leaves were used by the Aborigines for making tea. Today it is the source of the spicy-scented tea tree essential oil, which has excellent antiseptic and bactericidal properties. Several species of the *Melaleuca* genus are used in aromatherapy, notably *M. linariifolia* (T) and *M. viridiflora* (T).

7 aromatic plant portraits

the working garden

Having assessed your garden and planned the overall structure, your
attention can be turned to the plants themselves. The ideal aromatic
garden should not only be a scented sanctuary, but also a working area
where plants are chosen carefully for their scent, color, and usage,
whether medicinal, culinary, or decorative. The following species have
been selected specifically for the modern aromatic garden on the basis of
their esthetic appeal and variety of applications.

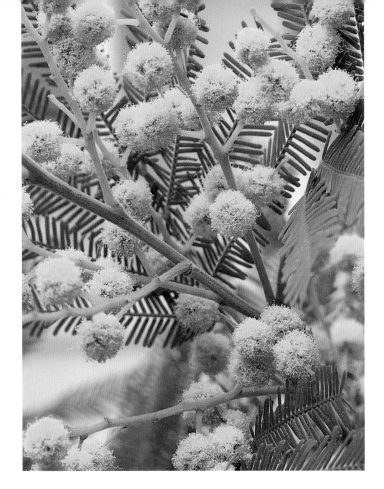

ABOVE: MIMOSA (*A. DEALBATA*)

Acacia dealbata

MIMOSA (Mimosaceae)

Scent – violetlike, woody-floral, slightly green, rich, sweet, uplifting, soothing.

DESCRIPTION AND CULTIVATION

Acacias, or wattle, are attractive evergreen or semi-evergreen trees, with strongly scented, fluffy yellow flowers that bloom in either spring or winter. There are more than 400 varieties, many of which are found in the tropics or subtropics of Australia, South America, or Africa. Mimosa (*A. dealbata*), also known as the silver wattle, is a native of Australia, but has naturalized across much of Africa and southern Europe. It was first introduced into Europe in the early nineteenth century as an ornamental evergreen plant for its delicate silvery-green foliage and fragrant lemony yellow flowers, produced from late winter to early spring. Mimosa is now cultivated in France and Spain especially for its perfumery value.

Mimosa can withstand a minimum temperature of 23°F (-5°C): with the right protection it can be grown outside in a sheltered position in colder climates, provided the plant is wrapped up in horticultural fleece if there is danger of a hard frost. If mimosa is grown in a container, it needs vigorous pruning to keep it from growing too tall – trees can reach heights of more than 40ft (12m). Conservatory specimens can be moved outside to a sunny position during the summer. Acacias like well-drained soil and full sun, and are best propagated by seed sown in spring or by semi-ripe cuttings in summer.

RECOMMENDED SPECIES

A. ulicifolia (zones 9–11) is a frost-hardy dwarf variety (3ft/1m high) with clusters of pale yellow flowers in spring. Some of the more outstanding wattle trees for a conservatory are undoubtedly *A. baileyana* (zones 10–11), the Cootamundra wattle from New South Wales, Australia, which has striking blue-green foliage, and Oven's wattle (*A. pravissima*) (zones 10–11) with bright yellow flowers – both reach about 16ft (5m) high. A deeper yellow flower is found on the Queensland silver wattle, *A. podalyriifolia* (zones 10-11), which flowers both in winter and spring, as does *A. retinodes* (zones 10–11), which is sweetly scented.

HOME USES

• *Aromatherapy applications* – An absolute is produced from the fresh flowers and twigs of *A. dealbata*, mainly for use in expensive perfumes. It also has excellent fixative properties. In aromatherapy, mimosa is used in astringent skin ointments and for treating stress-related conditions such as anxiety, over-sensitivity, and depression. *A. farnesiana* (zones 8–10) or sweet acacia is used to produce the perfumery material cassie. In India, its dried flowers are added to baths for their skin-toning properties. They are also prepared in the form of an infusion as a cosmetic aid – see page 73.

• *Drying and decorative uses* – Fresh mimosa flowers look beautiful in naturalistic arrangements; the dried bark can be burned to produce a musky, leatherlike incense, while the dried flowers of sweet acacia and mimosa can be added to potpourris.

• *Culinary suggestions* – Cassie is used in minute amounts for flavoring confectionery and soft drinks; the ripe seeds are pressed for cooking oil.

• *Health-giving properties* – The bark of mimosa contains 42 percent tannins and is employed medicinally for the treatment of diarrhea and as an astringent gargle and ointment. Many acacia species have native medicinal uses: for example, the Senegal acacia (*A. senegal*) (zones 10–11) yields a sticky exudation from its trunk known as gum arabic, which is used extensively as a demulcent.

Achillea millefolium

YARROW (Asteraceae)

Scent – fresh, green, sweet, herblike, slightly camphoraceous, restorative, revitalizing, tonic.

DESCRIPTION AND CULTIVATION

Yarrow is one of the oldest known medicinal plants, named after the heroic warrior Achilles, due to its outstanding healing qualities. Its dried straight stems are used to make the divination sticks for the Chinese "I Ching" oracle, and in the West, too, it has also traditionally been associated with divination and magic. Yarrow is an unassuming perennial herb, with a straight stem up to 3ft (1m) high and finely dissected grayish-silver leaves, giving it a lacy appearance. It bears numerous pinkish-white dense flower heads from summer into fall.

Common throughout Europe, Asia, and North America, where it can be found growing wild on wastelands, yarrow is an easy plant to grow

BELOW: COMMON YARROW (*A. MILLEFOLIUM*) WITH MARIGOLD. ABOVE: *ACHILLEA* 'MOONSHINE.'

and will survive even the most inhospitable conditions, such as very dry, salty, or windswept situations – though it does not like heavy soils. It is a prolific grower and spreads rapidly via its creeping rootstock, but although it is invasive, it is not hard to control by digging up established clumps each spring and dividing or discarding surplus growth. Yarrow thrives in a sunny position where the warmth of the sun draws out the plant's aroma: both the flowers and the leaves are richly pungent.

RECOMMENDED SPECIES

The cultivars 'Cerise Queen' (deep pink), 'Fire King' (rich red), and 'Moonshine' (bright yellow) are particularly striking, the latter being smaller in stature (2ft/60cm), making it suitable for the front of a bed. Plants from *A. ptarmica* (zones 3–8) The Pearl Group have very pretty, pomponlike white flowers and are mid-height with glossy green leaves; *A. filipendulina* (zones 3–9) makes a lovely tall plant for the back of the bed with stiff erect stems and yellow flowers; *A. grandifolia* (zones 4–8) is the giant of the yarrows and makes a dramatic statement.

HOME USES

• *Aromatherapy applications* – An essential oil is made by steam distillation from the dried flowering herb. The oil is used with massage to reduce hypertension and insomnia, and to treat stress-related conditions. Yarrow also tones the blood vessels and is used to treat varicose veins, arteriosclerosis, and high blood pressure. The flower water has an astringent and toning effect on the skin and is good for a wide range of skin conditions including acne, eczema, inflammations, and scars – see page 72.

• *Drying and decorative uses* – The flowers of all forms of yarrow dry well and can be used in potpourris, sweet bags, etc. The cut stems are ideal for fresh and dried flower arrangements. An infusion of yarrow makes a good hair rinse and promotes hair growth.

• *Culinary suggestions* – Try adding the young leaves of *A. millefolium* sparingly to early summer salads.

• *Health-giving properties* – Highly valued, particularly for its anti-inflammatory, antiseptic, and wound-healing qualities, yarrow is also one of the best herbal remedies for fever. For an uplifting tonic tea, add 1 tablespoon of dried flowers to 1 pint (500ml) of boiling water, infuse well, and add honey to taste.

NOTE: Avoid during pregnancy.

Allium schoenoprasum

CHIVES (Alliaceae)

Scent – sharp, slightly acrid, onionlike, green, stimulating, fresh.

DESCRIPTION AND CULTIVATION

Some of the most invaluable plants In the herb or kitchen garden are alliums, better known as garlic, onions, and chives. Besides being valuable for cooking, garlic (*A. sativum*) (zones 4–9) has traditional medicinal properties and was used extensively throughout history by the ancient Egyptians, Greeks, and Romans, and right across the Middle and Far East and Europe. Onions (*A. cepa*) (zones 3–9), of which numerous cultivars are now available, also possess outstanding medicinal and culinary qualities.

Chives (*A. schoenoprasum*) demonstrate many of the same properties as garlic and onions, and are mentioned in early Chinese herbals. They have a

milder flavor and a less intense aroma than either garlic or onions, making them more versatile as garden plants. A clump of chives makes a colorful addition to any herb garden or bed, with their striking mauve or rose-pink clustered heads. Native to Europe, Australia, and North America, they thrive in hot sun and like a rich, moist soil – they also enjoy the addition of leftover coffee grounds to their soil. Without nutrients and plenty of water, the leaves soon begin to turn yellow and wilt.

Planted under roses, chives, like garlic, act as an aphid repellent, prevent black spot, and help intensify the perfume of the roses; planted next to apple trees, they help prevent scab. Chives make very attractive edging plants and will flourish in windowboxes or in pots. A heavy frost will make them die back in winter, so bring a pot into the house for a fresh all-year-round supply. Easy to grow from seed, chives can also be propagated by bulb division – indeed, it is best to lift established clumps every few years and divide them.

• *Culinary suggestions* – Chives can be cut to within 2in (5cm) of the ground up to four times a year for culinary use. Because the flavor is relatively mild, they are best added at the end of the cooking or chopped as a fresh garnish onto egg or potato dishes, soft cheeses, salads, or soups, or scattered over broiled fish and meat.

• *Health-giving properties* – Like garlic, chives can help to boost energy, detoxify the system, and aid digestion. They also possess mild antiseptic properties. For medicinal purposes, the most effective and convenient way to get the benefit of alliums is in the form of garlic capsules, taken internally.

RECOMMENDED SPECIES

There is also a white form, a fine-leaved variety, and a pink form of *A. schoenoprasum*. The so-called garlic chives (*A. tuberosum*) (zones 4–8) have starry white flowers and a sweet garlic flavor. Instead of chives, the larger evergreen Welsh onion (*A. fistulosum*) (zones 4–9) can be grown and used in the winter months; the tree onion (*A. cepa* Proliferum Group) is useful in salads and stews. There are also several ornamental allium species that have scented flowers, such as *A. stipitatum* (zones 4–9).

HOME USES

• *Aromatherapy applications* – Essential oils are produced from many allium species, including onions (*A. cepa* and *A. fistulosum*), garlic, chives, and garlic chives. Valuable for flavoring, they are rarely used in aromatherapy work because of their pungent smell.

• *Drying and decorative uses* – Flower heads can be dried and used in potpourris, but the leaves of chives do not dry well. Instead, a pot of fresh chives makes a useful and colorful kitchen addition. The more decorative allium species are valuable for use in fresh flower arrangements.

Aloysia triphylla

LEMON VERBENA
(Verbenaceae)

Scent – lemony, fruity-floral, fresh, sweet, uplifting, refreshing, soothing.

DESCRIPTION AND CULTIVATION

This is one of the most beautiful semi-hardy deciduous shrubs for a sheltered spot in the garden or for a cool conservatory. Lemon verbena has bright green foliage and delicate pale purple flowers. It produces woody stems with long, lush, graceful branches bearing very fragrant, lemon-scented narrow leaves. Because of its delightful scent, it is a lovely plant to position near an entrance or by a seat where it can be appreciated. A native of South America, it was first taken to Europe by the Spaniards in the seventeenth century. In tropical conditions, it will reach a height of 16ft (5m) or more, but in cooler climates it will not usually grow higher than 6ft 6in (2m). If it is grown outside, in temperate regions lemon verbena needs the warmth of a sheltered wall to survive, for it will not tolerate temperatures below 14°F (−10°C), and even so will benefit from being protected over winter with thin spun polyester. After winter, new growth can often be slow, and it is best to wait until late spring to see if a plant has survived or not.

Alternatively, lemon verbena can be grown as a container plant and simply moved under glass at the end of the summer. It thrives in a rich but free-draining soil, in a sunny position, and likes to be kept moist during the growing season. Trim the branches to about half their length in the fall to encourage bushy growth the following season. Plants are best propagated by softwood cuttings taken in late spring or by semi-hardwood cuttings taken in late summer (the seeds do not set well in cool climates).

NOTE: Lemon verbena is not to be confused with *Verbena officinalis*, a hardy herb known as vervain, or with the herb lemon balm (*Melissa officinalis*).

HOME USES

• *Aromatherapy applications* – An essential oil is produced by steam distillation from the fresh leaves, mainly for use in perfumery and particularly to produce *eau de verveine*. However, the oil is phototoxic and also is frequently adulterated with other lemon-scented oils, such as that from the plant *Litsea cubeba* (zones 8–10). Hence, it is little used in aromatherapy for these reasons, although it does have value therapeutically for stress-related disorders and digestive complaints. To make a flower water at home, see page 72.

• *Drying and decorative uses* – Dried leaves will retain their fragrance for several years and are ideal for use in potpourris, bath bags (fresh or dried), herb pillows, and for all kinds of scented sachets

• *Culinary suggestions* – Use fresh leaves to flavor oil or vinegar (see page 35), to add to salads, and as a garnish for all sorts of fruit drinks, desserts, ice cream, etc.

• *Health-giving properties* – Sharing similar medicinal properties to lemon balm, the fresh or dried leaves make a deliciously uplifting yet soothing tea that is also good for digestive upsets of nervous origin.

NOTE: Prolonged use of the herb can cause stomach irritation.

Angelica archangelica

ANGELICA (Apiaceae)

Scent: rich, herby-earthy, fresh-green, spicy, fortifying, pungent, purifying, warming.

DESCRIPTION AND CULTIVATION

Angelica is one of the most striking sculptural plants in the herb garden. The whole plant is powerfully aromatic: the ferny leaves have a pungent, fresh green scent while the large rhizome or root has a musky-earthy aroma. In early summer, umbels of sweet-scented greenish-white flowers rise from tall branches, which later in the year bear many spicy-scented seedheads. This is one of the earliest herbs known and comes from the cold climates of Russia, Lithuania, and Iceland. The whole plant can reach a height of about 8ft (2.5m) with a 3ft (1m) spread, so it needs to be positioned at the back of a bed. Best planted in dappled shade, it likes rich soil with plenty of moisture. Although angelica is a hardy biennial (a perennial if it is prevented from flowering), it dies down completely over the winter. It can easily be grown from seed sown in early fall, although this is hardly necessary since it is a great self-seeder and will propagate itself year after year. Plants can also be propagated by root division, which should be carried out at the end of the growing season.

LEFT: LEMON VERBENA (*ALOYSIA TRIPHYLLA*), IF POTTED, CAN BE OVER-WINTERED UNDER GLASS.

ABOVE: ANGELICA (*ANGELICA ARCHANGELICA*) MAKES A
DRAMATIC SCULPTURAL STATEMENT IN A BED.

RECOMMENDED SPECIES

The American angelica (*A. atropurpurea*) (zones 4–9)
shares similar properties with *A. archangelica*, but only
grows up to 5ft (1.5m) high, making it more suitable for
smaller gardens. Wild angelica (*A. sylvestris*) (zones 4–9)
is also a smaller plant, but is not suitable for culinary use.

HOME USES

• *Aromatherapy applications* – The seed oil is mainly
used for "damp" conditions such as arthritis, gout,
rheumatism, edema, colds, and coughs; also for
digestive disorders and nervous debility. An aromatic
water made from the distilled leaves revitalizes dull
and congested skin. See page 72 for instruction on
making flower waters.
• *Drying and decorative uses* – The dried chopped
root or root latex makes an excellent potpourri fixative;
seedheads can be used in dried arrangements.
• *Culinary suggestions* – The leaves, stem, root, and
seeds can all be used in cooking, and the fresh leaves
add zest to salads, soups, and stews. The tender
stems are traditionally candied and used to decorate
cakes, while the dried root is used in breadmaking and
the seeds for flavoring pastry.

• *Health-giving properties* – An infusion made from the
fresh leaves or seeds has soothing digestive and
restorative properties. The Chinese angelica (*A.
sinensis*) (zones 4–9) is a very effective tonic,
comparable to ginseng, but specifically for women.
NOTE: Best avoided during pregnancy and by
diabetics.

Artemisia dracunculus

FRENCH TARRAGON
(Asteraceae)

*Scent – bitter-sweet, peppery, warm,
herby, sharp, slightly aniselike,
stimulating.*

DESCRIPTION AND CULTIVATION

Artemisia is a large genus that contains some of the
bitterest aromatic herbs known, including tarragon,
wormwood (*A. absinthium*) (zones 4–8),
southernwood (*A. abrotanum*) (zones 5–8), and
sagebrush (*A. californica*) (zones 5–9). Many have
pronounced medicinal properties, but it is the unique
scent and sharp herby-green flavor of tarragon that
makes it indispensable for the fragrant herb garden.

LEFT: WORMWOOD (*A. ABSINTHIUM*).
RIGHT: FRENCH TARRAGON (*A. DRACUNCULUS*).

French tarragon (*A. dracunculus*) is a half-hardy perennial herb, with narrow green aromatic leaves and small yellowish flowers. In warm climates it will grow all year round, but in colder regions it will die back after the first frosts. As a native of southern Europe, French tarragon is slightly tender, and in cold areas it is a good idea to cover the roots with a mulch before winter sets in. Alternatively, it is happy to be grown outside in big pots over summer and then moved to the protection of a cold frame or greenhouse in the fall. It likes plenty of warmth and a free-draining soil, so plants grown in pots need plenty of drainage.

French tarragon grows to about 3ft (1m) tall in a single season, and although it does not have the most decorative of flowers, its fine dark green leaves and bushy shape contrast well with the foliage of other kitchen herbs, such as sage or chives. For culinary use, the flowers should be pinched out to encourage leafy growth. It is best to propagate French tarragon from cuttings or by root division, since it does not seed itself readily, and much of the commercial seed sold as French is actually the Russian species (*A. dracunculus dracunculoides*) (zones 3–7). French tarragon plants should be replaced every three or four years as the flavor gradually deteriorates.

RECOMMENDED SPECIES

Russian tarragon (*A. dracunculoides*) is a taller, more straggly plant 4ft (1.2m) high, with thinner, paler leaves and a milder, less refined flavor. It is, however, a completely hardy plant and will survive even the coldest of winters. Many of the other *Artemisia* species have decorative value for the herb garden or flowerbed. Wormwood (*A. absinthium*) has finely divided, silvery evergreen leaves with a pungent bitter aroma; the cultivar 'Lambrook Silver' is smaller with even more finely divided leaves. Southernwood (*A. abrotanum*) is a very attractive semi-evergreen plant with feathery olive-green leaves and a fruity-green scent. It grows to about 3ft (1m) high and bears yellow flowers in spring and early summer. It even does well in polluted cities. California sagebrush (*A. californica*) has delightfully citrus-scented leaves. Mugwort (*A. vulgaris*) (zones 4–8) is a renowned "magical" herb used for female ailments, while white mugwort (*A. lactiflora*) (zones 5–8) is valuable for dried flower arrangements.

HOME USES

• *Aromatherapy applications* – An essential oil (estragon) is produced by steam distillation from the leaves of French and Russian tarragon. In aromatherapy it is used in moderation for digestive and genitourinary problems. Essential oils are also produced from a wide selection of artemisias for use in perfumery and flavoring, including wormwood, southernwood, davana (*A. pallens*) (zones 5–8), and mugwort. All contain relatively large amounts of estragole, a moderately toxic constituent, and should therefore be used with caution.

• *Drying and decorative uses* – Apart from tarragon, many of the artemisias dry well for use in decorative arrangements. In addition, all the species mentioned here have moth-, flea-, and insect-repellent properties, making them ideal for linen sachets and posies.

• *Culinary suggestions* – One of the most valuable culinary herbs, tarragon can be used fresh all year round if protected. Apart from being the main flavor in sauce Béarnaise, it complements many dishes, especially fish, rice, chicken, egg, and salads. Good for infusing in oil or vinegar.

• *Health-giving properties* – Many species have powerful antiseptic and anti-infectious properties, and were previously used to combat epidemics such as the plague or jail fever. Due to their potency, however, they should only be administered by a professional herbalist. But a mild tea made from the leaves of French tarragon can be safely used to boost the whole system and to stimulate the appetite.

NOTE: Avoid using all species during pregnancy.

Calendula officinalis

MARIGOLD (Asteraceae)

Scent – green-herby, sharp, pungent, refreshing, cleansing.

DESCRIPTION AND CULTIVATION

This familiar herb of ancient medical repute is now more often cultivated as a decorative plant than for its practical uses. Its bright golden-orange, daisylike flowers are in bloom almost continually and will bring a splash of color to the herb garden or flowerbed, whatever the time of the year. In fact, the marigold is named *Calendula* from the Latin *calendae*, the first day of the month, since it is said that the plants can be found in flower at the beginning of every month.

The common marigold is a hardy annual, growing up to 2ft (60cm) high with soft, bright green leaves and many cheerful flowers. The whole plant is strongly aromatic, especially the leaves. Found growing wild right across the Mediterranean region, it will tolerate most situations, but prefers a well-drained, loamy soil and a sunny position. A single plant will flower over a long period if it is dead-headed regularly, but will eventually die down in winter. Marigolds self-seed readily, but can easily be propagated if required by seed sown in the fall (for early spring flowers) or in spring (for a later show). Some gardeners find it makes an excellent companion plant, as it helps to keep away insect

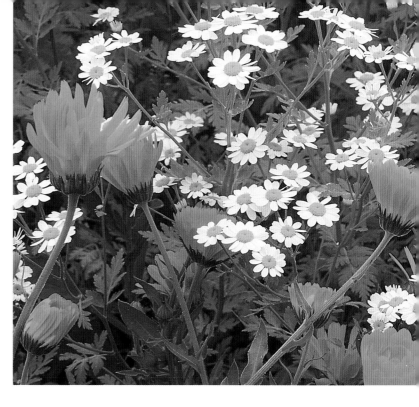

ABOVE: THE COMMON MARIGOLD (*CALENDULA OFFICINALIS*) WITH FEVERFEW.

pests (especially whitefly) from surrounding flowers, herbs, and vegetables.

RECOMMENDED SPECIES

There are many cultivars of the common marigold now available with yellow, red, or double flowers, including 'Prolifera,' which has multiheaded flower stems. Not to be confused with the so-called French marigold (*Tagetes patula*), a strongly scented half-hardy annual about 1ft (30cm) high with bright orange daisylike flowers and deeply cut green leaves.

HOME USES

• *Aromatherapy applications* – True calendula absolute is produced from the fresh flowers of *C. officinalis*. It is, however, an expensive product and difficult to get hold of. In aromatherapy, the infused oil or cream is more commonly used for the treatment of a wide range of skin complaints and injuries including cracked skin, scars, eczema, rashes, viral infections, and inflammations. To make your own infused oil at home, see page 73. An essential oil is also produced from *Tagetes patula*, and – confusingly – it is also called calendula oil. It has a bitter-green odor and is moderately toxic and of limited use, but is sometimes used in the treatment of bunions, calluses, corns, and fungal infections.

• *Drying and decorative uses* – The dried flower heads add zest to potpourri and impart a golden tint to brown hair if used as a final rinse. Use the fresh flowers in bath bags as a skin healer. In the East, marigolds are commonly used in garlands and at festivals for their bright, decorative effect.

• *Culinary suggestions* – Add fresh petals to fish dishes and to salads; the flowers can also be cooked with rice to add a golden color (they are often used as a saffron substitute). The leaves were once used in soups and stews to "comfort the heart and spirits," and gave rise to the name pot marigolds (as they were added to the cooking pot).

• *Health-giving properties* – Applied externally, *C. officinalis* was used extensively during World War II and in the Civil War to treat wounds and to prevent sepsis: the flowers were made into a poultice or used to produce an infused oil. A standard infusion or tea can help heal internal wounds – such as those caused by canker sores, stomach ulcers, or colitis. The infusion stimulates the lymphatic system, reduces glandular swellings, and helps cleanse the body of impurities. **NOTE**: Avoid during pregnancy.

Chamaemelum nobile
ROMAN CHAMOMILE
(Asteraceae)

Scent – warm, sweet, fruity-herby, earthy-green, applelike, profoundly soothing, relaxing.

DESCRIPTION AND CULTIVATION
Roman chamomile is a low-growing evergreen

ABOVE: THERE ARE MANY VARIETIES OF *TAGETES*, SOME OF WHICH ARE USED TO PRODUCE ESSENTIAL OILS.

perennial with feathery leaves and sweet-scented, daisylike white flowers. The whole plant has an apple-like scent and is in flower all summer. It is an ancient medicinal plant and was one of the nine sacred herbs of the Saxons. Chamomile is renowned historically for the fragrant lawns and seats so beloved of the Elizabethans, and examples can still be enjoyed in several historic gardens today, including Buckingham Palace in London. The best chamomile for a lawn is the non-flowering, miniature variety 'Treneague;' otherwise, the flowers require constant cutting. Although it only grows about 4in (10cm) high, it has a spread of 18in (45cm), making it an ideal ground-cover plant.

Chamomile is best planted in the sun and prefers a well-drained soil. It has a beneficial effect on other plants growing nearby and is thus known as the physician's plant. Even cut flowers last longer if chamomile tea is added to their water. Plants can be propagated by seed planted in spring (both Roman and German species), by cuttings, or by division of established plants. See page 84 for instructions on how to plant a chamomile seat.

RECOMMENDED SPECIES
Low-growing *C. nobile* 'Treneague' and the double-flowered cultivar *C. n.* 'Flore Pleno' are very compact – ideal for lawns or for planting between paving. German chamomile (*Matricaria recutita*) is an annual hay-scented herb, up to 2ft (60cm) tall with delicate

feathery leaves and simple, daisylike white flowers that are smaller than those of Roman chamomile. This herb has potent medicinal properties. The short-lived perennial dyer's chamomile (*Anthemis tinctoria*) (zones 3–7) is an attractive plant for the bed, and it grows up to 3ft (1m) tall, with bright yellow daisylike flowers and a mossy-green scent.

HOME USES

• *Aromatherapy applications* – Essential oils are produced from several species of chamomile including Roman, German, and Moroccan chamomile (*C. mixta*). The most valuable oil in aromatherapy is known as chamomile blue, extracted from the flower heads of German chamomile (*Matricaria recutita*). It's an inky-blue viscous liquid with a strong sweet-herby odor. It contains the powerful anti-inflammatory and sedative constituent chamazulene, which is not present in the fresh flower, but is produced only during the process of distillation. In aromatherapy, both Roman and German types are used for a wide range of skin complaints, including acne, allergies, eczema, and inflammations. They are also extremely valuable herbs for soothing pain caused by headaches, periods, indigestion, earache, inflamed joints, muscular sprains or spasm, and for treating stress-related complaints. A soothing massage oil and a flower water that helps heal the skin can be made from the fresh flower heads – see pages 72–3.

• *Drying and decorative uses* – Dry flowers of all species for potpourris and herb pillows. The dried or fresh flowers can be used to make soothing bath bags; chamomile water can also be used on fair hair to keep it light and in good condition.

• *Culinary suggestions* – Chamomile flowers steeped in boiling water and served with a spoonful of honey make a soothing nightcap.

• *Health-giving properties* – The healing properties of chamomile are too numerous to list here, although it is best known for its antispasmodic, digestive,

RIGHT: DAISYLIKE FLOWERS OF ROMAN CHAMOMILE (*CHAMAEMELUM NOBILE*).

sedative, and tonic effects. A very safe and mild herb, it is often used for children's complaints, such as insomnia, teething pain, colic, or upset stomach – either in the form of a weak tea or as a massage oil.

Cistus ladanifer

ROCK ROSE (Cistaceae)

Scent – rich, sweet, balsamic, resinous, herby, slightly musky, warming, restorative, soothing, comforting.

DESCRIPTION AND CULTIVATION

Cistus, otherwise known as rock or sun roses, have open cup-shaped white, yellow, or pink flowers and bloom profusely throughout the summer. As fast-growing evergreens, they make ideal rockery or flowerbed plants, but they do need some shelter since they resent frost – a free-draining bed beneath a sunny wall is ideal. These plants are found in the Mediterranean areas right up to the Caucasus.

Gertrude Jekyll wrote: *Among the sweet shrubs from the nearer of these southern regions, one of the best for English gardens is* Cistus. laurifolius *(zones 8–10). Its wholesome, aromatic sweetness is given off even in winter. In this, as in its near relative,* C. ladaniferus, *the scent seems to come from the gummy surface, and not from the body of the leaf.* (*The Gardener's Essential Gertrude Jekyll*)

Her observation is hardly surprising since it is the sticky resinous gum, known as labdanum, which gives these plants their characteristic balsamic scent. The resin (found on the leaves and stem) was formerly collected by shepherds on the island of Crete by combing the sticky gum from the fleeces of sheep and goats that had brushed against it while grazing.

C. ladanifer will grow up to 10ft (3m) tall in a protected position and has soft lance-shaped gray-green leaves (white on the underside) and white flowers with crimson blotches. Plants should be

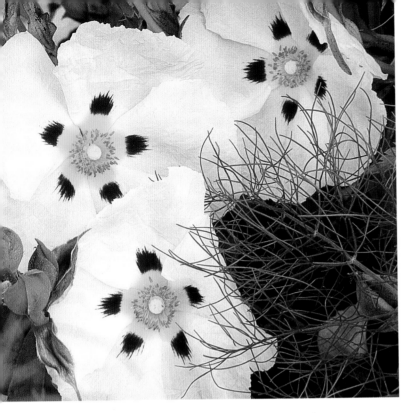

ABOVE: ROCK ROSE (*CISTUS LADANIFER*).

trimmed lightly in spring and after flowering to maintain a compact shape and to prevent them from getting too woody – but avoid hard pruning, which can prove fatal. Cistus are best propagated by seed sown in spring or fall, or by softwood cuttings taken in summer.

RECOMMENDED SPECIES

An exceptionally hardy pink cistus is *C.* 'Silver Pink' (zones 8–10); other hardy species are *C. laurifolius*, which has white flowers with a yellow center, and *C.* x *cyprius* (zones 8–10), which is white with crimson blotches. *C.* x *aguilarii* (zones 9–10) produces huge white flowers that are very impressive, but the plant is not hardy in severe winters. *C.* 'Peggy Sammons' (zones 9–10), has delicate pink flowers and green-gray foliage; another pale pink cistus, also very beautiful, is *C.* x *skanbergii* (zones 9–10), a small shrub that grows wild in Greece. *C.* x *pulverulentus* 'Sunset' (zones 9–10) is a short compact shrub with vivid magenta flowers and an orange center.

HOME USES

• *Aromatherapy applications* – An essential oil is produced by steam distillation of labdanum gum or from the leaves and twigs directly. The oil (and absolute) is an important perfumery material (similar to ambergris), and many species are used, notably *C. ladanifer* and *C. creticus* subsp. *incanus* (zones 9–10). In aromatherapy, the oil is valued for its warming,

mildly erotic qualities – good for depression, grief, or shock. The dark brown crude oleo-resin or gum can be obtained by simply boiling the plant material in water at home.

• *Drying and decorative uses* – The dried leaves (or the oleo-resin) can be burned as a fumigant or incense. Dried leaves can be added to potpourris for their tenacious scent.

• *Culinary suggestions* – The oil is used commercially for flavoring a wide variety of foods, especially meat products – but is little used in home cooking.

• *Health-giving properties* – Labdanum gum is an ancient aromatic material, traditionally used in skin-care ointments because of its antiseptic and astringent properties.

NOTE: Avoid use during pregnancy.

Citrus aurantium

BITTER ORANGE TREE
(Rutaceae)

Scent – fruit: fresh, citrus, rich, sweet, warm, comforting.
flowers: sweet-floral, honey, delicate, soothing, aphrodisiac, sedative, uplifting.
leaves: fresh-green, citrus, slightly herby, refreshing.

DESCRIPTION AND CULTIVATION

The bitter orange tree or Seville orange is one of the most versatile aromatic species. It produces three different types of essential oil, each with a distinct perfume, from various parts of the plant: orange oil from the fruit, neroli oil from the flowers, and petitgrain oil from the leaves. The bitter orange is a very handsome evergreen tree up to 33ft (10m) high with dark green, glossy oval leaves, and long but not very sharp spines. It has a smooth grayish trunk and branches, and very fragrant large white flowers. The bitter fruits have an aromatic rind and are smaller and darker than the sweet orange.

Native to China and northeastern India, the Seville orange is now cultivated all over the world, especially in the Mediterranean. It was the first citrus species to be taken to Europe by the Portuguese in the twelfth century. In colder northern European climes, most citrus species need protection against frost and must be overwintered under glass. They require a minimum temperature of 45°F (7°C), plus rich but well-drained soil, plenty of sun, and like to be well watered during the growing season but sparingly in winter. Plants can be propagated by seed (although cultivars do not come true from seed) or by semi-ripe cuttings taken in summer.

RECOMMENDED SPECIES

There are now numerous different citrus species available to the gardener. The sweet orange tree (*C. sinensis*) (zones 9–11) is a smaller evergreen tree than the bitter variety and is less hardy with fewer or no spines. The lemon tree (*C. limon*) (zones 9–11) makes an excellent conservatory plant and has various cultivars suitable for pot culture – 'Variegata' has interesting yellow-margined leaves. The mandarin tree (*C. reticulata*) (zones 9–11) can grow up to 26ft (8m) high and has very attractive miniature fruits, while the lime (*C. aurantiifolia*) (zones 9–11) is a smaller tree growing up to 16ft (5m) high with clusters of very fragrant white flowers in spring and summer.

HOME USES

• *Aromatherapy applications* – Orange essential oil is produced by cold expression from the outer peel of the almost ripe fruit; petitgrain oil by steam expression from the leaves; neroli oil by steam distillation from the freshly picked flowers. In aromatherapy, the most valuable oil is that from the flowers, for it has a

profoundly soothing effect on the entire nervous system and is used to treat anxiety, depression, nervous tension, PMS, shock, and other emotional problems. Petitgrain and neroli oil also all have excellent skin-care qualities: they tone the complexion and are beneficial for all skin types, scars, stretch marks,

ABOVE AND BELOW: THE FRUIT, LEAVES, AND FLOWERS OF THE ORANGE TREE ARE ALL HIGHLY FRAGRANT.

thread veins, and wrinkles. The distillation water, known as orange-flower water, is a popular cosmetic and household article; petitgrain oil is also a classic ingredient of eau de cologne. See pages 72–3. for making flower waters and eau de colognes.

NOTE: many citrus peel oils are phototoxic – that is, they discolor the skin under UV light – and their use on the skin should be avoided if there is danger of exposure to direct sunlight.

• *Drying and decorative uses* – Orange flowers have many folk associations. Neroli oil was named after a princess of Nerola in Italy, who loved to wear it as a perfume (see page 73 for making a natural perfume). The fresh flowers were used in bridal bouquets and wreaths, and are good for small posies and arrangements. Dried peel from all citrus species can be used in potpourris. Dried oranges, either sliced or whole, have many decorative uses, especially at festive occasions. Oranges are, of course, the traditional base for pomanders.

• *Culinary suggestions* – Orange-flower water is used in cake making; the fruits and rinds of all the citrus species have flavoring and nutritional value.

• *Health-giving properties* – It is well known that

oranges, lemons, and most citrus fruit varieties are rich in vitamin C. Dried bitter orange peel is also used as a tonic and carminative in treating dyspepsia. In Europe, an infusion of dried citrus flowers is used as a mild tonic for the nervous system and also as a blood cleanser.

Convallaria majalis
LILY-OF-THE-VALLEY
(Convallariaceae)

Scent – very sweet, floral, spicy, strong, strengthening, heart warming, restorative.

DESCRIPTION AND CULTIVATION
In the seventeenth century, the herbalist Nicholas Culpeper evocatively described sweetly scented lily-of-the-valley, as having "white flowers like little bells with turned-up edges." It has been known by a number of charming names such as fairies' bells, ladder to heaven, or lady's tears. The white blossoms are traditionally associated with purity and the Virgin Mary, and they are still used in bridal bouquets today – they are indispensable for their delicate scent, which is not too cloying. *Convallaria* is a single-species genus, native to Britain, northern Europe, and North America, especially in woodlands. Lily-of-the-valley is a hardy rhizomatous perennial that flowers in late spring. It prefers to be planted in shade or semi-shade, ideally where it can enjoy rich, moist earth that has been thoroughly manured and is free-draining. It has bright green, lance-shaped leaves, and its creeping rootstock increases annually; although the plant can be divided after flowering in the fall, in general it dislikes being disturbed. Lily-of-the-valley is a small plant, growing only 9–12in (23–30cm) high, but once settled, its rootstock spreads rapidly to form clumps.

RECOMMENDED SPECIES
There are a couple of varieties of *C. majalis* with blooms that are predominantly white. *C. majalis* 'Flore Pleno' is a double variety with small, very fragrant

ABOVE: LILY-OF-THE-VALLEY (*CONVALARIA MAJALIS*).

flowers, while the larger-flowered *C. m.* 'Fortin's Giant' blooms slightly earlier in the spring. The leaves of *C. m.* 'Variegata' are attractively golden-striped. Two hundred years ago, there was reputedly a double form with flowers variegated purple and white, as well as a red. Of all the varieties, the rosy-pink *C. m.* var. *rosea* has the sweetest scent of all.

HOME USES
• *Aromatherapy applications* – As all parts of the plant are toxic, the oil is not used in aromatherapy. Today it is used (mainly in synthetic form) as a basis for perfume and toilet waters, although in the Middle Ages, great healing qualities were attributed to the water distilled from the flowers, known as "aqua aurea," and renowned as an astringent, beautifying skin tonic that also "comforteth the heart… and strengthen the memorie."
• *Drying and decorative uses* – The fresh flowers have traditionally been used for posies and last well in water. The fragrant flowers can also be dried for use in potpourris.

• *Culinary suggestions* – Lily-of-the-valley is potentially poisonous and should not be used in cooking at all.

• *Health-giving properties* – Lily-of-the-valley was used for centuries in herbal medicine, especially as a heart tonic. According to a seventeenth century herbal, the distilled flowers in wine were considered "more precious than gold." It was thought to be particularly effective against palsy and gout, for it has diuretic properties when infused with water. *C. majalis* is still used by professional herbalists to regulate heartbeat, as the dried plant contains a similar substance to digitalin extracted from foxgloves, but it is not suitable for home use..

NOTE: Lily-of-the-valley should not be used at home for therapeutic purposes due to its toxicity.

Coriandrum sativum

CORIANDER (Apiaceae)

Scent – leaves: pungent, sweet, woody-spicy, revitalizing, stimulating. seeds: warm, spicy, earthy, musky, aphrodisiac, sedative, slightly narcotic.

DESCRIPTION AND CULTIVATION

Coriander is a strongly aromatic herb with bright green, filigree leaves and umbels of lacelike white flowers, followed by a mass of round green seeds that ripen to brown. It has been cultivated for at least 3,000 years as a medicinal and culinary herb, although today it is best known as cilantro, a flavoring in Middle Eastern dishes. Coriander is an annual that is easy to grow and can reach about 3ft (1m) high, but its delicate structure requires a sheltered position and protection from strong winds. It prefers full sun and rich, light, well-drained soil – it does not like damp conditions. Try it in an herb garden, or in a naturalistic setting, planted in drifts. Coriander can also be grown in pots either outside or indoors. Plant the seeds in the fall or late spring (or early spring under glass) and water regularly until established. Coriander self-seeds readily, but seedlings do not transplant well, so it is best to sow *in situ* and thin them out later. The seeds can be harvested once they turn brown, by shaking them from the flower heads.

NOTE: Coriander should not be planted alongside fennel, as the latter's seed production will suffer.

HOME USES

• *Aromatherapy applications* – An infused oil can be made using the crushed seeds for massage purposes – see page 73. An essential oil produced from the seeds is used in aromatherapy primarily for digestive upsets and to stimulate the circulation and eliminate toxins. As a perfumery ingredient, it is used mainly for scenting soaps and toiletries, especially to provide a masculine note. It is also used in quality perfumes, for example, Coriandre by Jean Coutourier.

• *Drying and decorative uses* – The dried seeds were once called dizzycorn, because when freshly crushed, their scent can promote dizziness. Use them in sachets and potpourris.

• *Culinary suggestions* – The leaves and seeds have two distinct flavors. The seeds can be dried and stored whole for use in curries, chutney, meat dishes, sweet puddings, and for flavoring vinegar. The fresh young leaves can be used in salads, curries, stews, and as a spicy garnish for oriental-style dishes.

• *Health-giving properties* – A tea made from the fresh leaves helps relieve indigestion and flatulence. If breastfeeding mothers drink coriander tea, it can help prevent colic in the baby.

BELOW: CORIANDER LEAVES (*CORIANDRUM SATIVUM*).

Dianthus caryophyllus

CARNATIONS AND PINKS
(Caryophyllaceae)

Scent – floral, clovelike, exotic, chocolate, warming, uplifting, aphrodisiac, intoxicating, comforting.

DESCRIPTION AND CULTIVATION

Carnations or clove gilliflowers, also known as pinks, are one of the most popular and ancient scented flowers in cultivation. In the seventeenth century they were a favorite with gardeners and one of the best-loved florists' flowers (see page 25). Theophrastus, in the fourth century B.C., honored carnations, calling them *Dios-anthos*, literally "flower of Zeus" or "flower of the gods," from which they took their Latin name. They were used to make garlands at festivals and crowns for coronations, hence their common name, carnations. It is thought that they were taken to England from southern Europe by the Normans in the Middle Ages.

BELOW: THERE ARE NUMEROUS FORMS OF *DIANTHUS* INCLUDING THE LOVELY *D.* 'LONDON GLOW' (ZONES 5–9).

Carnations and pinks are low-growing evergreen or semi-evergreen perennials, annuals, and biennials, mainly grown for their scented pink, white, or purplish flowers. Although not all species are scented, the majority are, and they provide an abundance of perfumed flowers for cutting. Native to the Mediterranean and generally hardy, they prefer being planted in semi-alkaline soil in the sunshine. In an herbaceous bed, it may be necessary to renew plants every couple of years, since they die from excessively kind treatment.

In late summer, bed carnations can be propagated by layering; others can be propagated by cuttings in late spring or by seed. *D. caryophyllus*, the original wild rose-pink carnation, is the parent of today's hardy bed carnations. In midsummer, they carry double (or semi-double) flowers that are richly perfumed with a spicy clove scent.

RECOMMENDED SPECIES

A number of modern carnations have lost their scent, but one of the best fragrant varieties is the rosy-pink double *D. caryophyllus* 'Chabaud Giant Double' (zones 6–9), while the deep crimson *D.* 'Bookham Perfume' (zones 6–9) is thought to have the strongest clove fragrance. The source of most scented cottage pinks is the hardy *D. plumarius* (zones 4–9).

D. barbatus (zones 3–7), the perennial sweet william from eastern Europe, is a very old garden plant first described in the sixteenth century, and ranges in color from white through to pink and crimson-purple. Highly fragrant, with a sweet, spicy, clovelike scent especially pronounced in the evenings, it also has the virtue of flowering all summer.

The strongly fragrant white double garden pink 'Mrs Sinkins' (zones 5–9) is an old favorite, as is 'Sops-in-Wine' (zones 5–9), another old-fashioned fragrant variety known since the fourteenth century, which has single maroon flowers, marked white. Modern pinks derive from the hybrid group *D.* x *allwoodii* (zones 5–9), which is a cross between the old-fashioned pink and perpetual-flowering carnations. They are generally hardier and more vigorous than the old-fashioned pinks.

HOME USES

• *Aromatherapy applications* – Oil distilled from the

fresh flowers of *D. caryophyllus* is produced mainly in France and Egypt. The richly perfumed oil is honey-scented with a touch of clove, and its effect is simultaneously warming and aphrodisiac. As its actions are uplifting, it is suitable as an anti-depressant, but it also has antibacterial and antifungal properties. Although not specifically used in aromatherapy, it can be burned to scent a room or used as a perfume.

• *Drying and decorative uses* – Use fresh flowers in tussie mussies – traditional Elizabethan posies of aromatic herbs and flowers (see page 77) – and decorative arrangements. The scented dried petals of pinks make an attractive addition to potpourris; use them combined with other dried aromatic flowers in scented pillows and bags. Bunches of dried pinks also burn well on an open fire, fragrancing the room.

• *Culinary suggestions* – The flower petals can be used in salads (but be sure first to remove the white heel, which is extremely bitter). Their clove flavor can also be used to flavor soups, wine, liqueurs, and syrups, and to add a spicy flavor to wine vinegars. Additionally, the flowers can be crystallized in sugar or simply used decoratively in desserts.

• *Health-giving properties* – Reputedly good for the nerves, the flower petals of *D. caryophyllus*, infused in wine, can be used to make a simple health-giving medicinal tonic.

Dictamnus albus

BURNING BUSH
(Rutaceae)

Scent – citrus, lemon-peel, balsamic, resinous, minty, astringent, refreshing.

DESCRIPTION AND CULTIVATION
Burning bush or dittany is an upright, long-lived herbaceous hardy perennial native to southwestern Europe and Asia Minor. The plant's most common popular name derives from the inflammable lemon-scented oil vapors given off by the flowers in hot weather. These either ignite spontaneously or can be

PREVIOUS PAGE AND
LEFT: BURNING BUSH
(*D. ALBUS var.
PURPUREUS*)

lit with a match, producing a blue flame. Not only the flowers, but also the leaves have an aroma reminiscent of lemonpeel when rubbed. They can cause a rash to those with sensitive skins. The oregano species *Origanum dictamnus* (zones 8–10) has a similar scent, and this is probably the source of its nomenclature.

Burning bush is a striking plant, growing to 3ft (1m), with hairy stems and light green divided leaves. It makes an unusual and attractive addition to a flowerbed, especially grown in large clumps, but can look equally stunning in a more naturalistic setting – in its native conditions, it grows wild in dry scrub and pine woods. Although it requires some patience, plants can be grown from seed planted in open ground in late summer. It is preferable to plant i*n situ*, but if you choose to transplant seedlings, do so in the fall or the following spring, and prepare to wait a few years before the plants flower. Generally, the plants do not like transplanting or any disturbance, especially once they are established. Burning bush likes fertile, well-drained or dry alkaline soil and should be planted in full sun or only partial shade in warm sheltered areas. Young plants need protection from slugs.

RECOMMENDED SPECIES

There is only one species in this genus. *D. albus* produces star-shaped fragrant white flowers in summer, occasionally marked with purple. The mauve-pink variety *D. albus* var. *purpureus* (syn. *D. fraxinella*) produces fragrant flower spires, streaked deeper purplish pink.

HOME USES

• *Aromatherapy applications* – An essential oil is produced for perfumery use from the leaves and flowers, but it is not employed in aromatherapy. A perfumed distilled water using an infusion of scented flowers can be used as an astringent skin tonic – see page 72.

• *Drying and decorative uses* – The leaves and flowers of burning bush can be dried and used in potpourris.

• *Culinary suggestions* – The scented leaves can be infused to make a fragrant uplifting tea.

• *Health-giving properties* – The bark from the roots of burning bush is used in Chinese medicine for dispelling pathogenic heat – an unnaturally high temperature, as in a fever. In the West, an infusion of its leaves was used to ameliorate nervous conditions, a root decocotion to treat fevers and stomach cramps, and the root together with the seeds in the treatment of kidney stones. But none of these treatments is recommended today, and burning bush is not suitable for medicinal home use **NOTE:** Avoid during pregnancy.

BELOW: THE PURE WHITE VARIETY OF THE BURNING BUSH, *DICTAMNUS ALBUS*.

Foeniculum vulgare var. *dulce*

SWEET FENNEL
(Apiaceae)

Scent – sweet, aniselike, slightly earthy-peppery, restorative, purifying.

DESCRIPTION AND CULTIVATION

Sweet fennel is a lovely plant for the back of a bed or the herb garden. Its tall growth and bright green feathery leaves lend an air of softness to more defined bushes, such as old roses or woody herbs like lavenders or santolinas. It is not dissimilar to dill in appearance, though taller in stature, reaching up to 6ft 6in (2m) high, with umbels of tiny golden-yellow flowers that ripen into aromatic seeds.

Sweet fennel is native to the Mediterranean region and is naturally a biennial or perennial herb, although generally cultivated as an annual. It prefers a well-drained sunny position, but will grow almost anywhere and will seed itself freely. Otherwise, sow the seeds in spring directly in the ground after all frosts have passed, or earlier under glass; fennel can also be propagated by root division in the fall. If stems are cut right down in the summer, there will be a second flush of leaves.

CAPTION: AROMATIC SEED HEADS OF SWEET FENNEL (*FOENICULUM VULGARE* var. *DULCE*)

NOTE: Avoid growing fennel near dill or coriander since they can cross-pollinate and reduce overall seed production.

RECOMMENDED SPECIES

There are two main varieties of fennel. Bitter or common fennel (*F. vulgare*) is slightly taller with less divided leaves. The cultivated sweet or Roman fennel is *F. vulgare* var. *dulce*. There is also a coppery-bronze variety, *F. v.* 'Purpureum,' which is particularly striking.

HOME USES

• *Aromatherapy applications* – An essential oil made from the seed is mainly used for congestive problems of the circulation, muscles, and joints, notably cellulitis, obesity, edema, and arthritis. It is also valuable for the digestive system and for easing cramps. A flower water (for dull and congested skin) or infused oil for massage can be made from the fresh leaves and seeds – see pages 72–30.

• *Drying and decorative uses* – The fresh leaves are valuable for naturalistic flower arrangements. Fresh fennel also repels fleas and other insects. Harvest and dry the whole herb in bunches once the seeds have turned brown, and use the dried seeds in potpourris.

• *Culinary suggestions* – Both the leaves and seeds have a strong aniseed flavor: fresh or dried leaves are delicious in fish dishes or salads; the seeds are traditionally used in chutneys and pickles. They also can enhance the flavor of borscht soup, Scandinavian-style bread, and even some desserts. Bronze fennel gives vinegar a rich claret color. Sweet fennel is also grown as a vegetable.

• *Health-giving properties* – Fennel seed (use 1 teaspoon of seeds per cup of boiling water) is a powerful tonic and nervine, and also a traditional digestive, taken after eating rich fare. A weak fennel seed infusion is the main ingredient in gripe water and can be used for colic in babies. Drinking fennel tea can help remedy insufficient milk in nursing mothers.

NOTE: Fennel should be avoided by epileptics.

Gardenia augusta

GARDENIA (Rubiaceae)

Scent – heady, exotic, sweet-floral, slightly spicy, aphrodisiac.

DESCRIPTION AND CULTIVATION

This tender evergreen shrub, with its glossy green leaves and pale ivory flowers, is one of the most

beautiful conservatory or patio plants. Its waxy double flowers emit a heavy, spicy-sweet fragrance and, like freesias, they can perfume an entire room. Originally *G. augusta* came from China, so in cold climates it needs to spend the winter under glass. Although it requires more careful attention than many other pot plants, it's well worth the effort.

Ideally, a gardenia plant needs to be kept at a minimum temperature of 61°F (16°C) in a light position, yet protected from direct sunlight. The soil should be kept moist at all times (using rainwater only) but not waterlogged. Indoor plants enjoy a regular misting, which helps to prevent the newly formed flower buds from dropping off; they also benefit from being moved outdoors once the weather is warm enough. With constant humidity and warmth, a bush can grow up to 5ft (1.5m), flowering from mid- to late summer. After flowering, all the old shoots should be reduced by about half and new shoots pinched out to encourage bushy growth. Repot (if required) or top dress in spring using lime-free, peaty soil. Gardenias can be propagated by softwood cuttings in spring or by semi-mature cuttings in summer.

RECOMMENDED SPECIES

G. augusta is the most commonly available species.

HOME USES

• *Aromatherapy applications* – A natural essential oil made from the flower is still occasionally used in high-class oriental perfumes; most gardenia oil produced today, however, is synthetic. Occasionally used in aromatherapy, the oil is considered to have similar properties to jasmine. A "true" gardenia perfume can be made at home using the enfleurage method – see page 73. Like ylang ylang and lavender, it is considered to be a perfect perfume in its own right, having a correct balance of top, middle, and base notes (see page 70).

• *Drying and decorative uses* – The petals retain scent well: use them in moist potpourris. The round fruits can also be dried for decorative use, while a few flowers will add an exotic touch to any bouquet.

LEFT: THE ELEGANT PALE IVORY FLOWERS OF GARDENIA (*GARDENIA AUGUSTA*).

• *Culinary suggestions* – Like jasmine, gardenia flowers are used in China to flavor tea.

• *Health-giving properties* – The berries are occasionally still used in herbal medicine for their bactericidal, fungicidal, anti-inflammatory, and febrifuge properties.

Helichrysum italicum
CURRY PLANT
(Asteraceae)

Scent – pungent, honey-rich, currylike, sweet, restorative, uplifting, tonic, cleansing.

DESCRIPTION AND CULTIVATION

The curry plant (*H. italicum*, syn. *H. angustifolium*) is an evergreen aromatic herb, with fine silvery foliage and a mass of small yellow flowers, both of which have a pervasive, sweet currylike scent – even stronger after rain. The flowers have a papery texture and are used a great deal in dried flower arrangements – several members of the *Helichrysum* genus are grown as *immortelles*, or everlasting flowers. Although it is a native of southern Europe, the curry plant is hardy enough to withstand most frosts and has become a popular addition to ornamental herb gardens and beds of more northerly countries in recent years.

ABOVE: CURRY PLANT (*HELICHRYSUM ITALICUM*).

Reaching a height of 2ft (60cm), the curry plant can make a striking visual impact all year round, especially when its bright silvery leaves are contrasted with darker foliage plants such as rosemary or blue-leaved rue. It needs to be grown in a sunny position in well-drained soil, for it dislikes cold, wet conditions and will die if the temperature drops below 14°F (-10°C). If there is danger of severe frost, it is worth lifting a plant from the open ground and overwintering it in a cold greenhouse.

Like santolina, the curry plant can make an attractive hedge, but it should not be clipped back as vigorously as the former. Nevertheless, it is essential to trim all bushes back in late spring and again after they have flowered to stop them from getting woody and shapeless. The plants grow happily in pots or tubs on a sunny patio. They are best propagated by softwood cuttings in spring or by semi-ripe ones taken in late summer.

RECOMMENDED SPECIES

The cultivar *H. i.* 'Dartington' is a compact plant with mustard-yellow buttonlike flowers; *H. i.* 'Nanum' is a dwarf herb 12in (30cm) high, ideal for knot gardens or edging. *H. arenarium* (zones 9–10) is an ornamental species favored by florists; *H. stoechas* (zones 9–10) and *H. orientale* (zones 8–10) are both highly aromatic, decorative species that are also used for producing essential oils for the perfume and flavoring industries.

HOME USES

• *Aromatherapy applications* – An essential oil is produced by steam distillation from the fresh flowers. In aromatherapy, the oil is used for treating nervous debility and, in massage, for easing muscular aches and pains. The oil also has an antiseptic, cleansing, and astringent effect on the skin – see pages 72–3 for making flower water and home skin-care treatments.

• *Drying and decorative uses* – Many helichrysums are extremely valuable for dried flower arrangements, since they retain their color and fragrance long after they have been cut. Use dried flower heads in potpourris, while a spray of fresh curry plant hung in a closet will help deter moths.

• *Culinary suggestions* – Add a few leaves to egg, vegetable, rice, or chicken dishes to give them a mild curry flavor.

• *Health-giving properties* – In southern Europe, the herb is used mainly for respiratory infections, digestive disorders, and skin complaints, usually in the form of an infusion or tea.

Humulus lupulus

HOPS (Cannabaceae)

Scent – rich, warm, spicy-sweet, hypnotic, slightly narcotic, soporific.

DESCRIPTION AND CULTIVATION

This perennial hardy climber with deciduous, heart-shaped leaves and aromatic greenish-yellow flowers is grown commercially in vast quantities for the production of beer. Male and female flowers or cones are produced on separate plants, and it is the female cones or strobiles that are used for brewing. Although it is not a showy garden plant, it has many endearing characteristics, not least the fact that it is a very quick grower and can cover a trellis or wall in a single season. It is also useful for hiding unsightly spots, to create summer shade over an arbor, and for instant ground cover. Thus, the hop is a very versatile plant for the aromatic garden, although its rampant nature

needs to be kept well in check.

The common hop is an important medicinal plant and has a long history of being grown as a pot herb. Plants need to be adequately supported and require moist but well-drained soil in sun or partial shade. They can eventually reach over 26ft (8m) high. After the flowers are harvested in the fall, the twining stems should be cut right back to stimulate new growth. Hops can be propagated by taking cuttings of young shoot tips from female plants in early spring.

RECOMMENDED VARIETIES

The golden-leaved variety *H. lupulus* 'Aureus' is particularly attractive.

HOME USES:

• *Aromatherapy applications* – The essential oil is used in *chypre* and *fougère* type perfumes. In aromatherapy, it is recommended mainly for its profoundly soothing effect. An infused oil for massage as well as a flower water can be produced at home from the dried cones – see page 72–3.

• *Drying and decorative uses* – The heady scent of hop flowers on a hot summer's day is unmistakable, and in its dried form it is an especially valuable herb for the still room. The dried flowers or cones can be used to make sleep pillows, in bath bags, added to potpourris, or used in dried arrangements. Simply hung from old beams or hooks, the twining stems

ABOVE AND LEFT: HOPS (*HUMULUS LUPULUS*) IS A VERSATILE AND FAST-GROWING GARDEN PLANT.

antispasmodic properties. A herbal tisane can be made at home using the fresh flowers – add honey to taste to produce an excellent nightcap.

NOTE: Hop tisanes are not recommended to be taken for those suffering from clinical depression.

Hyacinthus orientalis

HYACINTH
(Hyacinthaceae)

Scent – sweet, mellow, balsamic, rich, floral, heady, narcotic, intoxicating, soothing, sedative, comforting, uplifting.

DESCRIPTION AND CULTIVATION

Hyacinths originated in the southeastern Mediterranean, in countries such as Turkey, Syria, and Persia. Legend tells of how the flowers supposedly grew from the blood of a Greek youth, Hyacinthus, who was killed accidentally by Apollo, and to modern Greeks they denote remembrance. At the end of the eighteenth century, the hyacinth was one of the eight florists' flowers (see page 25). It is a powerfully perfumed plant, producing spires of fragrant waxy flowers in the middle of spring that last for two to three weeks.

make attractive household decorations – they also help to dispel unpleasant odors, such as cigarette smoke or cooking smells. Fresh sprays can be used in naturalistic arrangements.

• *Culinary suggestions* – In spring the young shoots may be eaten raw or cooked like asparagus.

• *Health-giving properties* – The flowers are still widely used in herbal medicine for their sedative, slightly narcotic, hormonal, bactericidal, digestive, tonic, and

The different cultivars of *H. orientalis* range in color from white, yellow, pink, and blue through to red, violet, and purple, and are frost hardy. They require well-drained soil and like to be planted in a sunny or semi-shaded position. For impact, they look best clustered in groups. Plant the bulbs outdoors in the fall, using new bulbs each year for the most impressive display. The flowering stem from a new bulb can produce dense flower heads with as many as 60 individual flowerets. In the fall, bulbs that were planted the previous season can be moved to less prominent positions in the garden as their flowering is less showy.

ABOVE: HYACINTHS (*HYACINTHUS ORIENTALIS*) CAN BE FOUND IN A WHOLE RANGE OF JEWELLIKE COLORS.

Pot-grown plants make a welcome fragrant addition to the Christmas season by forcing them into flower early. Plant in pots the largest bulbs you can find that have been specially treated for forcing in a cool environment. Do this in the early fall. Place three or four bulbs in a pot filled with fiber or potting mixture, making sure the bulbs are almost touching each other and that the tops of the bulbs are just showing. To allow the root system to develop, keep the bulbs cool and damp for some weeks: a garage or shed is ideal for this. Once the first shoots appear and the flower spires are a couple of inches high, they can be brought indoors.

Another decorative way to grow hyacinths indoors – a method that was popular in earlier centuries – is to place a bulb in a vase of rain water, allowing the hyacinth to root. The base of the bulb should rest just above the water to avoid rotting. Keep the vase in a dark place until small shoots have formed.

RECOMMENDED SPECIES

The parent of many cultivars, *H. orientalis* bears pale mauve fragrant flowers and is closely related to the wild bluebell (*Hyacinthoides non-scripta*). Highly perfumed cultivars include the striking 'White Pearl,' exquisitely perfumed ivory-white 'L'Innocence,' which is also grown extensively indoors, and 'Ben Nevis,' one of the best double white balsamic-scented flowers. Familiar blues include 'Delft Blue' and 'Blue Jacket,' while 'King of the Blues' is a magnificent, strongly scented variety

deep purple-indigo. 'Amethyst' is a late-flowering mauve variety.

HOME USES

• *Aromatherapy applications* – The essential oil (and absolute) of hyacinth flowers are used extensively in perfumery – but today these are often synthetically produced. In aromatherapy, the essential oil is used to treat nervous exhaustion or fatigue, where its soothing, calming properties are useful for combating stress. It is also helpful in overcoming sadness and grief, and is used to boost a sense of self-worth.

• *Drying and decorative uses* – Dried hyacinth flowers can be used in potpourris. The fresh flowers make very decorative festive displays – see above.

• *Domestic Use* – The bulbs are poisonous, but the white sap is used traditionally as a substitute for starch or glue.

• *Health-giving properties* – The Greeks described the fragrance of hyacinth as being "refreshing and invigorating to a tired mind." The bulbs are balsamic – that is, soothing, especially to the respiratory system – with some styptic properties (they can halt bleeding), but should not be used at home.

NOTE: Do not use at home as the bulbs are toxic.

Hyssopus officinalis

BLUE HYSSOP
(Lamiaceae)

Scent – sweet, slightly camphoraceous, warm, spicy-herby, purifying, restorative, refreshing.

DESCRIPTION AND CULTIVATION

Hyssop is a most attractive, highly scented evergreen perennial that comes originally from the Mediterranean and Asia. With its decorative, vivid blue flowers and small lance-shaped leaves, hyssop forms a neat compact bush that is equally at home in an herb garden, rockery, or bed. Since in its natural habitat it is found on dry, rocky hillsides or on old walls, it will thrive in containers placed on a sheltered patio or on a sunny windowsill – in fact, it needs hot sunshine to really flourish.

Hyssop can also make a neat low hedge or edging plant if it is kept clipped into shape during the growing season. Reaching a maximum of 3ft (1m) high, it flowers continuously throughout the summer and early fall, especially if it is dead-headed. To maintain a compact shape, trim plants back to 8in (20cm) after flowering (or in spring in cold areas). Hyssop grows easily from seed sown under cover in spring or later directly into the soil once it is warm, or can be propagated by softwood cuttings in early summer. The whole plant is much loved by butterflies and bees for its strong, aromatic fragrance.

RECOMMENDED SPECIES

The white hyssop (*H. officinalis* f. *albus*) and pink hyssop (*H. o. roseus*) are similar in height and spread although slightly less hardy than the blue hyssop – they are, however, especially valuable for blending in with specific color schemes. Rock hyssop (*H. o.* subsp. *aristatus*) has darker blue-purple flowers and reaches a height of only 12in (30cm).

HOME USES

• *Aromatherapy applications* – An essential oil from the leaves and flowering tops of the blue hyssop is used mainly to reduce high blood pressure and ease stress-related conditions through massage. The vaporized oil is especially good for respiratory infections. A home-distilled hyssop water – see page 72 – improves skin tone and can reduce inflammation and discoloration caused by bruises or wounds.

• *Drying and decorative uses* – Harvest the flowers when in bud: the dried leaves and flowers can be used in decorative arrangements and potpourris. Fresh leaves and flowers made into bath bags are good as a pick-me-up for nervous exhaustion.

• *Culinary suggestions* – Fresh or dried leaves can be used to flavor stews or soups and are good with oily fish, game, and fatty meats. Use blue flowers and chopped leaves sparingly in salads.

ABOVE: BLUE HYSSOP (*HYSSOPUS OFFICINALIS*).

• *Health-giving properties* – A tea made from the leaves and flowers of hyssop is one of the best remedies for nasal and lung congestion, sore throats, bronchitis, and other respiratory complaints, as it is an excellent antiseptic and antiviral agent. A tonic for the heart and circulation, the tea can also help those suffering from nervous debility and during convalescence.

NOTE: Best avoided in pregnancy, by epileptics, and by those with high blood pressure.

Inula helenium

ELECAMPANE
(Asteraceae)

Scent – bitter, pungent, slightly camphoraceous, stimulating, purifying.

DESCRIPTION AND CULTIVATION
This ancient medicinal herb is a tall, bold perennial that grows about 5ft (1.5m) high, flowering over midsummer. It has oval, velvety green leaves and

large yellow daisy-like flowers, similar to a sunflower. It is spectacular planted in a group at the back of an herbaceous bed or in a corner of the herb garden, but may look awkward grown as a single specimen. Native to Asia, elecampane is now naturalized across much of

LEFT: ELECAMPAGNE (*INULA HELENIUM*) IS A TALL, BOLD PERENNIAL PLANT AND A VALUBLE MEDICINAL HERB.

Europe and America, having spread through its cultivation as a medicinal herb. In the East particularly, it is highly valued as an incense, medicine, and spice. It prefers moist soil and a sunny position, although it will tolerate most conditions, and may need staking if unprotected from strong winds. Cut the stems down after flowering and remove the leaves in the fall before they start to look ragged – the whole plant dies down completely over winter. Elecampane is best propagated by taking offsets from the large fleshy rhizomes in early fall.

RECOMMENDED SPECIES
I. hookeri (zones 4–8) is a smaller plant, 30in (75cm) high, with ragged daisylike flowers; *I. magnifica* (zones 5–8) is the giant of the species and can reach more than 6ft (1.8m) high with large dark green leaves; *I. ensifolia* (zones 4–9) is a species suitable for American gardens.

HOME USES
• *Aromatherapy applications* – An essential oil produced by steam distillation of the dried roots is much used in perfumery – it has a soft, woody, honey-like aroma. Unfortunately, the oil from *I. helenium* can cause a severe allergic skin reaction in some individuals, so it is not recommended for aromatherapy use. Sweet inula (*I. odora*) (zones 5–8), however, yields an oil that can be used to treat respiratory complaints in the form of an inhalation.

• *Drying and decorative uses* – The flowers look good in naturalistic arrangements, either fresh or dried. The whole plant dries well, including the roots (see below), which should be lifted in the fall.

• *Culinary suggestions* – The root of *I. helenium* can be cooked whole and eaten as a vegetable. It can also be crystallized or made into cordial.

• *Health-giving properties* – Elecampane's main use in herbal medicine is as a remedy for respiratory complaints, specifically tuberculosis. A decoction of the root is also used externally for the treatment of persistent skin conditions such as acne, scabies, and herpes. A tea made from the sliced root steeped in boiling water is beneficial for soothing dry, irritating coughs and bronchitis.

NOTE: Avoid during pregnancy.

Iris florentina – usually known as IRIS GERMANICA var. Florentina or Orris Root

FLORENTINE IRIS
(Iridaceae)

Scent – flowers: sweet, honey-floral, slightly spicy, uplifting.–
roots: violetlike, woody, fruity, very tenacious, warming, soothing.

DESCRIPTION AND CULTIVATION

This much-loved flower is one of the oldest cultivated plants – it is depicted on Egyptian temple walls dating from 1500 B.C. The Greek word "iris" means rainbow and refers to the variable nature of the flowers' coloring: from white, yellow, or red through to the deepest purple, violets, and blues.

The *Iris* genus can be subdivided into those species that have a rhizome and those that grow from a bulb. Some species, such as the stately bearded irises, can reach over 4ft (1.2m) tall; others like the

petite *I. reticulata* (zones 5–8) are only 3in (8cm) high.

The Florentine iris is a beardless iris that has dark green sword-shaped leaves, a creeping fleshy rootstock, and grows to about 3ft (1m) high. It has delicate, highly scented white flowers tinged with blue and a yellow "fall," which are borne in summer. It is also known as orris because its large rhizomes are used for making orris powder, a very valuable fixative and perfumery material with a distinctive violetlike scent.

Like most iris species, the Florentine iris is a native of southern Europe and prefers to grow in a rich but well-drained sunny position and benefits from having some lime in the soil. It should not be planted too deep, for it likes the surface of its rhizomes to bake in the sun. It is best propagated by removing offsets in late summer or by seed sown in the fall. The roots should be lifted in early fall if they are to be used for drying.

RECOMMENDED SPECIES

The common flag iris (*I. germanica*) (zones 4–8) has a rich fruity scent and prefers moist soil; *I. pallida* (zones

5–8), an ancient white to pale blue species has vanilla-scented flowers (especially pronounced in the variegated form); *I. reticulata* is an exquisite miniature purple iris that flowers in winter and has a violetlike fragrance (many cultivars in a range of colors are now available); I. *graminea* has grassy leaves and small purple flowers with a very strong "plum tart" scent. Then there are the tall bearded irises, many of which have a fine scent.

HOME USES

• *Aromatherapy applications* – An essential oil and absolute is produced from the dried rhizomes of *I. florentina*, *I. pallida*, and *I. germanica* for perfumery use. It is, however, extremely expensive and often adulterated – the oil is also a skin irritant, so it is not suited to aromatherapy work. The powdered root can be used as a dry shampoo and body powder.

• *Drying and decorative uses* – The rhizomes develop their violetlike aroma only after they have been dried for more than three years. Use powdered orris to scent sachets, linen, clothes, etc., and as a fixative for potpourris.

• *Culinary suggestions* – The dried rhizome has a bitter taste that is used in minute quantities to flavor some liqueurs. The fresh leaves and roots of all irises are harmful if eaten.

• *Health-giving properties* – In traditional herbal medicine, orris root was used to treat coughs and rhinitis. It also has emetic and purgative properties. The blue flag iris (*I. versicolor*) (zones 3–9) and *I. pallida* also have an ancient history of medicinal usage – however, iris species should not be used in home remedies because of their toxicity.

NOTE: Avoid during pregnancy.

Jasminum officinale (zones 9–10)

COMMON JASMINE
(Oleaceae)

Scent – intensely sweet, rich, honey-·floral, tealike, warm, exotic, uplifting, aphrodisiac, narcotic.

DESCRIPTION AND CULTIVATION

Jasmine is undoubtedly one of the most sweetly

ABOVE: JASMINIUM OFFICINALE HAS AN EXQUISITE SCENT.

intoxicating perfumed plants with a wide range of species, some tender and others hardy. The common jasmine is native to the Himalayas. It is a deciduous or semi-evergreen vine with delicate bright green leaves, bearing hundreds of tiny star-shaped, very fragrant white flowers from summer through to fall. The scent of the flowers increases at dusk – in India, jasmine is known as queen of the night – and it is often planted in courtyards, on verandas, or beneath windows where it can be enjoyed in the evening. Despite its fragile appearance, a jasmine vine can climb more than 33ft (10m) high, and care must be taken if it is grown against a house that it does not lift the shingles.

It looks lovely when allowed to scramble over a porch or arbor, its flexible twining stems combining well with clematis, akebia, roses, or honeysuckle. Outdoor varieties like full sun and a fertile, well-drained soil; tender species require a minimum temperature of 50°F (10°C). Most species need to be pruned back vigorously after flowering. Propagate plants by semi-ripe cuttings taken in late spring or by seeds sown in early spring.

RECOMMENDED SPECIES

Other hardy, outdoor jasmines include *J. officinale* 'Aureum' with yellow-variegated leaves; *J. x stephanense* (zones 8–10), a less vigorous climber with pinkish flowers; and the less well-known *J. humile* 'Revolutum' (zones 7–9), an evergreen shrub 8ft (2.5m) high, with scented yellow flowers from spring through to fall. The climber *J. mesnyi* (zones 8–10) also has yellow scented flowers and is almost hardy, as is the beautiful evergreen Chinese jasmine (*J. polyanthum*) (zones 8–10), which has masses of heavily scented white flowers and is best grown in a cool greenhouse or in a sheltered sunny position. Similar in appearance is the Spanish jasmine (*J.*

grandiflorum 'De Grasse') (zones 9–10), flowering in late summer and fall, but it is a smaller plant and frost tender. All should be pruned lightly after flowering.

HOME USES

• *Aromatherapy applications* – An essential oil is produced by steam distillation from the flower absolute. It is very costly to buy, but is priceless as a perfumery material: it has the ability to round off any rough notes and blends with virtually everything. In aromatherapy, the oil is used mainly for sensitive skin conditions and for nervous complaints, especially depression and nervous exhaustion where there is apathy, indifference, or listlessness, since the scent helps promote feelings of optimism and confidence. A flower perfume can be made at home – see page 73.

• *Drying and decorative uses* – In the East, especially in India, fresh flowers are worn in the hair, and made into wreaths and posies at religious festivals.

• *Culinary suggestions* – Flowers from *J. sambac* (T), the tender Arabian jasmine, may be used to flavor tea.

• *Health-giving properties* – The flowers of *J. officinale* are used for their antidepressant and antispasmodic properties, and for their tonic effect on the womb – they strenghten and stimulate the uterus.

Juniperus communis
JUNIPER (Cupressaceae)

Scent – sweet, fresh, warm, green-resinous, woody-balsamic, smoky, purifying, stimulating, restorative.

DESCRIPTION AND CULTIVATION

J. communis is a small evergreen tree that can be found growing wild from the Mediterranean to as far north as the Arctic Circle, in the Soviet Union and Canada. It is a tenacious plant that can thrive on bare rocky mountain slopes, moorland, and in cold conditions where few other shrubs survive. It has small flowers and little round berries, which are green in the first year and turn blue-

black in the second and third. Only the female tree bears berries. The flowers of the female tree are green and the male, yellow: both male and female plants are necessary for berries to be produced.

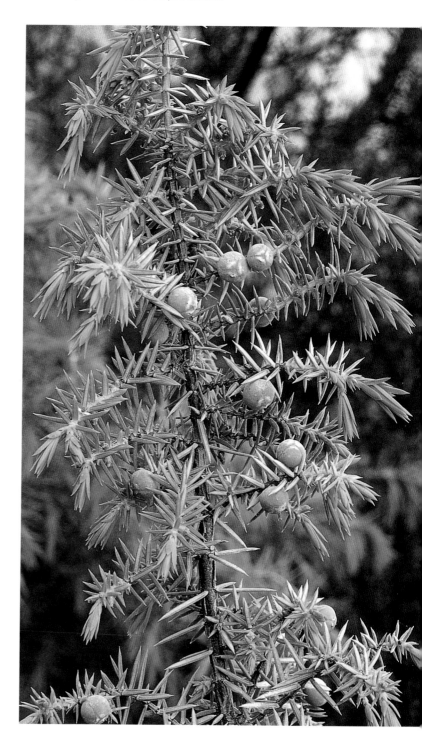

RIGHT: THE BERRIES OF JUNIPER (*JUNIPERUS COMMUNIS*) TAKE TWO YEARS TO RIPEN.

Juniper prefers to grow in an exposed, sunny site, but it will tolerate stony, dry, or shady conditions in both acid and alkaline soils. It is also very hardy and can survive strong winds, ice, and snow, so it is an extremely useful garden shrub for awkward places where little else will grow. Growing up to 20ft (6m) high, with bluish-green narrow, stiff needles, the whole plant exudes a lovely fresh resinous aroma. Although it is possible to propagate a juniper tree from seed, it may take two to three years to germinate. Since they are such slow growers, it is more practical to take semi-hardwood cuttings in late summer – this method also guarantees plant gender.

RECOMMENDED SPECIES

There are a great many cultivars of *J. communis*, including the Irish juniper 'Hibernica,' which forms a narrow pointed column up to 16ft (5m) high. 'Depressa Aurea' has golden needles and is ideal for ground cover. 'Prostrata' reaches only 1ft (30cm) high, but has a vast spread of 6ft (1.8m), while the miniature 'Compressa' grows only 30in (75cm) high and is ideal for rock gardens or containers. Several other species including *J. oxycedrus* (zones 7–9), *J. virginiana* (zones 3–9), and *J. sabina* (zones 4–7) are used commercially for essential oil production, mainly for perfumery usage.

HOME USES

• *Aromatherapy applications* – An essential oil is produced from the berries, needles, and wood of *J. communis*, although the most highly prized oil is from the berries. It is used therapeutically in skin care for acne, dermatitis, eczema, hair loss, oily complexions, and for conditions where there is an accumulation of toxins, such as arteriosclerosis, cellulitis, obesity, and rheumatism. It is also used to combat respiratory infections and to treat nervous tension and stress-related conditions. Make a warming massage oil using the fresh berries – see page 73.

• *Drying and decorative uses* – Harvest the berries when they turn blue and store them in airtight jars. They can be added to potpourris. Dry the needles for burning as a purifying incense.

• *Culinary suggestions* – The berries are wonderful used sparingly in marinades, sauces, pickles, and when cooking game or poultry – and of course they are famous for flavoring gin. Make a juniper-flavored vinegar or oil – see page 35.

• *Health-giving properties* – Juniper has a long history of herbal use, notably as a purification incense. Both the Tibetans and Native American burned sprigs of dried juniper in ritual cleansing ceremonies, while in Europe the burnt twigs were used to combat infectious epidemics and to keep demons at bay.

NOTE: Avoid using juniper during pregnancy and if there is kidney weakness.

Laurus nobilis

BAY (Lauraceae)

Scent – strong, spicy-medicinal, clean, fresh, warm, penetrating, purifying.

DESCRIPTION AND CULTIVATION

Bay is a handsome evergreen shrub with glossy, dark green, aromatic leaves and small black berries. In spring, it bears many small yellow tufted flowers, smelling sweetly of honey. As a native of the Mediterranean region, the sweet or true bay thrives in well-drained soil

in a sunny position, although it will tolerate some shade. As such, bay can be slightly tender, and young bushes may be cut to the ground by a hard frost, although they will usually shoot up again. In cold areas, it is best grown in a container and put under glass for the winter. However, in a warm site, sheltered from cold winds, a mature shrub can reach more than 20ft (6m) high with an equal spread if its roots are not confined. New shrubs can be propagated by semi-ripe cuttings in summer or by fall-sown seeds.

A bay tree can make a good structural focal point in a shrubbery or at the back of an herbaceous bed. It can also be clipped into all kinds of shapes or trained into a

BELOW LEFT AND ABOVE: LEAVES AND FLOWERS OF THE EVERGREEN BAY TREE (*LAURUS NOBILIS*).

standard specimen by removing the lower shoots of a new plant. Regular clipping throughout the summer months also encourages bushy growth. A clipped bay can make an ideal centerpiece for a formal herb garden, while a pair of standard bay trees grown in large tubs and placed on either side of the front door makes a traditional and dignified statement. Sweet bay is also at home in a warm environment such as a conservatory or greenhouse.

RECOMMENDED SPECIES

L. nobilis 'Aurea,' golden bay, has golden-edged leaves, while *L. azorica* (zones 9–10) (syn. *L. canariensis*) is a rare, more tender species. Several other species are also commonly called bay, including the California bay (*Umbellularia californica*) (zones 8–10) and the West Indian bay (*Pimenta racemosa*) (T) or bay rum tree, so called because its essential oil is used to produce the famous hair tonic. The cherry laurel (*Prunus laurocerasus*) (zones 6–9) is a useful garden shrub that has a similar leaf to common bay, but it is poisonous.

HOME USES

• *Aromatherapy applications* – In aromatherapy, the essential oil is recommended for infections, digestive complaints, and muscular aches and pains; in perfumery, the oil is used principally in aftershaves and colognes. An essential oil can be made at home from the fresh leaves, using the distillation method. An infused oil can also be produced for massage purposes – see pages 72–3.

• *Drying and decorative uses* – The leaves retain their shape, color, and scent very well upon drying. Harvest in summer for use in dried arrangements of all kinds, including potpourris. The leaves were once used for strewing on floors, especially in churches – the oil and leaves also repel weevils. Sprays of fresh bay last well in water (crush the bottom of the stem first) and look good in large, naturalistic arrangements. A wreath made up of fresh bay leaves hung on the front door at New Year is a traditional symbol of protection and courage.

• *Culinary suggestions* – Dried or fresh bay leaves are essential for any *bouquet garni* (together with parsley and thyme), especially for flavoring fish, beef, lamb, liver, game, and occasionally desserts.

• *Health-giving properties* – The leaves and berries are used in herbal medicine mainly for their powerful digestive and antiseptic properties. An infusion of the fresh leaves steeped in boiling water can be drunk to stimulate the digestion or can be added to bath water to soothe aching limbs.

Lavandula angustifolia (zones 5–8) (syn. L. officinalis)

LAVENDER (Lamiaceae)

Scent: sweet, floral-herby, balsamic-green, slightly camphoraceous, soothing, relaxing.

DESCRIPTION AND CULTIVATION

Lavender is both a classical and vital contemporary ingredient in any aromatic garden. Its hazy bluish-purple flowers, soft silver foliage, and dreamy yet pungent sharp-floral scent seem to capture the very essence of summertime, evoking memories of balmy childhood days and vivid images of the plant's native sun-baked Mediterranean mountains. It is one of the few herbs that has never gone out of fashion and has

ABOVE: HAZY BLUE FIELDS OF LAVENDER ON THE
ISLAND OF JERSEY.

enjoyed widespread use from the earliest times to the
present day.

Lavender is extremely valuable as an ornamental
garden plant, and there is now a great range of
species
to choose from. The so-called true lavender (*L. angustifolia*) is a relatively hardy, evergreen woody
shrub, up to 3ft (1m) tall, with pale green, narrow linear
leaves and flowers of a beautiful, violet-blue color on
blunt spikes. The whole plant is highly aromatic and
combines well with old rose species and other
subshrubs. All lavender species like full sun and well-
drained soil, but will tolerate partial shade.

The more compact species make good hedging
plants for the front of a bed or for lining a path. In colder
climates, tender species are best grown in pots that can
be moved to a greenhouse or conservatory for the
winter months.

Cut bushes back after flowering to maintain their
shape and prevent them from getting woody (but avoid
cutting into the old wood), then trim them again in the
spring. Seed can be sown in the spring, but this method
does not tend to result in plants that are true to species.
Instead take softwood cuttings in spring or semi-ripe
cuttings later in summer or early fall, and keep the young
plants protected over winter before planting the
following year.

RECOMMENDED SPECIES

There are many cultivars of *L. angustifolia*, notably
'Alba' with white flowers and 'Nana Alba,' a dwarf
white; 'Rosea' has pink flowers; 'Hidcote' is compact
with silver leaves and dark purple flowers, and
'Munstead' has mauve flowers and grows just 14in

(35cm) high. Another traditional hardy species is spike lavender (*L. latifolia*) (zones 6–8), an aromatic evergreen subshrub up to 3ft (1m) high, broader leaved than true lavender with gray-blue flowers. Less hardy are French lavender (*L. stoechas*) (zones 8–9) with purple bracts and *L. s.* subsp. *pedunculata* with magenta-purple bracts; wooly lavender (*L. lanata*), which is balsamic-scented with bright purple flowers, and 'Sawyers,' which is relatively hardy with large blue flowers. The unusual green-flowered lavender (*L. viridis*) (zones 9–10) and *L. dentata* (zones 8–9), a winter-flowering variety with finely toothed green leaves, are tender but well worth growing.

HOME USES

• *Aromatherapy applications* – It is the fresh flowering tops that are used to produce the well-known lavender essential oil, by far the most popular aromatic oil used in aromatherapy and generally regarded as the most versatile essence therapeutically. It is very valuable for skin care and all types of inflamed or infected skin conditions such as acne, allergies, burns, eczema, insect bites, and stings. It is also used for muscle and joint problems, respiratory infections, digestive cramps, and genito-urinary infections. Its most common use, however, is as a nerve sedative in cases of depression, headaches, hypertension, insomnia, migraine, nervous tension, and all stress-related conditions. A traditional lavender water/eau-de-cologne and massage oil can be made from the fresh flowers at home – see pages 72.

• *Drying and decorative uses* – Lavender is also one of the most reliable and versatile herbs of the still room. Harvest the flowers just as they open and hang up to dry in small bunches or lay them out on trays. The dried flowers can then be used in potpourris, bath sachets, and sleep pillows, while the dried twigs make a good burning incense or can be bound together in bundles to scent household drawers and keep moths at bay. See Chapter 5 (page 66) for more ideas for decorative uses.

• *Culinary suggestions* – Small amounts of the flowers added to vinegars, *provençale* stews, and lamb stuffing impart a bitter-sweet flavor.

• *Health-Giving properties* – Lavender tea is drunk in France for its tonic effect and for its antidepressant, antispasmodic, nervine, and sedative properties.

Lilium candidum

MADONNA LILY
(Liliaceae)

Scent – heavy, honeylike, rich, exotic, floral, sweet, intoxicating, euphoric, aphrodisiac.

DESCRIPTION AND CULTIVATION

The Madonna lily is one of the very earliest exotic garden plants taken to Britain by the Romans. As its name suggests, it is startlingly white with golden stamens and is symbolically associated with the Virgin Mary. The oldest of the cultivated lilies, it originally came from ancient Egypt and Greece, and is now an endangered species in the wild.

The bulb produces a rosette of dark green base leaves in the fall, then in spring a flowering stem shoots up to 5ft (1.5m) high with as many as 20 trumpet-shaped flowers that bloom around midsummer. Despite its stately appearance, it is relatively easy to grow, although it can be temperamental, and prefers to have some shade at its the base.

RIGHT: THE EXOTIC LILY IS UNDER-STANDABLY FAVORED BY FLORISTS.

It will naturalize in a semi-shaded position, and is equally at home in a bed, *potager*, or herb garden, infusing the surrounding air with a heavy honeyed fragrance akin to honeysuckle.

The lilies also make ideal container specimens for a patio or conservatory; the pots can then be moved around so their scent can be enjoyed to the maximum – especially after dark. Plant the bulbs in early fall with no more than 2in (5cm) of light alkaline soil covering them. Plants can be propagated by seed sown in spring or fall, or by division of mature bulbs, using the offsets or outer scales, in late summer. The Madonna lily resents disturbance once it has become established.

RECOMMENDED SPECIES

The golden-rayed lily from Japan (*L. auratum*) (zones 5–8), known as the queen of lilies, is easier to grow than the Madonna lily. In the late summer, it carries more flower heads on each stem than any other lily, sometimes as many as 30. This is one of the most outstanding species with an intoxicating, spicy perfume. The regal lily (*L. regale*) (zones 4–7), discovered in western China in 1908, is a long-standing favorite with gardeners as well as florists. Equally attractive is *L. regale* 'Album,' a pure white version, with a greenish

exterior; *L. longiflorum* (zones 7–9) is also pure white and makes an excellent easy-to-grow potted plant, but needs frost-free conditions. The oriental lilies are a beautiful and highly scented group as a whole, but the creamy cultivar 'Casa Blanca' (zones 5–8) has possibly the most pervasive perfume of all.

HOME USES

• *Aromatherapy applications* – The fresh flowers of *L. candidum* are used to produce a costly essential oil used in exclusive perfumery work. *L. regale* also yields an essential oil used to make an exotic high-quality perfume in Bermuda. Fresh lily flowers can be used at home to make a perfume using the enfleurage method, while the distilled flower water possesses toning and astringent properties. An infused oil of lilies can be used to treat dry eczema and chapped skin as well as making an exotic and sensual massage treatment. See pages 72–3 for instructions on how to make these preparations at home.

• *Drying and decorative uses* – Fresh lilies are one of the most long-lasting and attractive flowers for indoor arrangements with a pervasive, perfume – the scent of some species can be overpowering. Beware of the pollen, though, which can stain surfaces or clothes.

• *Culinary suggestions* – Various lilies have edible bulbs, including *L. candidum*, and are commonly used as vegetables in China and Japan where they are cultivated specifically for food.

• *Health-giving properties* – The Madonna lily has an ancient history of medicinal usage in both the East and West. The soothing mucilage obtained from the bulbs in late summer is used for irritated skin conditions, including burns, acne, chilblains, ulcers, chapped skin, etc., usually prepared in the form of an ointment.

Lonicera periclymenum

HONEYSUCKLE
(Caprifoliaceae)

Scent – rich, fruity, slightly spicy, honey-sweet, floral, refreshing, uplifting.

DESCRIPTION AND CULTIVATION
The pervasive perfume of honeysuckle is one of the great pleasures of the summer, both in the garden and in the wild. This familiar hedge and country-garden plant is an essential feature in any aromatic garden. The common honeysuckle is a deciduous plant that can reach 20ft (6m) high, bearing its pinkish-yellow flowers right through the summer. It is also a very hardy plant (although some species and varieties are tender) and will tolerate most soils, although it likes to be shaded at the base.

Most honeysuckles look best when they are left to scramble up walls or trees in a naturalistic fashion,

combining well with clematis or climbing roses. They also make good semi-transparent screens for dividing up different areas of the garden, climbing up arbors, and for covering unsightly stumps or stone ruins. Most honeysuckles will tolerate being grown in a container. In the fall, or after flowering, give plants a light pruning or tidying to remove surplus shoots. Propagate them from seed sown in spring or fall, soft or semi-hardwood cuttings taken in summer, or root division in the fall.

RECOMMENDED SPECIES
There is a wide range of different species and cultivars that flower at different times of the year, some even in the depths of winter, for example *L. fragrantissima* (zones 5–8). Slightly tender species such as *L. etrusca* (zones 7–9), which grows 13ft (4m) high, make excellent plants for a large conservatory. Other highly scented forms include the invasive and often woody Japanese honeysuckle (*L. japonica*) (zones 4–10), which is semi-evergreen with creamy-white flowers, and *L. j.* var. *repens*, a beautiful tall climber with purplish evergreen leaves.

HOME USES
• *Aromatherapy applications* – An essential oil from *L. periclymenum* and *L. etrusca* is produced in minute quantities for high-class perfumery work, but it is rarely used in aromatherapy. A natural perfume and a skin-cleansing toilet water can be made at home from the fresh flowers – see pages 72–3.

• *Drying and decorative uses* – The flexible stems can be used to make dried wreath bases. Wild honeysuckle is suited to naturalistic arrangements – winter honeysuckle is especially valuable for fresh arrangements when other flowers are scarce. Crush the bottom of the woody stem before placing in water; once indoors, it releases its spicy-sweet fragrance. The dried flowers can be used in herb pillows and potpourris.

- *Culinary Applications* – The fresh flowers can be added to salads or infused in apple jelly. The black berries are poisonous.
- *Health-giving properties* – An infusion of the flowers

ABOVE AND LEFT: HONEYSUCKLE (*LONICERA PERICLYMENUM*) HAS A SWEET FRUITY FRAGRANCE.

can be drunk as a tea or as a remedy for coughs, colds, and rhinitis. Recent research suggests that honeysuckle may be a valuable herb for use in the treatment of colitis.

Melissa officinalis

LEMON BALM
(Lamiaceae)

Scent – light, fresh-green, lemony, uplifting, refreshing, restorative.

DESCRIPTION AND CULTIVATION

Lemon balm, as its name indicates, is a delightfully citrus-scented herb, soft and bushy, with bright green, serrated leaves and tiny white or pink flowers. A native of Europe and the Mediterranean region, this herb will thrive in virtually any soil or situation (though it prefers light shade) and can be very invasive if it is not kept in check. Not only does it seed itself readily, it can also spread rapidly by root runners to form new clumps. Unlike mint, however, it is easy to pull up and control, so it is not necessary to keep it confined.

Despite its rampant nature, lemon balm remains a first choice for the herb garden since it is both decorative and useful. Growing up to 3ft (1m) high, the bright foliage of lemon balm looks best when planted next to herbs of a contrasting color and texture, such as purple sage or blue-leaved rue. It also grows happily in a container, where it forms a compact shape if it is trimmed regularly. The flowers are very attractive to bees, which explains one of its folk names of bee balm. Planted in orchards or among other fruit trees, it encourages in bees for rapid pollination. Lemon balm is easy to propagate by root division or by cuttings taking from mature shoots. Cut to ground level after flowering, it will produce a new crop of leaves before the whole plant finally dies back in winter.

RECOMMENDED SPECIES

M. officinalis 'Aurea' has variegated leaves and is slightly smaller; *M. o.* 'All Gold' (zones 4–9) has striking golden leaves.

HOME USES

• *Aromatherapy applications* – An essential oil is made from the leaves and flowering tops in minute quantities, but most so-called melissa oil, however, contains some or all of the following: lemon, lemongrass, or citronella oil. In aromatherapy, the oil is used mainly for nervous conditions, including anxiety, depression, hypertension, insomnia, migraines, shock, and vertigo. Melissa is the main ingredient of a traditional eau-de-cologne called Carmelite water, and a toilet water can be made from the fresh leaves – see page 72.

• *Drying and decorative uses* – Leaves should be harvested just before flowering, then used to make herb sachets or added to potpourris. Leaves stuffed in bath bags release a really refreshing citrus aroma, especially when used fresh; they also make a good hair rinse. The juice of the stems was at one time rubbed over oak furniture for the shine and lemony fragrance it imparted.

• *Culinary suggestions* – The leaves were originally added to ale: use them fresh in summer drinks and tea; add chopped leaves to fish, poultry, and mushroom dishes; serve with fruit salads, gelatines, ice cream, and custard as decoration.

• *Health-giving properties* – Lemon balm has a long history of medicinal use, most famously as a cure for melancholy and to promote longevity. It has been called the elixir of life, and several people who have lived to more than 100 years old swear their good health is due to drinking lemon balm tea daily. Tea made from fresh or dried leaves is good for headaches or insomnia, and for easing cramps

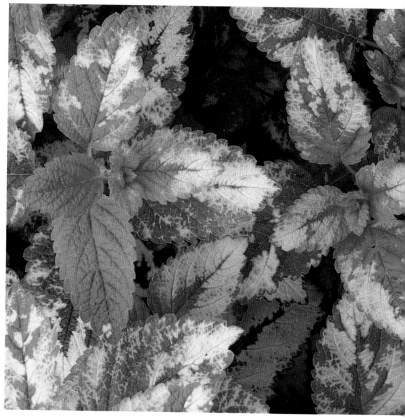

ABOVE: LEMON BALM (*MELISSA OFFICINALIS*) SEEN HERE IN ITS PLAIN AND VARIAGATED FORM.

caused by indigestion or period pains. Rub fresh leaves on wasp stings for pain relief.

Mentha x piperita

PEPPERMINT (Lamiaceae)

Scent – minty, refreshing invigorating, green-herby, fresh, slightly camphoraceous.

DESCRIPTION AND CULTIVATION

Mint has been cultivated since ancient times and is still one of the most popular and familiar aromatic herbs. Peppermint is a perennial plant up to 3ft (1m) high and dies down over the winter period. White peppermint has soft, green stems and leaves; black peppermint has dark green serrated leaves, purplish stems, and reddish-violet flowers. Most mints will quickly take over an area of the garden via their spreading underground runners if they are not confined. Peppermint will thrive in a pot on the terrace or in a windowbox; it can also be grown in the herb garden by first sinking a container into the soil to ground level, then planting the mint inside. It is easy to propagate new plants from root cuttings at any time during the growing season. Most mints prefer rich, moist soil in sun or partial shade.

RECOMMENDED SPECIES

There are many varieties of mint that are grown commercially for the production of essential oils, including water mint (*M. aquatica*), corn mint (*M. canadensis*) (zones 4–9), and pennyroyal (*M. pulegium*) – all attractive garden varieties. At home, choose the species according to your requirements: apple mint (*M. suaveolens*) (zones 7–9) is good for cooking; spearmint (*M. spicata*) (zones 4–9) is useful for children used therapeutically; buddleia mint (*M. longifolia*) (zones 6–9) is a decorative plant for the flowerbed.

HOME USES

• *Aromatherapy applications* – In aromatherapy, peppermint oil is mainly used as an insect repellent and as an inhalation for colds, bronchitis, and asthma; in perfumery it is employed principally in colognes and toiletries. A eau-de-cologne water can be produced at home using young fresh leaves – see pages 72–3.
• *Drying and decorative uses* – Harvest the whole plant as it begins to flower; the leaves retain their color and scent well for use in potpourris. Use fresh sprigs in tiny bouquets, known as tussie mussies (see page 77), and the leaves in bath bags, especially those of the eau-de-cologne mint (*M. piperita* f. *citrata*) for their refreshing effect.
• *Culinary suggestions* – Cook with potatoes to add flavor. Make mint sauce to serve with lamb by finely chopping the leaves and adding to vinegar; use young leaves for decorating desserts and in iced drinks. Middle Eastern dishes use lots of chopped fresh mint.
• *Health-giving properties* – Use the fresh or dried leaves to make a herbal tea for indigestion, nausea, nervous fatigue, and respiratory infections such as colds and 'flu.

Monarda didyma

BERGAMOT (Lamiaceae)

Scent – lemony, sweet, uplifting, minty-fresh, stimulating.

DESCRIPTION AND CULTIVATION

This hardy perennial woodland herb is a native of North America and has become a popular garden flower with numerous cultivars available. The name

RIGHT: IN FLOWER ALL SUMMER, LARGE CLUMPS OF BERGAMOT GRACE THE LONG BEDS AT WEST GREEN GARDENS, ENGLAND.

Monarda honors the Spanish botanist Dr. Nicholas Monardes, who wrote an herbal on the flora of America in 1569 and who named the plant bergamot because its scent reminded him of that of the Italian bergamot orange (*Citrus bergamia*) (zones 9–11).

Bergamot is a useful herb for planting along paths so it releases its scent when the leaves are brushed. The flamboyant flowers, which are now available in a range of colors from white through pink to scarlet, add interest to the herb garden or herbaceous bed over a long period, flowering throughout the summer. The flowers will also attract bees and butterflies to the garden, hence its folk name of bee balm. Although bergamot will tolerate hot sun, it prefers partial shade, requiring rich, light, and moist soil. Sow seed in spring, then thin or plant out to about 18in (45cm) apart in summer. Plants will grow to about 3ft (1m) high. Divide them every three years, or take new root cuttings in spring or softwood cuttings in summer. Seed can be collected for sowing the following year. It is not suitable for growing indoors.

RECOMMENDED SPECIES

More than five species of bergamot are used for producing essential oils for perfumery work – for eau-de-colognes and hair preparations – including *M. didyma*, *M. citriodora* (A), *M. fistulosa* (zones 3–9), *M. clinopodia* (zones 5–9), and *M. pectinata* (A).

HOME USES

• *Aromatherapy applications* – A flower water can be made at home using the fresh leaves and flowers – see page 72. The oil is little used in

ABOVE: BERGAMOT (*MONARDA DIDYMA*).

aromatherapy, despite the fact that it possesses powerful antiseptic properties.

• *Drying and decorative uses* – Collect whole plants during flowering: the leaves and flowers can then be dried for use in potpourris, dried flower arrangements, and herb teas. The flowers retain their color well when dried.

• *Culinary suggestions* – Young leaves can be added to pork stuffing, fruit salads, jams, homemade lemonade, and to give tea an Earl Grey flavor. Add fresh flowers to salads.

• *Health-giving properties* – The wild purple bergamot (*M. fistulosa*) was used by Native Americans as a remedy for colds and bronchial complaints, while the scarlet bee balm (*M. didyma*), which grew by the Oswego River, was used to make a digestive tea – thus its folk name Oswego tea. A tea made from the fresh young leaves of *M. didyma* can be drunk for minor digestive complaints, menstrual pain, and nausea.

Myrtus communis

MYRTLE (Myrtaceae)

Scent: clear, fresh, balsamic, green-floral, camphoraceous, sweet-herby, uplifting, clarifying, aphrodisiac.

DESCRIPTION AND CULTIVATION

Myrtle forms a beautiful shrub or small tree up to 10ft (3m) tall, with many tough but slender branches, brownish-red bark, and small evergreen pointed leaves. It has simple, five-petaled ivory flowers with dense golden stamens, followed by small blue-black berries; and both leaves and flowers are very fragrant.

ABOVE: MYRTLE FLOWERS (*MYRTUS COMMUNIS*).

According to myth, the goddess Aphrodite hid her nakedness behind a sweet myrtle bush, and the plant has always been associated with the qualities of beauty, innocence, and love. Its name is derived from the Greek *myrtos*, the "herb of love."

Myrtle is a Mediterranean plant and is almost frost hardy: it can survive outdoors in a warm, sheltered position (covered with thin spun polyester if a hard frost is forecast), but it prefers a minimum average temperature of 40°F (5°C). In colder climates, it is best grown as a conservatory plant or brought under glass for the winter where it makes a lovely specimen shrub, especially as a topiary plant. Trimming back growth in late spring will maintain a pleasing shape. Myrtle is easily propagated by softwood cuttings in spring or hardwood cuttings in mid- or late summer, set in free-draining potting mixture.

RECOMMENDED VARIETIES

M. communis 'Variegata' is slightly smaller than sweet myrtle with variegated leaves; *M. c.* 'Flore Pleno' has long-lasting, fully double white flowers; the dwarf subspecies *M. c.* subsp. *tarentina* makes an ideal specimen or container plant.

HOME USES

• *Aromatherapy applications* – Valued primarily as an antiseptic and skin-care agent, myrtle leaf oil is mainly used for acne, oily skin, asthma, bronchitis, catarrhal conditions, chronic coughs, colds, 'flu, and infectious conditions – especially children's coughs and chest complaints. The fresh leaves and flowers can be used to make a refreshing facial lotion – myrtle is a major ingredient in the classical angel flower water – and a fragrant body oil, traditionally used for beautifying the skin (see pages 72–3 for making flower waters).

• *Drying and decorative uses* – The berries can be dried and used as a spice, much like juniper. Dried leaves and flowers can also be included in sweet pillows and potpourris, and hung up in bunches as an insect repellent. The fresh flowers are popular in bridal bouquets, as a symbol of love and chastity.

• *Culinary suggestions* – Dip fresh leaves in water and lay on the grill for 10 minutes when barbecuing meat to impart a sweet smoky flavor. Preserve the fresh leaves in oil or vinegar for cooking – see page 35.

• *Health-giving properties* – A tea made from the leaves is said to preserve love and youth – the reason why some French women still drink myrtle tea.

Narcissus poeticus
POET'S NARCISSUS
(Amaryllidaceae)

Scent – sweet, heavy, honeylike, floral-green, rich, intoxicating, narcotic, aphrodisiac.

DESCRIPTION AND CULTIVATION
An orchard or meadow full of poet's narcissi is one of the most welcome sights in late spring, each dainty head displaying its starlike, pure white petals, which in turn reveal a small yellow inner cup trimmed with red. The name is derived from the Greek term *narkao* meaning "to numb," due to the plant's paralyzing effect on the nervous system. The legend of the handsome Greek youth who fell in love with his own image and was changed into a narcissus flower also tells us something about their intoxicating quality. The scent is certainly very powerful and can even cause headaches if the flowers are present in any quantity in a closed room.

Native to the Middle East and the eastern Mediterranean region, *N. poeticus* has also become naturalized in southern France and can be found growing wild in the mountains – this is known as *des montagnes* type, as opposed to the cultivated *des plaines* variety. The cultivated variety grows to about

ABOVE: POET'S NARCISSUS (*NARCISSUS POETICUS*).

20in (50cm) high and has long, narrow swordlike leaves and single flowering stems.

Bulbs should be planted about one and a half times deeper than their size in moist but well-drained soil in early fall. They are best suited to growing in dappled shade in woodlands, grouped in beds, or naturalized in grass, in which case the leaves should not be cut back for at least four weeks after flowering, or the next season's show will be diminished. Narcissi are also well adapted for growing in containers: plant them in a double layer for an *en masse* effect.

RECOMMENDED SPECIES
There are several types of *N. poeticus* commonly available: *N. p.* var. *recurvus* (pheasant's eye) is smaller with a deeper red eye; 'Plenus' is a double version that is very striking. Of other species, *N. jonquilla* has an orangelike scent and *N. tazetta* (zones 7–9) subsp. *lacticolor* (syn. *N. canaliculatus*) has a very sweet floral perfume.

HOME USES
• *Aromatherapy applications* – Both cultivated and wild species of *N. poeticus* are used for producing an absolute in France. Jonquil (*N. jonquilla*) (zones 5–9) and campernella (*N. x odorus*) (zones 7–9) are also used to produce an absolute for perfumery use. In aromatherapy, narcissus oil is used in moderation for its euphoric and inspirational effect. Sensual and hypnotic, it can also be profoundly relaxing. Use flowers to produce an enfleurage-style perfume at home – see page 73.

- *Drying and decorative uses* – Narcissus make excellent cut flowers on their own – like daffodils, they are best not mixed with other species due to their poisonous sap. Some Tazetta varieties such as the orange-cupped 'Soleil d'Or' and the popular paperwhite narcissus (*N. papyraceus*) (zones 8–10) can be forced for very early indoor flowering. The latter will flower a month or two after planting and is easy to grow.
- *Culinary suggestions* – Narcissus bulbs are potentially fatal if eaten: they have a paralyzing effect on the nervous system.
- *Health-giving properties* – Juice from the bulbs was once used by Roman soldiers to numb the pain of battle wounds. The flowers have been used in France for their antispasmodic effects and to treat epilepsy.

NOTE: Narcissus should not be used medicinally at home because of its high toxicity.

Nepeta cataria

CATNIP (Lamiaceae)

Scent – minty, slightly camphoraceous, herby-woody, pungent, mildly narcotic.

DESCRIPTION AND CULTIVATION

Catnip is an attractive perennial herb: its tumbling gray-green, aromatic foliage and pale mauve flowers add an air of softness to any bed. Native to Europe, North Africa, and Asia, there are now many species and varieties to be found growing in temperate zones worldwide. Most of the herbaceous, decorative varieties have a loose, spreading habit, making them ideal for planting at the front of beds or alongside paths, especially since the whole plant releases its fragrance when brushed against. The wild species *N. cataria* has long been cultivated specifically for its medicinal and seasoning properties, and is so-called because cats find the scent irresistible and love to roll in the leaves. It grows to about 3ft (1m) high, and flowers over the whole midsummer period. Like most catnips, it is a hardy plant, although rather short-lived, and will tolerate most conditions apart from boggy or very wet conditions.

Ideally catnip prefers light, well-drained soil in a sunny position, which is why it will also thrive in terracotta pots. Cut plants right back after the first flush of flowers to encourage a second crop of blooms. They can easily be propagated by taking softwood cuttings in spring or early summer, or by dividing an established clump. Sow seed in early spring or late summer.

RECOMMENDED SPECIES

N. cataria 'Citriodora' has light blue flowers and is lemon scented; *N. racemosa* (zones 4–9) has decorative purple-blue flowers, grows up to 20in (50cm) high and combines well with old roses; *N.* x *faassenii* (zones 4–9) has loose spikes of lavender-blue flowers and grows up to 18in (45cm) high. The stunning cultivar 'Six Hills Giant' has deeper purple flowers and grows 3ft (1m) high. *Calamintha officinalis* (zones 5–9), also known as catmint, is mainly used to produce nepeta oil commercially.

HOME USES

• *Aromatherapy applications* – The leaf oil is occasionally used for stress-related conditions, digestive complaints, and muscular aches and pains. A flower water can be made at home from the fresh leaves – see page 72.

• *Drying and decorative uses* – The leaves of *N. racemosa* retain their lemony scent especially well when dried and may be used together with lemon balm and verbena to make delightfully fresh-scented potpourris or bath bags. The blossoms of all nepetas will add soft color to flower arrangements, either fresh or dried.

• *Culinary suggestions* – Add freshly picked young shoots of *N. cataria* to salads or use them to give meat a minty flavor.

• *Health-giving properties* – the leaves of *N. cataria* are

LEFT: *N. CATARIA*

still used in herbal medicine for digestive and nervous complaints, and as a specific remedy for colic in children and for the common cold. An infusion of the fresh leaves steeped in boiling water makes a delicious tonic tea or can be used as a traditional cold remedy. Served cold with ice, it also makes a refreshing summer drink.

NOTE: Avoid using catnip during pregnancy.

Ocimum basilicum

SWEET BASIL (Lamiaceae)

Scent: light, fresh, sweet-spicy, balsamic, clovelike, uplifting, purifying, reviving, warming.

DESCRIPTION AND CULTIVATION

Basil is one of the most valued aromatic herbs, and there are some 160 different varieties found worldwide. Native to India, the richly balsamic-scented species known as holy basil (*O. sanctum*) (A) is held sacred by the Hindus and frequently grown outside their temples for its protective influence, but it is not used in cooking. When other types of basil later spread throughout the Mediterranean region, it became used extensively as a culinary herb, especially in Italy. Sweet or French basil (*O. basilicum*) is a tender annual herb with green, shiny ovate leaves, up to 2ft (60cm) high bearing spikes of two-lipped greenish or pinkish-white flowers throughout the summer. It is perhaps the best variety for general culinary and therapeutic usage – both its leaves and flowers emitting a warm, powerful clovelike scent. It is best planted in a warm, sunny, sheltered site in well-drained, rich soil after all danger of frost has passed.

Basil makes a good companion plant in the vegetable garden, especially alongside tomatoes. Most basil species will also thrive grown in pots on a sunny windowsill or in a cool greenhouse, where they can be treated as short-lived perennials. Keep pots moist but

ABOVE: SWEET BASIL (*OCIMUM BASILICUM*).

not waterlogged. Sow seed thinly in late spring as soon as the soil has warmed up – it dislikes being transplanted. Always protect plants from scorching sun and pinch out tops to encourage bushy growth.

RECOMMENDED SPECIES

Bush basil (*O. minimum*) (A) is slightly hardier and more compact in shape than sweet basil; it has smaller leaves and is well suited to growing on a windowsill. The pink flowers and purple leaves of *O. basilicum* 'Dark Opal' and 'Purple Ruffles' contrast well with the bright green leaves of sweet basil, combined in a hanging basket or as a feature in the herb garden. *O. x citriodorum* (A) is a tender, small variety with lemon-scented, bright yellowish-green leaves, valuable in the kitchen and still room.

HOME USES

• *Aromatherapy applications* – Basil oil is mainly used for muscular aches and pains, cramp, rheumatism, and respiratory and infectious diseases. In addition, basil is one of the best aromatic nerve tonics for conditions such as anxiety, depression, insomnia, migraine, nervous tension. The scent alone can help to clear the head, relieve intellectual fatigue, and give the mind greater clarity. An infused oil for massage can be prepared from the fresh leaves – see page 73.

• *Drying and decorative uses* – Fresh pots of basil grown in the kitchen look decorative and will help keep flies away. Dried basil leaves and flowers can be used in potpourris.

• *Culinary suggestions* – The leaves are best picked fresh for cooking. Add them at the very last minute since they can become bitter if they are cooked for a long time. Leaves should always be picked from the top to prevent the plant from flowering and then torn, not chopped. They can be used in all sorts of dishes especially pasta, egg, chicken, or shellfish recipes, combining delightfully well with garlic, tomatoes, or eggplant. They can also be added to soups, salads, and sauces to give a fresh, tangy flavor or to make flavored oils and vinegars – see page 35.

• *Health-giving properties* – A tonic tea made from fresh basil leaves aids indigestion, nausea, and mild digestive upsets.

NOTE: Avoid basil tea during pregnancy

Origanum vulgare

WILD MARJORAM
(Lamiaceae)

Scent – warm, woody, spicy-camphoraceous, herby, stimulating, refreshing

DESCRIPTION AND CULTIVATION

There is much confusion surrounding the naming and identification of the various members of the oregano and marjoram family, for they are closely related. To confuse matters still further, common oregano, which is also known as wild marjoram, is very variable in scent and appearance, according to where it is growing. Generally speaking, wild marjoram (*O. vulgare*) is a bushy perennial herb, 18in (45cm) high, with upright purplish stems and oval leaves that are sometimes flushed with red, and dark purple-pink flowers. The whole plant is highly aromatic, with a warm, sweetly spicy flavor. *O. vulgare* is found growing wild from Europe right across to central Asia and thrives in the warm Mediterranean region – where it is called oregano, or joy of the mountains. The same plant sometimes has paler pink flowers and the scent is less pronounced.

With the exception of sweet marjoram (*O. majorana*) (zones 9–10), most oregano species are hardy and will tolerate a range of situations, as long as the soil is not waterlogged. Plants are best propagated by softwood cuttings taken in spring or by root division after the plant has flowered. Trim the plants back after flowering to maintain their shape.

RECOMMENDED SPECIES

There are numerous cultivars of *O. vulgare*, including the lovely golden-leaved marjoram *O. v.* 'Aureum,' which adds luster to any herb garden with its bright, fresh foliage. It forms a compact low-growing mound and has a mass of mauve flowers. 'Aureum Crispum' also has golden-green leaves that are slightly crinkled; 'Compactum' is a dwarf form with pink-violet flowers; *O. v.* var. *album* is a bushy, white-flowered, naturally occurring variety; while 'Polyphant' has white-variegated foliage and is good for containers and edging. The most highly scented marjoram, however, is the pot marjoram (*O. onites*) (zones 8–10), which has erect stems bearing white to pink flowers and very aromatic leaves. The "knotted" sweet marjoram (*O. majorana)*, is a slightly tender bushy perennial plant (cultivated as an annual in colder climates), up to 12in (30cm) high with hairy stems, greenish-gray oval leaves, and small pinkish-white flowers in clusters or knots produced in late summer. It is perhaps the best species for culinary purposes, with a delicate, more refined flavor and scent. For similar reasons, it is also the favored species used in aromatherapy and perfumery work. Spanish oregano or conehead thyme (*Thymus capitatus*) (zones 9–10) is a perennial creeping herb with a woody stem, small dark green leaves, and pink or white flowers borne in clusters. Although this herb is strictly a thyme, it serves as the source for most so-called oregano oil.

HOME USES

• *Aromatherapy applications* – An essential oil is produced by steam distillation of the dried flowering herb. Used in massage, wild

RIGHT AND OVER PAGE: WILD MARJORAM (*O. VULGARE*) HAS VARIABLE COLORING.

marjoram oil helps relieve aching joints, stiffness, rheumatism, sprains, and strains. It is also used to help combat respiratory infections and digestive complaints. Sweet majoram oil, which has a more sedative effect, is used for headaches, hypertension, nervous tension, and stress-related conditions. A massage oil can be made at home from the fresh herb – see page 73.

• *Drying and decorative uses* – Infused in vinegar, wild marjoram was earlier used as a substitute for smelling salts; in baths, the fresh flowering tips are reviving and uplifting. The leaves and flowers of sweet marjoram also dry well and are good for cooking. The decorative marjoram species can be used in dried flower arrangements, wreaths, potpourris, etc.

• *Culinary suggestions* – Both marjoram and oregano are used extensively in cooking – they are one of the ingredients of *bouquet garni* – particularly in tomato-based or Italian dishes.

• *Health-giving properties* – Both marjoram and oregano have powerful antiseptic properties and were much favored by early herbalists such as Culpeper and Turner. They also have powerful antiviral and tonic properties: a tea made from sweet marjoram leaves helps combat colds and infections; marjoram leaves, chewed, can relieve toothache.
NOTE: Not to be used during pregnancy.

Pelargonium 'Graveolens'

ROSE GERANIUM
(Geraniaceae)

Scent – sweet, rosy, floral, slightly green, minty, harmonizing, balancing, uplifting, refreshing.

DESCRIPTION AND CULTIVATION
Pelargoniums are among the most obliging tender plants, needing little watering and protection in winter, and a bare minimum temperature of 34–41°F (1–5°C). They are equally happy in a cool conservatory or in a warm house, provided they have enough light. They do not, however, like hot moist conditions. Generally it is the leaves that are scented rather than the flowers, although there are exceptions such as *P. gibbosum* (T) and *P. triste* (T), those flowers are sweetly scented in the evening. *Pelargonium* is a large genus of shrublike perennials, mostly flowering in the summer and sometimes into the fall, although they are often cultivated as annuals. Besides the scented-leaved species, there are four other categories within the genus.

The scented-leaved varieties originally came from the Cape Province in South Africa, but the genus is also native to the Mediterranean and the Middle East. In England they were first grown by the rich in glasshouses and it was only in the nineteenth century that they gained wider popularity in North America as well.

The great number of scented pelargonium varieties available has guaranteed their widespread popularity. Pelargoniums are now frequently planted in pots and are a colorful addition to hanging baskets and window-boxes. They are also popular bedding plants: if planted outside, they like lots of sunshine and a well-drained soil. Beware of over-watering, especially in winter, when the plants should be kept dryish. To propagate, take softwood cuttings from mid spring right through to late summer.

RECOMMENDED SPECIES
It is important to differentiate between pelargoniums

BELOW: THE HARDY HERBACEOUS *GERANIUM ENDRESSII* (ZONES 5–8)

and geraniums, as they are frequently confused. The original wild pelargonium from South Africa had small leaves and flowers, but most we know today are hybrids – all need minimum winter protection. Geraniums, by contrast, are hardy perennials. Both, however, belong to the same family, Geraniaceae. One of the best scented pelargoniums is *P.* 'Graveolens' (T), a large variety with pink starry flowers and rose-scented leaves; it can grow 3ft (1m) high. 'Lady Plymouth' is a green and cream variegated variety with a delightful rose scent. Another excellent rose-scented species, bearing pale pink flowers, native to South Africa is *P. capitatum*, while the fragrance of the tiny 'Attar of Roses' is similar to the more expensive true of attar of roses and is sometimes used as a substitute. More of a balsamic fragrance is found in *P.* Fragrans Group 'Creamy Nutmeg,' which has a musky scent similar to nutmeg; another balsamic-scented variety is the oak-leaf pelargonium (*P. quercifolium*) (T). The showy rose-pink 'Clorinda' is eucalyptus scented with a touch of rose; *P. tomentosum* (T), a tall variety with a minty scent, was a favorite of Gertrude Jekyll and used by her to make peppermint jelly. An old variety of pelargonium with a definite nutmeg scent is 'Lady Mary,' while 'Pretty Polly' and 'Little Gem' are almond scented. Lemon scented-leaved pelargoniums include *P. crispum* 'Variegatum' (T), the Prince Rupert geranium, *P. c.* 'Major,' and *P.* 'Citriodorum', while *P.* 'Prince of Orange' has leaves sweetly scented with oranges. *P. odoratissimum* (T) is apple scented and is sometimes used to flavor apple jelly.

HOME USES
• *Aromatherapy applications* – An essential oil is extracted from *P.* 'Graveolens' by steam distillation of the flowers and leaves. It has antifungal, antiseptic, and astringent properties, and is much used in skin care and for the treatment of cellulitis and water retension. It is also used to treat sore throat and tonsillitis, poor circulation, menopausal problems, and stress-related conditions. A flower water can be made

ABOVE: THE SCENTED LEAVES OF ROSE GERANIUM (*P. GRAVEOLENS*) HAVE A DELIGHTFUL, UPLIFTING PERFUME.

at home from the scented leaves – see pages 72.
• *Drying and decorative uses* – Dried leaves are used in potpourris. Scented-leaf pelargoniums are perhaps some of the most pleasing insect-repellent plants.
• *Culinary suggestions* – Leaves of *P.* 'Graveolens' can be made into a refreshing tea, but avoid the lemon-scented varieties of *P. crispum*, which can act as an irritant. The leaves can also be used to flavor fruit syrups, preserves, and alcoholic and soft drinks.
• *Health-giving properties* – Various pelargonium and geranium species, such as *Geranium robertianum* (zones 4–8), have been used since antiquity for their medicinal applications, mainly for their styptic, tonic, and antiseptic properties.

Prostanthera cuneata
MINT BUSH (Lamiaceae)

Scent – aromatic, minty-green, slightly camphoraceous, stimulating, uplifting, fresh, astringent.

DESCRIPTION AND CULTIVATION
Mint bushes are evergreen shrubs native to Australasia. Both the leaves and flowers, which are carried in late spring or early summer, are aromatic, although the leaves are not always mint-scented. Some species can grow more than 13ft (4m) tall, and most are relatively hardy, although some require a minimum winter temperature of 41°F (5°C). It is best to

ABOVE: MINT BUSH BLOOMS (*PROSTANTHERA CUNEATA*).

plant them in full sunshine against a protected wall in fertile, well-drained acid or neutral rich soil – the bushes do not grow well in chalk. The dark green leaves of the hardy *P. cuneata* smell strongly of wintergreen, and its scented white or lilac orchidlike flowers are marked with purple. This species grows only about 3ft (1m) tall and can make an attractive feature as a patio plant or as a low evergreen hedge. Its attractive foliage, compact form, and mass of scented long-lasting flowers, make it a valuable addition to an herbaceous bed or rockery.

More tender species can be grown in containers in a conservatory and moved outside into full sunshine during the summer months. Propagate mint bushes by semi-ripe cuttings in the fall, or by seed sown in spring and protected under glass. Prune very lightly after flowering to maintain a compact shape. Take care not to overwater, which can kill young plants.

RECOMMENDED SPECIES
The thickly clustered fragrant violet flowers of *P. melissifolia* (zones 9–10) are most decorative and striking, as are those of the round-leaved mint bush (*P. rotundifolia rosea*), which carries lavender-purple flowers in early spring – it can reach a height of 13ft (4m) in its native country. The leaves of both these bushes are powerfully mint-scented. *P. rotundifolia* (zones 9–10) needs to be planted in peaty soil in a frost-free environment or have winter protection in a greenhouse or conservatory, as does the tender *P. ovalifolia* (zones 9–10).

HOME USES
• *Aromatherapy applications* – The essential oil extracted by steam distillation from the leaves is rich in menthol and cineole – much like peppermint oil – but is seldom available for use in aromatherapy practice.

• *Drying and decorative uses* – Use fresh sprays in posies. Dry the leaves and flowers for burning on an open fire – the dried leaves can also be used to liven up potpourris.

• *Culinary suggestions* – The leaves can be brewed to make a minty refreshing tea.

• *Health-giving properties* – Several species were used by Australian Aborigines to combat headaches and infections. The infused leaves have antibacterial and fungicidal properties, and can be used to relieve the common cold or a congested head, either drunk as tea or as a steam inhalation.

Reseda odorata

MIGNONETTE
(Resedaceae)

Scent – floral, sweet, spicy, raspberry-scented, violetlike, healing, pungent, powerful.

DESCRIPTION AND CULTIVATION
The genus *Reseda*, native to the Mediterranean and North Africa, includes hardy and half-hardy fragrant annuals and biennials. *R. odorata* is an annual. In Roman times, the plant reputedly had healing and protective properties: *reseda* means "to heal." By contrast, in Egypt it grew so freely and was so undistinguished that it was considered a weed. Mignonette, however, was much loved by the Empress Josephine who was sent the seeds by Napoleon during his campaign in Egypt. It

subsequently became very fashionable, especially planted in pots on Parisian balconies – its popular name mignonette signifies "little darling."

The plant was introduced into England at the beginning of the eighteenth century, when its powerful perfume was used to disguise unpleasant street smells. Legend says that if a lover rolls three times in mignonette, good fortune will follow. Although the plant has fallen out of fashion, it is well worth growing for its delightful sweet perfume if not for the success of aspirant lovers. Seed should be sown under glass in spring; then plant out the young seedlings in a bed that enjoys full sunshine, in fertile well-drained soil. The flowers themselves, although fragrant, are not overly attractive, being somewhat straggly. But what they lack in appearance, they make up for with their very intensely powerful perfume, which is greatly attractive to bees. Deadhead plants regularly for maximum flower production.

RECOMMENDED SPECIES

The best and most fragrant of the mignonettes is *R. odorata* (although other cultivars have been developed). Its semi-star-shaped greenish-white flowers, borne throughout summer into early fall, are deeply perfumed with a raspberry scent, pervasive throughout the day into the evening. It grows up to 2ft (60cm) tall.

ABOVE: *R. ODORATA.*

HOME USES

• *Aromatherapy applications* – The powerfully scented essential oil of mignonette is very expensive and used only in small amounts in perfumery. The oil is not employed for aromatherapy use.

• *Drying and decorative uses* – The flowers of mignonette can be dried and used in potpourris.

• *Culinary suggestions* – Not recommended for culinary use.

• *Health-giving properties* – The leaves were used by the Romans to treat bruising.

Ribes odoratum

FLOWERING CURRANT
(Grossulariaceae)

Scent: clovelike, fruity-spicy, musky, exotic, warming, uplifting, restorative.

DESCRIPTION AND CULTIVATION

The genus *Ribes* comprises about 60 species of shrubs, including many cultivated varieties of currants and gooseberries. *R. odoratum*, otherwise known as *R. aureum*, and popularly as the buffalo, golden, or clove currant, carries spicy, clove-scented golden flowers in arching clusters in the spring. The cultivar 'Crandall' is especially beautiful: in the fall the leaves are flushed with warm tints and the flowers transform into large yellow fruits. A native of North America, its name buffalo currant derives from the use of the berries, which were ground to flavor buffalo meat and make meat patties. It is a hardy deciduous shrub growing 6–8 ft (1.8–2.5m) high, and it prefers full sunshine or very light shade in fertile well-drained soil, although it is tolerant of most soils. Propagate the shrub by taking hardwood cuttings in the winter. Since flowers are carried on the previous season's growth, prune the older shoots after flowering; in winter or early spring, cut any straggling stems right down to ground level. This will promote better growth.

ABOVE: *RIBES SANGUINEUM* IS COMMONLY SEEN.

RECOMMENDED SPECIES

Not all currants are deciduous. Some are evergreen, such as *R. laurifolium* (zones 7–9), which is native to China. Its leaves are deep green, similar to laurel, and its

ABOVE: *RIBES ODORATUM* IS A MORE UNUSUAL SPECIES.

subtle sweetly scented, greenish-yellow flowers are borne in late winter and early spring. *R. viburnifolium* (zones 9–10) is another evergreen species, a California native that needs a certain amount of winter protection elsewhere. Try planting it against a warm wall. In spring it has lovely terracotta blossoms, and its evergreen leaves have a fragrant pine aroma when crushed. *R. gayanum* (zones 9–10), evergreen and native to South America, also requires some winter protection, but has the advantage of blooming in early summer with softly fragrant, pale yellow flowers. The best known of the flowering currants, *R. sanguineum* (zones 6–8), with its rose-red flowers, has a rather unpleasant musty scent and is not really recommended for its fragrance. The blackcurrant bush (*R. nigrum*) (zones 6–8) is the medicinal species and is used to produce an essential oil.

HOME USES

• *Aromatherapy applications* – An exotically scented absolute known as cassis and an essential oil (niribine oil) are derived from the fresh buds of the blackcurrant bush (*R. nigrum*). It is an expensive oil used in high-quality perfumery, but is little employed in aromatherapy practice.

• *Drying and decorative uses* – The flowering sprays of ornamental *Ribes* species can be used in fresh flower arrangements, but it is recommended that the tough stems are re-cut and sliced before putting them into water. Re-cutting will increase their absorbtion properies.

• *Culinary suggestions* – Blackcurrants are used for making jam and in tarts – they can also be steeped in

brandy for a tonifying winter liqueur! Redcurrant jelly complements game or lamb, and the fruit can be used in desserts, along with blackcurrants. Delicious homemade wine can also be made from both red- and blackcurrants.

• *Health-giving properties* – Blackcurrants are high in vitamin C: boil redcurrants or blackcurrants with honey to obtain a soothing syrup for sore throats. Blackcurrant tea is good for colds and urinary infections, as well as helping to lower blood pressure and strengthen capillaries. An infusion of blackcurrant can also relieve nervous tension. The young tender leaves of the blackcurrant are astringent and can be dried for use as tea on their own or blended with Indian teas.

Rosa gallica (plus R. damascena and R. centifolia)

ROSES (Rosaceae)

Scent – rich, deep, sweet-floral, slightly spicy, tenacious, soothing, uplifting, aphrodisiac, warming, euphoric.

DESCRIPTION AND CULTIVATION

Ancient Persia is thought to be the birthplace of the cultivated rose and the first country where roses were planted in formal gardens. Botanically speaking, however, it is difficult to locate the exact origin of the first wild roses because early records are far from complete. What is clear, is that from very early times there existed several distinct species of rose that were distributed over the northern hemisphere, having two main centers – one in Central Asia and the other in Western Europe. These became known as old roses, because they formed the basis of all the subsequent hybrids or new roses. The division between old and new roses is generally taken to be 1800, largely due to the influence of the Empress Josephine, a passionate rose grower.

Since then, many new varieties have been developed, and today there are numerous books available on the cultivation of garden roses, illustrating the diversity, beauty, and allure of the modern (but often scentless) new rose. In recent years, however, there has a been a nostalgic return to the appeal of the old scented rose varieties, largely through the efforts of David Austin, Peter Beales, and Graham Stuart Thomas in England.

The most significant of the original highly scented old roses, especially with regard to the production of essential oils, are the following: the Gallica rose (*Rosa gallica*, syn. *R. rubra*); the Damask rose (*R. damascena*) (zones 4–9); and the cabbage rose (*R. centifolia*) (zones 4–9). See Chapter 3 for more information.

Cultivars of the Gallica rose, such as 'Belle de Crécy' (zones 3–9), are still used today for the production of essential oils. The Damask rose (*R. damascena*) is still used to produce a very high quality essential oil known as attar of roses, and an absolute, mainly for use in perfumery.

The Cabbage rose or hundred-leaved rose produces a rich, sweet-scented oil or absolute, for which it is widely cultivated in Turkey and North Africa (Morocco and Tunisia). It has given rise to innumerable other subspecies, including the Moss rose. All these roses prefer an open, sunny position with shelter from strong winds and loamy rich soil. Most roses can be propagated by hardwood cuttings taken in the fall. Prune in spring and deadhead regularly to encourage a long flowering period.

RECOMMENDED SPECIES

Other ancient highly scented varieties that are still used for the production of essential oils but on a smaller scale include the dog rose (*R. canina*) (zones 5–8), a deciduous, rambling shrub that can reach 10ft (3m), bearing delicate pink or white, single five-petaled flowers. Sweet briar (*R. rubiginosa*) has lovely apple-scented leaves. The musk rose (*R. moschata*) (zones 7–9) is a snow-white rose, with a very fragrant scent; it grows into a vigorous bushy shrub, and is often planted as a windbreak or hedge. Tea roses are generally either climbers or small, sparse bushes bearing a continuous succession of large, beautiful flowers in shades of pink, buff, or light yellow. The

RIGHT: A MIXTURE OF PERFUMED CLASSICAL GALLICA ROSES, INCLUDING *ROSA MUNDI*.

rose (*R. gallica* var. *officinalis*) can be added to salads, exotic chicken and rice dishes, or used in jam-making.

• *Health-giving properties* – In early times, the petals of the apothecary's rose were often made into a fragrant powder and employed for their pharmaceutical properties. The leaves, but especially the hips of the common dog rose *(R. canina)*, were also once a common European folk remedy – the hips can be made into a syrup or tea at home which is very rich in vitamin C.

ABOVE: THE TEA ROSE HAS THE MOST PERFECT FORM.

essential oil of the Oriental or Tea rose is mainly produced in the East, where it is used as a perfume and remedy.

HOME USES

• *Aromatherapy applications* – An essential oil, otto or attar, is produced by water or steam distillation from the fresh petals of various types of rose (see above). A concrete (solid perfumed wax) and absolute (viscous liquid) are also made by solvent extraction from the fresh petals – the Bulgarian absolute (*R. damascena*) is considered superior for perfumery work, but in therapeutic practice rose maroc oil (*R. centifolia*) is more commonly used, having a pronounced euphoric and heart-warming effect. Rose oil and rosewater are also used extensively in skin care for broken capillaries, mature and sensitive complexions, and wrinkles; to help regulate the menstrual cycle; and more generally for stress-related complaints, such as anxiety, depression, impotence, insomnia, frigidity, and headaches. To make your own rosewater see page 72.

• *Drying and decorative uses* – Fresh roses are indispensable for all kinds of flower arrangements; dried rose buds and rose petals are the main classical ingredients for potpourris. Rosewater has traditionally been used to perfume a range of household items such as linen, paper, clothes, etc.

• *Culinary suggestions* – Petals of the apothecary's

Rosmarinus officinalis

ROSEMARY (Lamiaceae)

Scent: pungent, fresh, pinelike, herby, woody-balsamic, slightly camphoraceous, stimulating, restorative, purifying.

DESCRIPTION AND CULTIVATION

Rosemary has been called the prince of aromatic herbs. It is one of the most deliciously fragrant plants for the kitchen or herb garden, and a popular aromatic shrub for a traditional mixed bed. Gertrude Jekyll wrote in *House and Garden*: " ...ever blessed rosemary all over the garden, so that every few steps the passer-by can run his hand over the blue-flowered branchlets and smell the warm resinous incense in his palm."

This handsome evergreen bush has silvery-green needle-shaped leaves and pale blue scented flowers in late spring, and the whole plant is strongly aromatic. Rosemary has been much loved by gardeners throughout the ages. Historically, its pungent scent has been associated with the qualities of faithfulness and fidelity, as Shakespeare noted: "There's rosemary, that's for remembrance." It has also been used traditionally as an aid to memory or mental alertness.

Rosemary also has a very ancient history of medicinal usage. It was burned in early religious ceremonies to purify the air, and its powerful anti-infectious qualities were employed during the plagues of Europe to ward off illness. Of all the different rosemary varieties available, *R. officinalis* is still considered to be the most valuable species, medicinally and for culinary use.

The native habitat of the wild rosemary is Asia Minor and southern Europe and, like lavender, it thrives in the Mediterranean region. Given the right warmth and protection, it can grow up to 6ft (1.8m) high, but in more northerly climes it rarely grows taller than 4ft (1.2m). Rosemary can be slightly frost tender and is best grown in a sunny position, beneath the shelter of a wall if possible, in well-drained soil. In a protected situation it can be grown as a hedge or topiary specimen, but needs to be trimmed regularly to promote bushy growth and to retain its shape. In fact, all rosemary plants benefit from being clipped back, but avoid doing this in the fall or they may be killed by frost. Rosemary also looks good grown in pots or tubs, although it will not tolerate waterlogged conditions, so it is vital to provide good drainage. Growing rosemary from seed takes some skill: it is much easier and more reliable to propagate from either softwood cuttings taken in spring, or semi-hardwood cuttings in summer.

RECOMMENDED VARIETIES

There are many beautiful cultivars available to the gardener today. The flowers can range in color from bright blue, mauve-purple, pink, and grayish-blue to white, while the needlelike leaves can vary from a rich, dark green to a variegated, silver or golden form. *R. officinalis* var. *albiflorus* has white flowers; 'Primley Blue,' 'Tuscan Blue,' and 'Miss Jessopp's Upright' (a tall variety) have mauve-blue flowers and a dense upright habit, making them good hedging plants. Several cultivars have a trailing or arching habit including 'Severn Sea' (with brilliant blue flowers), 'Majorca Pink,' and prostrate rosemary (*R. o.* Prostatus Group) – good for edging, on walls, or in pots.

HOME USES

• *Aromatherapy applications* – A very popular essential oil is produced by steam distillation from the fresh

ABOVE: AZURE BLUE BRANCHES OF ROSEMARY.

flowering tops. In aromatherapy, it is invaluable in its capacity to raise the spirits and is used to treat listlessness, mental fatigue, and nervous exhaustion. Used in combination with massage, it is employed in the treatment of arteriosclerosis, muscular pain, poor circulation, and rheumatism; as an inhalation, it is highly efficient at combating colds, bronchitis, flu, and other infections. It is also highly effective for infected skin conditions and as a hair-conditioning agent, for it is antiseptic, promotes hair growth, and regulates seborrhea. Famous as the main ingredient in Hungary water, a youth-promoting elixir, and in eau-de-cologne, the water distilled from the seed or flowers also sweetens the breath. See pages 72–3 for instructions on how to make distilled rosemary water and oils for massage.

• *Drying and decorative uses* – Since rosemary is an evergreen, it can be harvested throughout the year for decorative use in bouquets or tussie mussies (see page 77). It is an indispensable ingredient of potpourris, retaining its scent and color well on drying. The dried twigs can be burned on barbecues or open fires for a lovely incenselike aroma; a bunch of fresh needles in a bath sachet gives a wonderful uplifting scent; use infused rosemary water as a final rinse for dark hair.

• *Culinary suggestions* – In the kitchen this strong-flavored, sturdy herb is often used with lamb, but is also delicious with roast chicken, fish, casseroles, and tomato dishes, plus rice, roast potatoes, and salads, using discretion. Rosemary is also good for flavoring oils and vinegars (see pages 35).

• *Health-giving properties* – Medicinally rosemary has been used to treat a wide range of complaints, mainly due to its outstanding antispasmodic, anti-infectious,

ABOVE: THE LEAVES OF GARDEN RUE (*RUTA GRAVEOLENS*) HAVE A VERY PUNGENT SMELL.

and tonic qualities. Rosemary tea made from the fresh flowering tips may be used as a gargle for mouth and throat infections, and can be drunk as a general tonic, especially for the nerves and circulation.

NOTE: Avoid this herb during pregnancy. Not to be used by epileptics.

Ruta graveolens
GARDEN RUE (Rutaceae)

Scent – bitter, pungent, herby-fruity, sharp, acrid, green, stimulating, purifying, warming.

DESCRIPTION AND CULTIVATION

Garden rue, which is also known as herb of grace, is an extremely ornamental evergreen herb with fine bluish-green, deeply cut leaves and a pungent, bitter scent. It has a woody stem and small greenish-yellow flowers borne in late summer, and forms a bushy shrub up to 2ft (60cm) high. It was a favorite remedy of the early herbalists, especially as an antidote to poison, and together with southernwood (*Artemisia abrotanum*), was once placed in courtrooms to keep jail fever at bay. It is often grown in traditional herb gardens alongside the other main medicinal plants. However, like bitter members of the *Artemisia* genus, such as wormwood (*A. absinthium*), rue is a potentially toxic herb if used in excess. Nevertheless, it is included here because, as a purely decorative foliage herb, it is hard to match. Equally at home in a mixed bed, it can also be clipped to form a low evergreen hedge or topiary ball.

Like many of the temperate aromatic herbs, it is a native of the Mediterranean region and can be found growing wild extensively in Spain, Corsica, Sardinia, and Morocco. It prefers a dry, well-drained sunny position and will tolerate very poor soil (and even drought conditions if necessary). Rue will thrive in a pot, as long as it is given good drainage, and can make a very attractive evergreen feature. It needs to be trimmed back regularly in early spring and again after it has flowered, to prevent it from becoming leggy. Propagate rue by seed sown in spring or by softwood cuttings.

RECOMMENDED SPECIES

The cultivar 'Jackman's Blue' has particularly attractive steely-blue foliage; 'Variegata' has unusual round-lobed leaves with white and cream markings – it is slightly tender and needs protection from hard frosts.

HOME USES

• *Aromatherapy applications* – R. graveolens is used to produce an essential oil by steam distillation from the fresh herb. Other species used for producing essential oils include summer rue (*R. montana*) (zones 7–9), winter rue (*R. chalepensis*) (zones 8–9), and Sardinian rue (*R. angustifolia*) (zones 8–9). The main constituent of the oil is methyl nonyl ketone (90%) which is a toxin and a severe skin

RIGHT: R. 'VARIEGATA' IS A MORE UNUSUAL SPECIES.

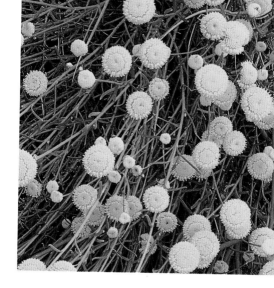

irritant. The oil should therefore never be used in perfumery or aromatherapy work.

• *Drying and decorative uses* – The decorative leaves are valuable in fresh flower arrangements, but the flowers are insignificant in this respect. The dried leaves can be used to repel insects and moths.

• *Culinary suggestions* – Not recommended in cooking.

• *Health-giving properties* – Rue is used by professional herbalists mainly for nervous disorders, weak eyesight, and for dispelling worms. It should not be used medicinally at home at all since it is toxic.

NOTE: Avoid altogether during pregnancy. Rue leaves can irritate the skin if they are handled without wearing gloves.

Santolina chamaecyparissus

COTTON LAVENDER
(Asteraceae)

Scent – pungent, slightly acrid, bitter, lemony-green, herby, stimulating, purifying.

DESCRIPTION AND CULTIVATION

This evergreen woody herb has silver-gray foliage and from midsummer until fall a mass of small bright yellow, ball-shaped flowers. Native to the Mediterranean region, it is a tough plant that likes full sun and can tolerate even very poor soil – indeed, the foliage color deteriorates if the soil is too rich. Cotton lavender was introduced to Britain during the sixteenth century as an ornamental plant, and became especially prized for creating intricate knot garden designs, which were very popular during the Elizabethan period. It grows just 18in (45cm) high and makes an ideal low hedging plant or edging herb. However, when grown as a hedge, it needs to be clipped frequently to prevent it from flowering and to maintain its compact shape.

Cotton lavender also looks good in a mixed herbal bed, in a dry Mediterranean gravel bed, or as a feature in its own right. It will thrive in pots, where its silver foliage can act as a foil for other ornamentals. The whole plant has a strong, slightly rank smell, a bit like Roman chamomile, to which it is related. Despite its common name, it is not a member of the lavender genus, although the finely cut corallike leaves closely resemble those of *Lavandula dentata*. Plants are best propagated by cuttings taken in spring or late summer.

RECOMMENDED SPECIES

S. chamaecyparissus var. *nana* is a dwarf form 6in (15cm) high, ideal for rock gardens or pots; another dwarf cultivar *S. c.* 'Lemon Queen' has narrow leaves and creamy flowers. *S. rosmarinifolia* subsp. *rosmarinifolia* (zones 7–9) has feathery greenish-gold foliage. *S. pinnata* subsp. *neapolitana* (zones 7–9) is a particulary good variety for drying.

HOME USES

• *Aromatherapy applications* – An essential oil can be produced by steam distillation from the seeds, but it is not often used in flavoring, perfumery, or aromatherapy due to its high toxicity level.

• *Drying and decorative uses* – Most *Santolina* species will dry well for use in arrangements or in potpourris. The dried herb also has excellent insecticidal properties and will help keep moths away from linen and clothes.

• *Culinary suggestions* – Cotton lavender is not recommended for flavoring because of its bitter taste and toxicity. it is, however, used in dried form as an ingredient in herbal tobacco.

• *Health-giving properties* – A decoction made from the flower and leaf of cotton lavender is used in herbal medicine to reduce skin inflammations and expel intestinal parasites.

NOTE: Not recommended for home use medicinally due to its toxicity.

LEFT: COMMON SAGE (*SALVIA OFFICINALIS*) WITH OTHER HERBS.

Salvia officinalis

COMMON SAGE
(Lamiaceae)

Scent – camphoraceous, slightly pine-like, spicy-herby, fresh, reviving, stimulating, warming, purifying.

DESCRIPTION AND CULTIVATION

There are more than 750 species in the *Salvia* genus, and no scented garden would be complete without a bush of common sage (*S. officinalis*). Invaluable in the kitchen, sage is also one of the most ancient medicinal plants – the name salvia derives from the Latin *salvere*, to save, indicating its well-established reputation as a healing herb. Native to the Mediterranean region, it has soft, silvery oval-shaped leaves and a mass of deep blue or pinkish-violet flowers in late summer. Like lavender and santolina, it has a woody base and evergreen leaves, and reaches a height of about 2ft (60cm), lending structure to the kitchen or herb garden when other plants die down in winter.

Sage is also a decorative shrub for the herbaceous bed, especially since there are numerous species to choose from. Most sages require full sun and well-drained soil to really flourish, although they are not fussy plants and will grow virtually anywhere. Clipping plants hard back every spring (after all danger of frost has passed), as well as later in the summer, helps keep them compact and stop them from becoming leggy. Still, it is best to replace plants every four years or so or when the stem becomes too woody. Sage is a fast grower and is easy to propagate from seed sown outdoors in spring or from softwood cuttings in late spring.

RECOMMENDED SPECIES

S. officinalis 'Albiflora' has white flowers; *S. o.* Purpurascens Group (zones 7–9) has dark purple leaves and is very ornamental; *S. o.* 'Tricolor' (zones 6–9) has leaves variegated purple, white, and green, and is slightly tender; while the leaves of *S. o.* 'Icterina' (zones 7–9) are colored gold. Clary sage (*S. sclarea*) (zones 4–9) is a stout biennial or perennial herb, far more bold in appearance than common sage. Its erect flowering spike grows up to 3ft (1m) high; it has large wooly gray leaves with a hint of purple, and small soft-lilac flowers with pinkish bracts add an immediate touch of drama to the herb garden. *S. s.* var. *turkestanica* has pale blue and white flowers with pink bracts and smells extremely unpleasant. Spanish sage (*S. lavandulifolia*) (zones 7–9) is an evergreen shrub, similar to common sage, but with narrower leaves and small blue-purple flowers; it is an excellent culinary sage with a scent reminiscent of spike lavender. There are also a wide range of tender or semi-tender varieties of sage with a range of intriguing scents; for example, *S. elegans* (zones 9–10) is a subtropical species with a pineapple scent and bright scarlet flowers. It makes a good pot plant, as do most sage species.

HOME USES

• *Aromatherapy applications* – Essential oils are produced from the flowering tops of several species of sage including *S. officinalis*, *S. lavandulifolia*, and *S. sclarea*, each having slightly different characteristics and properties. Clary sage oil has a sweet nutty-herbaceous scent and is used more frequently in

ABOVE: CLARY SAGE
(*S. SCLAREA*).

ABOVE: WINTER SAVORY (*S. MONTANA*) IS FAVORED FOR CULINARY USE FOR ITS REFINED FLAVOR.

aromatherapy than common sage oil, which is altogether harsher. Clary sage oil is used extensively for depression, nervous tension, and stress-related disorders, having a pronounced euphoric, restorative, and uplifting effect. Common and Spanish sage oil are both used primarily for respiratory infections, poor circulation, and hair care. The leaves of clary sage make a excellent eau-de-cologne or toilet water – see page 72–3.

• *Drying and decorative uses* – Use dried flowers and leaves (of all varieties) in potpourris. Clary sage is striking as a cut flower. Dried sage bundles thrown on the fire purify the air in a room, like rosemary or lavender. A sprig of leaves in the closet will help repel moths. Fresh sage makes a good conditioning hair rinse.

• *Culinary suggestions* – In the kitchen, sage is best known as a stuffing for poultry, but it can be used equally well with cheese dishes or vegetables.

• *Health-giving properties* – Sage leaves, boiled in water and drunk with honey and lemon juice, are excellent for relieving a sore throat and colds. A tonic tea made from the leaves is good for indigestion, cramps, and nervous exhaustion.

NOTE: Avoid sage during pregnancy. Do not use clary sage oil if you have been drinking alcohol or plan to do so, since it can induce a narcotic effect and exaggerated drunkenness.

Satureja hortensis (A) and S. montana (zones 6–9)

SAVORY (Lamiaceae)

Scent – fresh, herby, spicy, sharp, green-peppery, stimulating, warming, restorative, aphrodisiac.

CULTIVATION & GARDENING GUIDE:

Summer savory (*S. hortensis*) is a popular annual culinary herb with slender green leaves and small, pale lilac flowers. Although it is more delicate than winter savory (*S. montana*) and needs to be replanted each year, summer savory is preferred for cooking, since it has a more refined flavor – it is also favored for

medicinal purposes. Winter savory is the perennial version with white flowers and smaller, dark green leaves. It forms a neater, more compact plant, making it a good edging plant in the herb garden or bed, especially since it is semi-evergreen.

Winter savory is the best choice for container planting as it is an altogether tougher plant, requires less water, and will thrive even in poor soil – although it is best given some protection over winter. Natives to southern Europe and North Africa, both winter and summer savory will tolerate most conditions (except extreme cold and wet), but prefer light, well-drained soil in a sunny position. Both herbs will grow to a height of about 12in (30cm), although summer savory needs to be picked or trimmed regularly to prevent it from getting leggy. Both types can easily be grown from seed sown under glass in early spring, then planted outdoors once any danger of frost is past. Winter savory can also be propagated by softwood cuttings taken in spring.

RECOMMENDED SPECIES

The purple-flowered savory (*S. coerulea*) (zones 6–9) is a decorative garden plant with small purple flowers and dark green aromatic leaves. Creeping savory (*S. spicigera*) (zones 7–9) is a very attractive low-growing herb similar to thyme, with lime-green leaves and producing a mass of white flowers.

HOME USES

• *Aromatherapy applications* – An essential oil is produced by steam distillation from several savory species including *S. hortensis*, *S. montana*, *S. thymbra* (zones 7–9), and *S. douglasii* (zones 7–9), mainly for use in flavoring and occasionally in perfumery. It is not employed in aromatherapy because the oil causes skin irritation.

• *Drying and decorative uses* – The leaves of summer savory dry well for decorative and culinary use. Store them in an airtight container.

• *Culinary suggestions* – Summer savory is also known as the bean herb, since it enhances the flavor of all beans and helps prevent flatulence. It is also used for flavoring vegetable and egg dishes, and is often added to rich meat recipes, since it aids digestion.

• *Health-giving properties* – A tea made from the fresh leaves of summer savory is good for digestive complaints, menstrual irregularities, and respiratory conditions such as coughs, colds, and (as a gargle) sore throats. Applied externally, the fresh leaves help bring relief from bee or wasp stings.

NOTE: Avoid use during pregnancy.

Spartium junceum

BROOM (Papilionaceae)

Scent – floral, orange blossomlike, coconut, slightly citrus, sweet, evocative, warming.

DESCRIPTION AND CULTIVATION

The fragrant golden-yellow flowers of Spanish broom or weavers' broom (*S. junceum*), which are carried throughout summer, have a delightful sweet orange scent. It is a deciduous hardy shrub, with woody stems, almost without leaves, and the flowers are pea-like. Its height of 8–10 ft (2.5-3m) makes it a valuable plant at the back of the bed. Broom is native to southern Europe, and is a tolerant plant that grows best in sandy or alkaline soil and is therefore especially suited to coastal gardens, although it grows equally well in cities. Plant small bushes in spring or early fall in a spot that receives full sunshine. As Spanish broom self-seeds readily, it requires constant deadheading, but the ripe seed pods can be kept for propagation. For a supply of young seedlings, sow seeds in spring or fall into sandy medium for planting out after the second growing season. Spanish broom is fast growing: trim bushes lightly in both spring and fall to encourage growth and prevent them from becoming leggy.

RECOMMENDED SPECIES

The genus *Spartium* is generally considered to have only one species. Other recommended scented species include the Moroccan broom (*Cytisus battandieri*) (zones 7–9), a wonderful shrub found high up in the Atlas Mountains. It bears large, fragrant yellow pealike flowers that are pineapple scented. The yellow-flowered fragrant common broom (*C. scoparius*) (zones 6–8) grows wild in Britain and was once used medicinally. Members of the genus *Genista* have the advantage in that they are long-lived, unlike the *Cytisus* brooms. The medieval term *planta genista* – a sprig of broom – gave the name Plantagenet to English kings. Henry II even wore it on his cap. Mount Etna broom (*G. aetnensis*) (zones 8–10), has sweetly scented yellow flowers and grows up to 16ft (5m) high.

HOME USES

• *Aromatherapy applications* – Spanish broom is grown in southern France and Spain for the absolute obtained from the dried flowers, known as genet and included in high-quality floral perfumes. Spanish broom absolute is toxic and is not used in

LEFT: SPANISH BROOM (*SPARTIUM JUNCEUM*).

aromatherapy at all.

• *Drying and decorative uses* – Dried flexible branches of broom were once used for their namesakes, brooms, and today can be used for basket weaving. The dried flowers can be used in potpourris, but they must be kept away from young children, because of their toxicity.

• *Culinary suggestions* – Spanish broom should not be used for culinary purposes. The roasted ground seeds of common broom pods (*Cytisus scoparius*) can be used as a coffee substitute. Its pickled buds are considered similar to capers, while before the advent of hops, the new shoots were used to flavor ale. Wine can be made from the flowers of the common broom (*C. scoparius*), combined with citrus fruit.

• *Health-giving properties* – Spanish broom, *S. junceum*, should not be used as a herbal remedy at home at all. The common broom (*Cytisus scoparius*) was once considered an herbal cure for kidney and bladder complaints in the Middle Ages. An herbal tea made from common broom is used by medical herbalists as a diuretic, while the common broom tops boiled with dandelion root, flavored with juniper berries and a touch of cayenne pepper make a lively tonic.

NOTE: Do not use Spanish broom (*S. junceum*) flowers or shoots at home for culinary or therapeutic purposes at all due to their toxicity. If you have any doubts about distinguishing between different species, do not use them at all.

Thymus vulgaris (zones 4–8)
THYME COMMON
(Lamiaceae)

Scent – warm, spicy-herby, powerful, woody-green, refreshing, stimulating, purifying.

DESCRIPTION AND CULTIVATION

In the scented garden, thymes are essential for both their hardiness and their pungent, fresh, aromatic scent. A whole area of the garden can even be devoted to a specific thyme bed or a thyme lawn, for there are many species and varieties, mainly edible and nearly all with valuable medicinal properties. They are obligingly evergreen perennial subshrubs that thrive in dry sunny areas, in beds, or among paving and on the edges of paths, where they release their strong fragrance when trodden upon. Thyme walks were very popular from the fifteenth through to the seventeenth centuries: they require little to thrive except good drainage and sun, and need minimal nourishment.

Many thymes are native to the Mediterranean

ABOVE: A COLLAGE OF DIFFERENT THYME VARIETIES.

region. The common thyme (*T. vulgaris*) is a bushy evergreen herb up to 1ft (30cm) high with a woody root and stem, small gray-green, oval aromatic leaves and pale purple or white flowers. It will spread quickly to form a thick mass, especially if trimmed lightly after flowering – this will prevent it from becoming woody. Common thyme makes an excellent ground cover plant and is ideal for rockeries and all types of container planting. It is very popular with bees and makes a good companion for cabbages, since it helps keep away insect pests. Most are propagated by softwood cuttings in summer or by division in the fall.

RECOMMENDED SPECIES

There are a great many species and varieties of thyme, the leaves can be green, gray, silver, golden, or variegated. Cultivars of the common thyme include *T. vulgaris* 'Erectus' (zones 5–8), which is camphor-scented with upright growth and white flowers, and 'Silver Posie' (zones 7–8), with silvery-variegated leaves and a mass of mauve-pink flowers. The lemon-scented thyme (*T.* x *citriodorus*) (zones 5–9) is good for cooking and is frequently used in potpourris; *T. herba-barona* (zones 6–8) has a caraway scent, and *T.* 'Fragrantissimus' (zones 6–8) has orange-scented leaves. The wild creeping thyme (*T. serpyllum*) (zones 4–8), with its lilac-pink flowers, is perfect for a scented lawn or between paving stones. There are many cultivars of this wild thyme, such as *T. s.* 'Vey,' which is very compact; 'Annie Hall,' a popular pink variety; 'Elfin,' diminutive with magenta-pink flowers; and 'Russetings,' which has bronze-tinted foliage.

HOME USES

• *Aromatherapy applications* – An essential oil is made by water or steam distillation from the fresh or partially dried leaves and flowering tops of common thyme. The so-called red thyme oil is the crude distillate; white thyme oil is produced by further redistillation or rectification, to remove some of the less desirable chemical constituents. Essential oil of serpolet is made from wild thyme (*T. serpyllum*), a valuable medicinal oil that is milder in effect. Many chemotypes of thyme oil can be produced by a single species, since a plant's chemical makeup can vary according to growing conditions. Chemotypes include the thymol and carvacrol (warming and active); the thuyanol type (penetrating and anti-viral); and milder linalool or citral (sweet scented, non-irritant), depending on the specific species they are extracted from. In aromatherapy, common thyme oil is mainly used to combat problems of the circulation, muscles and joints, such as arthritis, cellulitis, muscular aches and pains, edema, poor circulation, rheumatism, and sprains; plus respiratory conditions such as bronchitis, coughs, mouth and gum infections, sore throats, and tonsillitis; and infectious diseases including chills, colds, and flu.

• *Drying and decorative uses* – Thymol, an active ingredient in common thyme oil, acts as a repellent to moths and flies; lay dried sprigs among linen. Used fresh in bath bags, thyme has a tonic, refreshing, and cleansing effect on the skin.

• *Culinary suggestions* – Thyme is an essential ingredient in *bouquet garni*, along with sage, rosemary, parsley, marjoram, and bay leaves. It is excellent with chicken and fish, in stuffings, and is used in many vegetable dishes. Use sprigs of the fresh herb in oils and vinegars and in mulled red wine.

• *Health-giving properties* – Medicinally, thyme has powerful antiseptic properties and was used as incense or to purify temples and homes. For centuries thyme was associated with the treatment of female ailments and used for nervous afflictions. Nicholas Culpeper recommended drinking a strong infusion of thyme as "a very effectual remedy for head-ache, giddiness and other disorders of that kind; and a certain remedy for that troublesome complaint, the nightmare." Thyme tea, drunk with honey, is good for sore throats, chesty coughs, and colds – it is also supposed to be useful in cases of drunkenness.

NOTE: Best avoided during pregnancy.

Tropaeolum majus

NASTURTIUM
(Tropaeolaceae)

Scent: sweet, delicate, floral, slightly spicy, uplifting, peppery, stimulating, refreshing.

DESCRIPTION AND CULTIVATION

T. majus, the common nasturtium, is also known as Indian cress. Although native to the West Indies and Central and South America, it had become a familiar garden plant in Europe by the early seventeenth century. *Tropaeolum* as a genus comprises hardy and half-hardy annuals and perennials, including climbers and scramblers that can reach up to 8ft (2.5m). They are grown for their brightly colored yellow, orange, or red sweet-scented, trumpet-shaped flowers, produced from the middle of summer into fall. There are also cream-colored varieties. As scramblers, they can be trained to climb over shrubs, through trellises, or against walls, and are also a welcome addition to hanging baskets.

Nasturtiums are also good for companion planting, as they attract hoverflies as well as repelling whitefly and wooly aphids. Plant them alongside vegetables such as cabbages. They prefer to be planted in bright sunshine, and *T. majus* in particular flowers best in poorer soil that is well drained. Planted in good soil, leaves are produced instead of an abundance of flowers. Grow common nasturtiums from seed in the spring; sow directly into the soil once the danger of frost is over.

RECOMMENDED SPECIES

T. majus is the common annual nasturtium: the 'Gleam' varieties have sweetly fragrant flowers and grow to 15in (38cm) high. These are semi-double plants with a trailing habit, bearing yellow, scarlet, and orange flowers. *T. majus* 'Empress of India' is a small hardy plant, a fast and prolific annual carrying dark crimson attractive flowers from early summer to early fall.

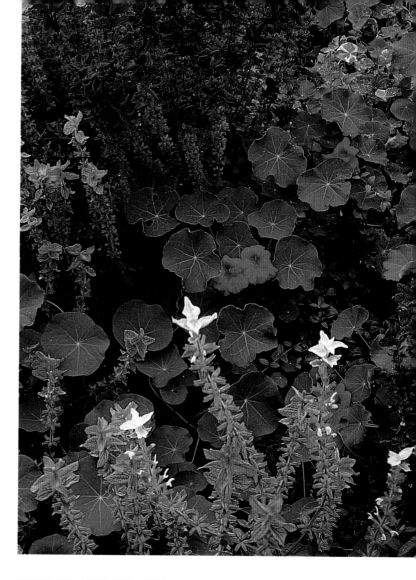

ABOVE AND LEFT: THE RAMPANT NASTURTIUM (*TROPAEOLUM MAJUS*) IS A GOOD COMPANION PLANT.

HOME USES

• *Aromatherapy applications* – The essential oil capucine extracted from common nasturtiums is used in modern seductive floral perfumes. It is not employed in aromatherapy.

• *Drying and decorative uses* – The fresh flowers last well in water and make simple posies. Dried nasturtium petals are colorful in potpourris: dry the petals in a low oven so they retain their color better.

• *Culinary suggestions* – Nasturtium leaves have a peppery taste like arugula and are delicious in salads. The flowers are also edible and make pretty decorations in salads or fruit punches. The green seeds can be pickled like capers, to which they are in fact related.

• *Health-giving properties* – Nasturtiums have medicinal benefits: the seeds have antibacterial properties, and medical herbalists use an infusion of the leaves to treat urinary infections and bronchitis.

Valeriana officinalis

VALERIAN
(Valerianaceae)

Scent – pungent, warm-woody, balsamic, musky, green, bitter-sweet, relaxing, narcotic.

DESCRIPTION AND CULTIVATION

Common valerian, also known as garden heliotrope, is a stately perennial herb up to 5ft (1.5m) high with a hollow stem, deeply dissected dark leaves, and dense clusters of small pink or white flowers. It has short, thick grayish roots, largely showing above ground, which have a strong odor. The scent of the roots, especially when dried, attracts cats who find their pungent-musky smell quite irresistible. They will also roll in the leaves, flattening the plant if given the chance.

Valerian root is one of the most powerful herbal remedies available for treating severe stress-related conditions, and was widely used in the treatment of shell-shock victims during World War I. It has a pronounced painkilling and tranquillizing effect on the entire nervous system and is mildly narcotic – however, in excess, it can cause hallucinations, dizziness, and agitation, so it must be used with caution.

Common valerian is widely distributed throughout Europe and western Asia. It prefers moist loamy soil and some sun, but will also tolerate a shady position. As an ornamental plant, *V. officinalis* forms an attractive backdrop to a floral bed or the herb garden, sending up tall elegant flowering shoots in midsummer that have a honey-sweet scent. By nature, it is also suited to woodland sites or naturalistic plantings, for it likes to be cool around its roots and

LEFT: VALERIAN (*VALERIANA OFFICINALIS*) IS A VERY VALUABLE MEDICINAL HERB. THE ESSENTIAL OIL IS USED ESPECIALLY FOR INSOMNIA.

prefers to grow near water. It is generally beneficial to the garden as it attracts earthworms. If valerian is being grown mainly for medicinal purposes, the flowers should be cut back so the herb's energy is diverted into the rhizomes. Propagate plants by seed sown in spring or by root division in spring or fall.

RECOMMENDED SPECIES

Common valerian (*V. officinalis*) should not be confused with red valerian (*Centranthus ruber*) (zones 5–8), a garden plant that seeds itself freely on sunny banks and walls. Spikenard (*V. jatamansi*) (zones 5–8) possesses similar medicinal properties to common valerian, while *V. phu* 'Aurea' (zones 5–9) is an attractive garden plant with rosettes of lemony-green foliage.

HOME USES:

• *Aromatherapy applications* – An essential oil is produced by steam distillation from the rhizomes. In aromatherapy, the oil is used in moderation, mainly in combination with massage, for nervous conditions including insomnia, nervous indigestion, migraines, stress, and nervous tension.

• *Drying and decorative uses* – Lift the rhizomes in the plant's second year after the leaves have died off, then clean, slice, and dry them, discarding all pale, fibrous roots. The root of spikenard is used in the East to scent cloth and bathwater. An infusion of the rhizome of *V. officinalis* added to the bath is good for unwinding. Try it in a bath bag – see page 77.

• *Culinary suggestions* – There are no culinary uses for valerian species.

• *Health-giving properties* – Valerian has powerful antispasmodic, carminative, hypnotic, hypotensive, and sedative effects; like hops, it is a depressant of the central nervous system. To make a soothing sedative tea, crush one teaspoon of the fresh or dried root in a cup of cold water and leave for 12 hours, then strain it well.

NOTE: Do not use valerian for more than two weeks at a time or in conjunction with sedatives or sleeping pills. Valerian is contra-indicated for those with liver problems.

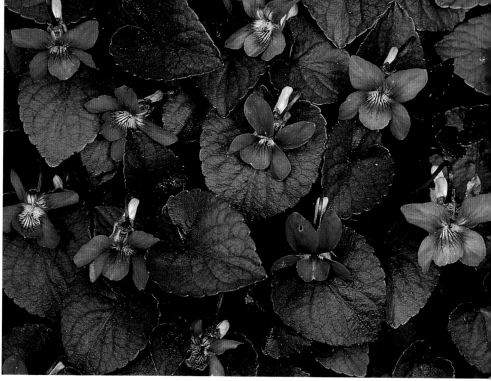

Viola odorata
SWEET VIOLET
(Violaceae)

Scent – sweet, rich, floral, intense, comforting, uplifting, soothing.

DESCRIPTION AND CULTIVATION
The sweet violet is one of our most popular early spring flowers. *V. odorata* is native to Britain and is very fragrant and easy to grow, making it an intrinsic part of any aromatic garden. The very scent of the flowers is said to "comfort and strengthen the heart." Both the Greeks and Romans loved the scent of violets – they were sacred to Aphrodite – and although the violet is a humble plant, it has captured many hearts. It was the symbol of love between Napoleon and the Empress Josephine, who had her wedding dress embroidered with violets.

The sweet violet is a small hardy perennial plant with dark green, heart-shaped leaves, fragrant violet-blue flowers, and an oblique rhizome root. Though barely 3in (8cm) high, it spreads rapidly by sending out root runners, eventually forming a sweetly scented green carpet. Violets thrive best in fairly rich, moist soil in semi-shade, and they do not like the heat. They are easy to propagate, either by seed sown in the fall under glass and planted out in spring, by dividing established clumps after flowering, or by taking root cuttings in late spring. Violets also display the additional blessing of self-seeding abundantly. Parma violets, such as 'Duchesse de Parme' (zones 6–8) and 'Marie Louise' (6–8), make good container plants for scenting a room or conservatory, especially as they are not reliably hardy.

RECOMMENDED SPECIES
Cultivars of *V. odorata* come in a variety of colors from white to pink and purple. Sweet violets often flower twice, in spring and again in the fall and sometimes through a mild winter. Parma violets have single or double flowers with a very sweet fragrance in a range of rich colors – as grown by Josephine at Malmaison. The double varieties are not fully hardy and are easily spoiled in wet weather, and therefore need to be

ABOVE: THE COY SWEET VIOLET (*VIOLA ODORATA*).

protected under glass. For Gertrude Jekyll, there was a unique beauty and delicate refinement in the subtle fragrance of the wild wood violet (*V. reichenbachiana*) (zones 5–8) which was "never overdone."

HOME USES
• *Aromatherapy applications* – An absolute perfume material is made from both the fresh leaves and the flowers: both are very valuable perfumery ingredients. The leaf absolute has a strong green odor with a delicate floral undertone and is used in aromatherapy for treating eczema, thread veins, and refining the pores. The flowers have a sedative effect, good for nervous exhaustion, dizziness, headaches, and insomnia. A scented water made from the fresh flowers and a perfume can be made at home – see pages 72–73.

• *Drying and decorative uses* – A posy of fresh violets is one of the traditional tokens of love. Dried flowers and leaves can be used in potpourris, especially combined with violet-scented orris root.

• *Culinary suggestions* – The fresh flowers can be added to salads, and crystallized violets can be used for decorating for cakes and desserts.

• *Health-giving properties* – A syrup made from the flowers has anti-inflammatory, antiseptic, expectorant, and laxative properties. The roots and leaves are also used in herbal medicine.

index

acknowledgements

First, I would like to thank Judith Allan for her extensive research – without her help I'm sure this book would never have been completed. I would also like to thank Mrs. Joan Allan, Jennie Brech, James Crowden, Natasha Lawless, Hetty MacLise, Fiona Meadley, and Paul Murphy for their kind assistance; John Elsley, Julia Hull, Hugh I'Ange, Jane Moseley, Joanna Pyliotis (of Aurora), and Diana Wells for their horticultural guidance; and Martyn Mason, Sue Minter, Richard Sneesby, and Viv Wiseman for their expertise in the field of garden design. Special thanks are also due to all those who offered their gardens for photographic purposes: Sir Michael and Lady Angus of 'Cerney House'; Guy and the Hon. Mrs. Acloque of Alderley Grange; John and Fiona Owen of 'The Old Chapel,' and last but not least the Robinson family at 'Rowleys' – for permission to photograph my former aromatic garden. Finally, I would like to acknowledge Clay Perry for his stunning photographic contribution to this book (and for his patience), plus the team at Kyle Cathie for being such a pleasure to work with – Kyle, Sheila, George, and Paul.

Photographic Acknowledgments

Ancient Art and Architecture Collection: p14 R. Sheridan, p17 M.Wellar **Bridgeman Art Gallery**: p11, Alhambra Palace; p12, Persian Garden by Persian School (15th century) Bibliotheque Nationale, Paris, France; p19,The Lady and the Unicorn, Musée National du Moyen Age et des Thermes de Cluny, Paris; p56 Sir Joseph Banks by Sir Joshua Reynolds, Agnew & Sons, London, UK **Garden Picture Library**: p135 Eric Crichton **HGL**: p61 Jerry Harpur (garden designed by P. Hobhouse) **Mary Evans Picture Library**: p13 **Marion Marjerus**: p100, 120, 156.

Barbara and Ian Pollard, Abbey House Gardens, Wilts; Southampton University Tudor Gardens; Fontreveux Abbey Garden, Loire; Hestercombe House and Gardens, Taunton, Somerset; Ernest B. Shultz, Palos Cerdes, CA; The Herb Garden, Chesterfield, Derbyshire; Head Gardener David Roberts and Martha Lytton Cobbold, Knebworth House, Herts; The late Rosemary Verey, Barnsley House, Cirencester, Wilts; Mr. and Mrs. More Molyneux, Loseley House, Surrey; Lady Ashcombe, Sudeley Castle; Sir Michael and Lady Angus, Cerney Manor, Gloucs; The Duke and Duchess of Devonshire, Chatsworth House, Derbyshire; Flintham Hall, Notts; Kew Gardens; Green End, Suffolk; Fulham Palace Garden Centre; The Swiss Garden, Herts; David and Shirley Cargill, Elsinge Hall, Norfolk; Northbourne Court, Kent; David Austin Roses. Albrighton, Shropshire; Green End, Suffolk; Simon Houghton, Hawley House, Tasmania; Anthony Lynam Dixon, Arne Herbs, Bristol; Marylynn Abbott, West Green House, Hampshire; Jersey Lavender; Madame Cargére, Varengville, Normandy; The Herb Society's Gardens; The Scented Garden, Surrey; Pantile's Plant and Garden Centre, Chertsey; Annie Huntington. The Old Rectory, North Hants.

THE AROMATHERAPY GARDEN AT ROWLEYS .